SAGA

ISRAEL AND THE DEMISE OF NATIONS

RAMON BENNETT

Colorado Springs — Jerusalem

All quotations within the text proper are enclosed within quotation marks, quotations set off do not require quotation marks. All direct quotations from the Bible are indicated by *italics* and are enclosed within quotation marks except for quotations set off. All **bold emphasis** within Bible quotations is the author's own. Proper names and lesser-known foreign words are *italicized*.

Unless noted otherwise, Scripture quotations are from THE NEW KING JAMES VERSION of the Bible. Copyright © 1979, 1980, 1982, Thomas Nelson, Inc., Publishers. Used by permission.

Copyright © 1993, 2016 Ramon Bennett
All Rights Reserved
ISBN 978-1-943423-12-5

Written permission must be secured from the author to use or reproduce, **by any means**, any part of this book, except for brief quotations in reviews or articles.

First Edition published September 1993

Second (Expanded) Edition January 2016

Published and Distributed in the **United States** by:
Shekinah Books LLC,
755 Engleby Drive, Colorado Springs, Colorado 80930, U.S.A.
Tel: (719) 645-7722. eMail: usa@shekinahbooks.com.
Website: http://www.ShekinahBooks.com.

Distributed in **Israel** by: Ramon Bennett,
P.O. Box 37111, Jerusalem 91370.
eMail: armofsalvation@mac.com.

Shekinah Books

A division of *Arm of Salvation Ministries* headquartered in Jerusalem, Israel.

This paperback is subject to discounts for orders of 10 or more copies when purchased through Shekinah Books. *SAGA* is also available as a Kindle e-Book or in PDF form. Further information can be obtained, and hard copy or PDF purchases made, by logging onto:

http://www.shekinahbooks.com

I know that whatever God does, It shall be forever. Nothing can be added to it, and nothing taken from it. God does it, that men should fear before Him. That which is has already been, and what is to be has already been; and God requires an account of what is past

(Ecclesiastes 3:14–15).

Dedication

To all the Israeli men and women who determine to succeed on their own land. To the men of the Israeli Defense Forces (IDF) who display immense courage when facing impossible odds. To the grieving parents, wives, children, sweethearts, sisters, brothers and friends, whose tears have watered the parched earth of *Eretz Yisrael*. To Israel—the fruit of great sacrifice—I humbly dedicate these pages.

Acknowledgments

I am indebted to Shlomo Berger, not only for his professional editing and advice for the first edition of this book, but mostly for keeping me on my toes by rechecking my facts and statistics. It taught me to always be sure about what I write, because someone, somewhere, will check out my stated facts.

I am grateful to my longtime Norwegian journalist friend, Lars-Toralf Storstrand, who provided me with translated information for the chapter on Norway. I am also grateful for having met, through Lars-Toralf, a new friend in Norway, Jeremy Hoff, who sent me a copy of his book *A Breach In The Wall*, which details the massacre on the Norwegian island of Utoeya, a massacre that historically was unprecedented by a lone gunman anywhere in the world. Without these two Nordic Christian friends the chapter on Norway would be found wanting.

A very big thank you goes to all those who helped support my wife and me prayerfully during the long, spiritually intense months that it takes to produce a book of this type. The book is rightfully as much theirs as it is mine—without them it would still be a heap of notes and clippings from newspapers, magazines and periodicals.

Most of all, I thank my dearly beloved "Zippy"—my wife, lover, companion, and my one true friend on earth:

many daughters have done well, but you excel them all
                                                              (Proverbs 31:29).

Contents

Dedication — V
Acknowledgments — VII
Introduction — XI

PART I

The God of Israel

1 Israel: God's Riddle — 17
2 Israel's God — 21
3 The Sovereignty of Israel's God — 31
4 Israel's Commander — 37
5 Israel's Prince — 43

PART II

Israel

6 Israel: The Nation — 51
7 Israel: The Key To Prosperity — 57
8 Israel: God's Superpower — 63

PART III

Judgment Executed

9	Judgment	77
10	Judged	79

PART IV

Judgment Pending

11	Prelude to Judgment	101
12	The Soviet Union (Case Study)	109
13	America	113
14	Britain	141
15	China	159
16	The Church	165
17	France	173
18	Germany	179
19	Iran	189
20	Iraq	201
21	Israel	207
22	Japan	213
23	New Zealand	219
24	Norway	227
25	Rome	245
26	Syria	251
27	Turkey	261
28	Armageddon	275
	For Your Information	285
	Other titles by Ramon Bennett	286
	Testimony book, music by Zipporah Bennett	290

Introduction

God, being who and what He is, has said everything He wants to say to man in the Scriptures. Man (the word man stands for humankind, not gender), being who and what he is, accepts or rejects all or part of the Scriptures according to his particular belief—be it theological, agnostic or atheistic. Two times the Bible tells us that, *The fool has said in his heart,"There is no God"* (Psalms 14:1, 53:1). Therefore, should we need to describe our modern world in general terms we must needs describe it as "a paradise of fools." The cosmic ignorance of the knowledge of God on the part of man is simply appalling. This is not the fault of the masses, but the fault of the leaders, the teachers, and the news media—the spokesmen of the world.

Unfortunately, ignorance and misconceptions concerning God and His Word are not confined to the secular world. Many Christians hold their own set of fables closely to their bosoms. Again, this is not their fault, but that of the leaders and teachers. To naively accept as truth everything the Church teaches is equally as dangerous as believing nothing at all.

Many traditional Church teachings expose Christians to only half of the coin. The Bible, if looked at from only one angle, is indeed a book of love, joy and hope. If looked at from an entirely different viewpoint, it is a book of wrath, judgment and doom. But the Bible is exclusively none of these—it is a combination of all of them. In these pages I present to the reader the reverse side of the traditional coin concerning God, Israel, and judgment. It is a side of God that some Christians would rather not know about. The pretty pictures of Jesus, too, that portray Him as rather effeminate with blue eyes and long, blond hair only belongs in story books, it has no place in the Bible. Jesus, in the days of His humanity—His sojourn on earth—was a Middle Eastern man who would have had dark hair, dark eyes and an olive complexion. And, except for those who had taken the Nazarite vow, long hair was considered an abomination on a male (1Corinthians 11:14). Neither does the storybook image of Jesus fit the One that spoke more about judgment than the majority of His Old Testament forerunners.

The Bible tells us that *God is Love* (1John 4:8), but it also tells us (equally as clearly and much more forcibly) that He is the *God of Vengeance and Recompense* (Deuteronomy 32:35); a *Consuming Fire* (Hebrews 12:29); and the *Habitation of Justice* (Jeremiah 50:7). His attributes never contradict—they always compliment.

My first book, *When Day and Night Cease,* generated many hundreds of letters extolling its virtues; only one person to my knowledge disliked the book. However, my second book, *SAGA,* garnered 50 percent

Introduction

negative letters from unhappy readers around the world, each saying virtually the same thing—I was wrong about their country. Americans were upset and asked if I understood that their country gave more money to the Church than all other nations combined? I was told repeatedly that I was wrong about America but correct about the other nations. British readers wanted to know why I was so hard on Britain and so soft on the other nations, that I was right about the other nations but wrong about Britain. Germans said they were "offended" by what I wrote about Germany but I was right about the other nations. A German Christian lady, who was organizing a speaking tour for me, was so outraged that she canceled the proposed tour. Conversely, a former SS officer requested 10 autographed copies to give to other former SS men—he said every German needed to read the book. As a matter of interest, the most copies of *SAGA* being sold anywhere today (2016) are being sold in Germany.

I received a five-page fax from the heads of the Catholic Church in Malta, offering me additional information for "the next edition." However, while the fax said that I was absolutely right in what I had written concerning the nations, it also said I was "absolutely wrong" about the Roman Catholic Church.

It takes little intelligence to understand from all this that the average person sees himself and his nation as being beyond judgment, that repentance is only for other people and other nations. It is for this reason that we are hurtling at full speed toward the final Book of the Bible—*Revelation*—often called the "Apocalypse" for reasons other than the Book's Greek title: *Apokolupsus*.

Our studies in the *Word* concerning *the* L ORD G OD *of Israel, Almighty Creator of heaven and earth*, His *Son*, and the angelic host, help to set the record straight concerning Himself, His *Word*, and His people Israel. There is a need to read, ruminate, and digest the contents of the early chapters in order to appreciate the import of the second half of the book. Some documentation of facts is from foreign sources. This is because I minister extensively overseas and endeavor to keep up with world events while traveling.

T HERE ARE MANY B IBLE PROPHECIES WHICH have yet to find their fulfillment. Our studies leave us in no doubt that the L ORD intends to make use of the nation of Israel to execute judgments on this "paradise of fools." Tens of millions of the earth's inhabitants consider this modern world something

Introduction

akin to the Titanic—unsinkable. But the true fact of the matter is that this world is coming apart at the seams; it is full of bloodshed, evil, and moral filth. And this ship of fools is on a collision course with an iceberg called *The Holy One of Israel*. A good number of nations have been destroyed over the millennia due to their treatment of Israel and the Jewish people. We shall explore the Biblical accounts of those nations and find the reason for their destruction—religious, political, social and moral sins. We find, too, a clear warning that any nation committing the same sin invites the same judgment. The warning needs to be heeded by modern nations because there is only a hair's-breadth between many of them and destruction. Some nations are in decline due to their sins of the past, but decline is merely a token judgment that points to apocalyptic judgments yet to come. It is thought-provoking to see which judgments predicted in the first edition of this book have taken, or are currently taking place.

Few nations are being exalted today. Almost all are experiencing difficulties and economic depression. And the reason that so many nations are experiencing so much difficulty is that Israel has so few friends. Israel is the country that the world loves to hate.

The Church cannot escape Scot-free from the effects of God's judgments upon the nations. True believers were never spared suffering during past catastrophes and it would be naive to think that they will be spared suffering during future ones. God only promises to deliver us out of tribulation, not, from it. Every true Christian knows that his well-being is solely dependent upon his relationship with the Eternal Son of God's love, Jesus Christ. It is to Him that we must give our hearts, turn our eyes and trust. He is faithful. He will deliver us safely into His heavenly kingdom. But it is time for Christians to stop explaining and start declaring. They must don their prophetic mantles and declare to this world, clearly, loudly, forcefully and persistently, the first recorded word of their Lord's ministry: **Repent!**

PART I

The God of Israel

1

Israel: God's Riddle

Israel is an inexplicable mystery—an enigma. It is the only nation in history to be resurrected after two thousand years—it cannot be explained politically. Its tiny, standing army, swollen to 300,000 men with all reserves mobilized, defeated, within days, a multiple of trained, well-equipped Arab armies with a combined fighting force of more than 1,200,000 men that launched a surprise attack in 1973 on Yom Kippur (the Day of Atonement), Israel's holiest day of the year—it cannot be explained militarily. With a world-wide economic boycott in place against it for nearly fifty years, Israel today is a leader of the industrial world in economic growth—it cannot be explained economically.

Israel's sons are credited with having more effect in the four major disciplines of life than any nation or race in history: Albert Einstein in the field of science, Karl Marx in the field of political thought, Sigmund Freud in the field of psychology and psychiatry and Abraham, Moses and Jesus in the field of religion and moral values.

The spiritual intensity of Israel is such that many visitors to its cities become temporarily mentally unbalanced. The aura of Jerusalem, especially, overwhelms them. Often a foreign visitor will set his hotel room alight, or is found banging his head against a wall. Dr Eli Witztum, of Jerusalem's Kfar Shaul psychiatric hospital, says they treat 50–200 foreign tourists each year. The person usually returns to complete normalcy within two weeks of being sent back to his own country. This condition is now known throughout the world's medical profession as "the Jerusalem Syndrome." Israel cannot be explained rationally any more than her most famous citizen, Jesus Christ, can be explained rationally.

Israel is God's inspiration. It is, He says, *the dearly beloved of My soul* (Jeremiah 12:7) and whoever touches it, touches *"the apple of His eye"* (Zechariah 2:8). Israel was birthed by God and is protected by God. We must turn our eyes to Him and be satisfied with what He has revealed in His word about Israel.

THE MIND OF MAN IS OFTEN like a slate that the sponge of time wipes clean, erasing what was once written there. There is a need to write again upon the mind of man certain facts that effect him and his progeny. God is the governing and central authority of men and nations. Believing that there is no God does not negate the presence of His intervention in the affairs of men and nations. Neither will believing that the character of God changed at the commencement of the Christian era negate His determination to judge certain nations for the acts that they have committed against Him, and against His people Israel. It is an undeniable Biblical fact that *"the LORD has a controversy with the nations"* (Jeremiah 25:31), which He intends to settle. And we only need look at the hundreds of Biblical prophecies that have already been fulfilled to understand that it is impossible for the unfulfilled prophecies not to be fulfilled. God's ability to predict the future with such accuracy means that He is also able to control the future. Looking at Scriptures dealing with the judgment of nations that are as yet unfulfilled, and at the reasons for God's controversy with nations in the past, we know that the days of many modem nations are numbered. The finger of God has again appeared and is writing on the walls of those nations:

> *mene, mene, tekel, upharsin—you have been weighed in the balances, and have been found wanting* (Daniel 5:25–27).

The size of the nation is completely immaterial. The greatest empires the world has ever known have been reduced to rubble or brought to nothing by the hand of the God of Israel. And unless God grants our modern nations, and particularly our leaders, a spirit of repentance like that in Nineveh of old, economic, natural, physical, and military catastrophes cannot be averted.

SINCE THE TIME OF THE APOSTLE Paul, there have been "End Times." In almost every generation there has been a major catastrophe that has had Christians believing they were in the "End Times." In the past century alone there have been a number of "signs" to signify the "End Times": World War I, the Great Depression, World War II, the re-establishment of the State of Israel, the alignment of the planets, etc. But certain events must be prophetically fulfilled before The End can come, and these events are taking place before our very eyes.

ISRAEL, IN MODERN TIMES AS IN ancient times, is central to God's controversy with the nations—it has a special place in God's heart. He knows that Israel has many flaws in its national character today, but He knows, too, that the nations guilty of judging Israel are also guilty of double standards. The God of Israel echoes to them what Jesus first spoke some two thousand years ago in Israel:

Hypocrite! First remove the plank from your own eye, and then you will see clearly to remove the speck out of your brother's eye (Matthew 7:5).

Israel is firmly in the hand of its God and remains the key to the prosperity and well-being, the survival or the demise of our nations.

2

Israel's God

For anything and everything there must be a first cause and the first cause of everything is God. The first cause of a simple loaf of bread, a staple food for much of the world, is not the farmer that planted the grain but God, the One who made the grain the farmer planted. He is the pre-existent One. He is the *Creator* and *"Possessor of the heavens, the earth, the seas, and everything in them."* Man, the ultimate creation of God, is a pauper, owning nothing apart from his sin.

The Bible, God's living, pulsating, written *Word* contains everything God ever wanted to say to man throughout the ages. And it reveals a great deal about the God of Israel Himself. A better understanding of His magnitude, influence and power, is attainable through the names by which He makes Himself known. In exploring His names, nature, character, and personality, we also understand that this unique Being is incomparably complex. No matter how exhaustive a study is done, and no matter how deeply we plumb the depths of His personality, He still eludes us, simply because He is infinite and we are finite; His complexity, immensity and capability are all beyond the limits of our intelligence.

In expanding our knowledge of God we should first differentiate between the Name of God and the names of God. The names of God are a series of titles by which He is known. The Name of God encompasses the entire gamut of His nature and personality and is an entranceway to the knowledge of the Almighty. Moses, the Prophet of Israel and a very great man of God, said to the LORD GOD of Israel, *"Teach me your ways so I may know you"* (Exodus 33:13 NIV). Moses personally knew God face to face (Exodus 33: 11), but he also knew that understanding the ways of God would allow him to know God more intimately. In response to Moses, God replies:

> *I will cause all my goodness to pass in front of you, and* **I will proclaim my name, the LORD,** *in your presence* (Exodus 33: 19 NIV):

> *Then the LORD descended in the cloud and stood with him there, and* **proclaimed the Name of the LORD.** *And the LORD passed before him and* **proclaimed: "The LORD, the LORD GOD, merciful and gracious,**

long-suffering, and abounding in goodness and truth, keeping mercy for thousands, forgiving iniquity and transgression and sin, by no means clearing the guilty, visiting the iniquity of the fathers upon the children and the children's children to the third and fourth generation" (Exodus 34:5–7).

From God's own proclamation of His Name we see that He is merciful, gracious, patient, forgiving, and truthful, but also just and a firm enforcer of discipline. We see, too, that His justice and judgment are also part and parcel of His goodness.

This proclamation is of great significance. There are four main Hebrew words used and these are, *rachoom* (merciful), *chanoon* (compassionate), *chesed* (goodness, kindness) and *emet* (truth). These appear throughout the Old Testament either separately or together on 396 occasions. Being mindful of these Hebrew words and their usage we can observe how the God of the Hebrew Old Testament makes the transition to the predominantly Greek New Testament. A direct quotation from the Old Testament, and the subsequent discourse on that passage by the Apostle Paul, brings *rachoom* (merciful), and *chanoon* (compassionate) into the New Testament:

> *For He says to Moses, "I will have **mercy** on whomever I will have **mercy**, and I will have **compassion** on whomever I will have **compassion**." So then it is not of him who wills, nor of him who runs, but of God who shows **mercy**. For the Scripture says to Pharaoh, "For this very purpose I have raised you up, that I may show My power in you, and that My name may be declared in all the earth." **Therefore He has mercy on whom He wills, and whom He wills He hardens*** (Romans 9:15–18).

Not only is there a direct introduction into the New Testament here of two Old Testament words forming an intricate part of the Name of God, but Paul, moved by the Holy Spirit, also confirms the revealed Old Testament character of God.

The two remaining Hebrew words that help make up the Name of God are found, not surprisingly, linked to the One who is the image of God:

> **Grace** and **truth** *came through Jesus Christ* (John 1:17).

> *And **the Word** became flesh and dwelt among us, and we beheld **His** glory, the glory as of the only begotten of the Father, full of **grace** and **truth*** (John 1:14).

The phrase *"grace and truth"* that is found in most popular English versions is, in the Hebrew translation of the New Testament, *chesed ve'emet*—(**chesed**

Israel's God — Chapter 2

<u>and</u> **emet**). And, *"full of grace and truth"* is, in the Hebrew translation, *rav chesed ve'emet*—the exact same phrase used in the proclamation of the Name before Moses! It literally means "full of goodness, kindness and truth" and, being applied to the Lord Jesus, it completes the transition of the Name and personality of God from the Old Testament into the New. Jesus said, *"I and My Father are one"* (John 10:30). And Jesus, being the *"image"* of God (2Corinthians 4:4; Colossians 1:15), and the *"express image of His person"* (Hebrews 1:3), bears the Name revealed to us in the Old Testament.

There is an apparent confusion among Christians concerning the immutability (unchanging nature) of God. On the one hand we have an oft-quoted Scripture in the Old Testament, *"I am the L*ORD*—I do not change"* (Malachi 3:6), and another in the New Testament, *"The Father ... with whom there is no variation or shadow due to change"* (James 1:17 RSV). On the other hand some Christians are inclined to believe that the Father of the New Testament, is not the LORD of the Old Testament—that He was subject to mutation and somehow changed from a somewhat bloodthirsty God in the Old Testament to a more mild and merciful God in the New. But God, being immutable, cannot change. He cannot change for the better any more than He can change for the worse and will forever be what He has forever been. God is merciful. This attribute is also subject to His immutability. Therefore He will never be less merciful than He is right now nor more merciful than He is now or has ever been in the past.

In actual fact, in the Old Testament the word "mercy" appears 232 times in the NKJ version, 226 times in the KJV, 131 times in the TLB, 91 times in the NAS, 77 times in the RSV and 70 times in the NIV. In the New Testament the word "mercy" appears in the NKJ and the KJV versions a total of 58 times, in the RSV 60 times, NIV 59 and the TLB 51. The New Testament contains 30.5 percent of the volume of the Old Testament and should, therefore, contain at least 70 usages of "mercy" if it is to even equal the Old Testament level of usage. Should we then conclude that God was actually more merciful in the Old Testamental period than He is in the New Testamental period? Of course not! But if the reader would like God to appear more merciful he can simply change his Bible for a different version.

The four Hebrew words, so integral to the revelation of the Name of God, confirm that the Old Testament God of Israel did not undergo a personality change when man entered the age of the New Testament. He remains immutable—ever the same, with the identical characteristics of mercy, grace, compassion and patience; He is forgiving and truthful, but also just, and a firm enforcer of discipline.

Jehovah, the God of the Bible, is not exclusively the God of Israel. The Apostle Paul makes this perfectly clear in his letter to the Romans when he says:

> *Is He the God of the Jews only? Is He not also the God of the Gentiles? Yes, of the Gentiles also"* (Romans 3:29).

He is also referred to by the Prophet Jeremiah as the *"king of the nations"* (Jeremiah 10:7). These two references, however, are the only ones directly describing the LORD as being the God of the Gentiles, out of a whole mass of descriptive names by which the LORD makes Himself known. It is obvious, therefore, that Jehovah is first and foremost the God of Israel.

In contrast to the two references mentioned above, we find that the LORD makes Himself known to us as: a) *the LORD GOD of Israel*, 110 times; b) *the God of Israel*, 90 times; c) *the Holy One of Israel*, 31 times; d) *Israel's God*, one time; e) *the Light of Israel*, one time; f) *the Rock of Israel*, one time; g) *the Creator of Israel*, one time; h) *the Redeemer of Israel*, one time; i) *the Stone of Israel*, one time; j) *the Shepherd of Israel*, two times; and k) *the Hope of Israel*, two times. He is also l) *the Mighty God of Jacob*, one time; m) *the Mighty One of Jacob*, four times; n) *the Portion of Jacob*, two times; and also o) *the Holy One of Jacob*, one time; p) *the LORD GOD of the Hebrews*, five times; and also q) *the God of the Hebrews*, one time, making a total of 255 direct references to the LORD being Israel's God.

WHEN WE SPEAK OF ISRAEL'S GOD or, the God of Israel, we speak of the God of the physical nation of Israel—the Jewish people, not the Church. Israel is not a synonym for the Church. The Church was never called to replace or displace Israel. By being grafted into the root and stock of the natural olive tree (Romans 11:17–18), the Gentile Christians become part of the Commonwealth of Israel and are supported and nourished by Israel. (I would here refer the reader to my detailed exposition on this subject in my book *When Day and Night Cease*, now in its fourth edition.)

IN THE PROCLAIMED NAME THE LORD'S overall personality was revealed to us. In the distinct names by which He makes Himself known we see His attributes unveiled. One of the most predominant names He chooses is *the LORD of hosts*. The God of Israel uses this name 219 times. Unfortunately, the traditional translation of "hosts" for the Hebrew word *tsava* does great violence to the meaning of the text, as does the NIV's use of "sovereign" or "Almighty." The word *tsava*, meaning "army," is used a total of 458 times in the Old Testament and only on nine occasions is the use outside that of a military setting. Four times it refers to the sun, the moon, and the stars, all

Israel's God — Chapter 2

the host of heaven. The other five refer to the Levites serving in the temple along with the thousands of their brethren. *The LORD of hosts*, therefore, literally means *the LORD of armies*. This is corroborated in both the Old and New Testaments:

And it came to pass, when Joshua was by Jericho, that he lifted his eyes and looked, and behold, a Man stood opposite him with His sword drawn in His hand. And Joshua went to Him and said to Him, "Are You for us or for our adversaries?" So He said, "No, but **as Commander of the army of the LORD I have now come**" (Joshua 5: 13–14).

Do you think that I cannot now pray to My Father, and **He will provide Me with more than twelve legions of angels**? (Matthew 26:53)

Israel's God is in control of immense angelic forces that carry out His will. The Man met by Joshua was the Commander of the LORD's army of warrior angels. In Hebrew, *tsava* means "army"—a "mighty force," but the LORD is not "the LORD of a host" but *"the LORD of hosts"*—plural. The plural of the Hebrew word *tsava* is *tsavaot*, and thus we find it used two times in New Testament Greek, *"the Lord of Sabaoth"* in Romans 9:29 and James 5:4—(KJV, NKJ, ASV, NAS, etc. Other editions render the Greek *Sabaoth* as "hosts" or as in the case of the NIV as "Almighty," both renderings are wrong. Bringing the Hebrew *tsavaot* into the New Testament corroborates what has been presented before, that the personality of Israel's God is the cohesive force of the New Testament. It is interesting to note that the first time the name *LORD of hosts* or, more correctly, *LORD of armies*, appears, is in 1Samuel 1:3, at the time when Israel's kingdom was about to be established and when wars were to become inevitable.

ANOTHER REVEALING NAME OF THE GOD of Israel is *"I AM"* (Exodus 3:14), which opens another facet of God's personality. The translation of the Hebrew into *"I AM"* is probably as good a translation as could be made. The Hebrew in the first part of the verse is *ehiyeh asher ehiyeh*, literally meaning "I will be what I will be," or "I will be that which I want to become." The LORD then tells Moses to inform the Israelites that *"I AM"* (*ehiyeh* - "I will be") has sent him. Thus we see that the LORD makes room for Himself to be, or become, whatsoever He desires without any limitations. *"And the Word* (which was God – John 1:1), **became flesh** *and dwelt among us"* (John 1:14). In Jesus dwelt *"all the fullness of God"* (Colossians 2:9). Therefore, whoever looked upon Jesus, looked upon Israel's God (John 14:9, 20:28), but in a different form (Philippians 2:6–7, Mark 16:12, etc.). We shall have more to say concerning Jesus appearing in a different form in another chapter.

WE COME NOW TO THE ONE name by which the LORD commanded men to both know and remember Him, but neither Israel nor the Church complies. Israel began with the proper name of God upon its lips; but as man's rules and regulations "fenced-in" the *Torah* (Law), and the Biblical religion gave way to the rabbinical religion that prevails until today, the proper name of God became the "incommunicable" name—the name that was never uttered. The Church does not use the proper name of God because the early translators of the Hebrew texts, not knowing about the "fence" the rabbis had placed around the name, translated it incorrectly. The rabbis, desiring that no one should ever take God's proper name in vain (Deuteronomy 5: 11), made a rule that every person was to say *"Adonai"*—Lord, when they read His proper name in the Scriptures or prayer book. They also punctuated the proper name with a system of vowel signs called *nikud*, making the proper name actually read as if it were "Lord." Tradition, both Jewish and Christian (tradition is often as great a curse as it is a blessing), subsequently robbed God of His proper name and the Church of the knowledge of it.

The name to which I refer is used no less than 6,375 times in the Bible and, apart from being translated seven times in the 1611 King James version as "Jehovah," and as "Jehovah" throughout the entire ASV, it is translated in every other popular English version as LORD. Having seen that God's personality is revealed in both His Name and His names, we should now quickly realize that, from the preponderance of usage alone, this name has a great deal of import.

WHAT IS TRANSLATED AS "LORD," OR "Jehovah," are the four Hebrew letters *Yod*, *Heh*, *Vav,* and *Heh*, making up what is commonly known as the Tetragrammaton—the proper name of God. The name has a very distinct meaning, but when the early Bible scholars translated the Hebrew Scriptures into an English version, they followed the Rabbinical tradition of using "Lord" as the name of God; knowing that it was not His proper name, the scholars capitalized it as "LORD" to distinguish it from "Lord"—the equivalent of "Sir." They also attempted to translate the proper name of God, but not realizing that the *nikud* punctuation assigned to the Tetragrammaton by the rabbis was that of "Lord," and not that of the proper name, they translated a totally spurious "Jehovah" in place of "Yahveh," the closest pronunciation of God's proper name.

THERE IS MUCH IN FAVOR OF invoking the proper name of God over the rather (I say this reverently and without disrespect) nebulous LORD. The modem meaning of "LORD" is far from that of the original, making our use of it a mere shadow of its former strength. The proper name of God, on the

Israel's God — Chapter 2

other hand, has lost none of its majestical import. Even though relatively little is found in scholarly works and Bible commentaries on the name, it is not too difficult to comprehend its meaning. The four letters that make up the Tetragrammaton—*Yod*, *Heh*, *Vav,* and *Heh*, are rearranged into three words: *Heh*, *Yod,* and *Heh* (*Hiyah*—meaning "was"); *Heh*, *Vav,* and *Heh* (*Hoveh*—meaning "is"); and *Yod*, *Heh*, *Yod,* and *Heh* (*Yeeheeyeh*—which means "will be"). The meaning of God's proper name is, therefore, both obvious and provocative, and confirmed three times in the book of Revelation. For example:

> *"I am the Alpha and the Omega, the Beginning and the End," say the Lord, "**who is** and **who was** and who **is to come**, the Almighty"*
> (Revelation 1:8).

When, through His Son, we are in a right relationship with *Yahveh* and invoke His name, we guarantee His involvement. We also declare to every principality and power—in heaven, on earth, and under the earth—that the Eternal God, the One who ever was, is now, and ever will be, is our God. It is a powerful proclamation and, in fact, we are admonished to use this majestic name of God:

> *God said to Moses, "Thus you shall say to the children of Israel: The LORD GOD of your fathers, the God of Abraham, the God of Isaac, and the God of Jacob, has sent me to you.* **This is My name forever, and this is My memorial to all generations**" (Exodus 3:15).

The translation above should read, *"Thus you will say to the sons of Israel: '**Yahveh**, God of your fathers, the God of Abraham, the God of Isaac and the God of Jacob ... '"* The name *Yahveh* is more than a name, it is a **memorial**—a "particular remembrance." It was not sufficient for God to continue being known as *El Shaddai*, God Almighty—He wants His timelessness known:

> *I appeared to Abraham, to Isaac, and to Jacob, as God Almighty, but by My name, LORD [**Yahveh**], I was not known to them* (Exodus 6:3).

We are enjoined to call upon Israel's God by His name *Yahveh*, but error, followed by tradition, has robbed Him of His proper name and us of the desire to be obedient to His wishes. If I were to use the name of *Yahveh* throughout these pages in place of the traditional LORD, I would almost certainly lose the greater portion of all potential readers who pick this book up at random, thus entirely defeating the purpose of writing it.

The names *Yahveh*, and *I AM* (itself an expansion of *Yahveh*, using repetitions of *Heh*, *Yod,* and *Heh*—three of the four letters of the Tetragrammaton)—

denote the personality, individuality, self-existence and immutability of the Divine Being who designates Himself as Israel's Creator, Sustainer, Protector and God.

OTHER NAMES THAT REVEAL THE PERSONALITY and nature of God are: *the Almighty*, used 48 times; *the Possessor of heaven and earth*, two times; *the Judge of all the earth*, one time; *the Habitation of justice*, one time; and *the God of recompense*, one time. The name *the Almighty* tells us that God is not just mighty, but all-mighty—power and authority being an attribute rather than a possession. As *the Possessor of heaven and earth*, the LORD is the Owner and Master of everything in heaven, on earth and in the seas, and can, therefore, do whatsoever He desires with His own. He is *the Judge of all the earth*—the ultimate decision of everything spiritual and physical rests with Him. He is *the Habitation of justice* and His every decision will, therefore, be just and true. And as *the God of recompense*, He will return to each according to his ways:

> *For the day of the LORD is near for all nations. As you have done, it shall be done to you; your dealings will return upon your own head*
> (Obadiah 1:15).

Nations and individuals will be recompensed with the exact same coin they offered to God—*Vengeance is Mine, I will repay* (Romans 12:19). And, as the LORD of "armies," He leaves us with no doubt as to how He will repay those who cared more for themselves than for Him:

> **If I whet My glittering sword**, *and My hand takes hold on judgment, I will render vengeance to My enemies, and repay those who hate Me*
> (Deuteronomy 32:41).

THE HEBREWS, LIKE OTHER ANCIENT CIVILIZATIONS, implicitly believe that a name reflects the character of the one bearing it. The names of the God of Israel are, therefore, pregnant with meaning. The utterance of a Divine name guarantees the presence, attention, and active intervention of the Divine character revealed in that name. Illustrations are provided throughout the Old Testament. For instance, King Hezekiah, under siege in Jerusalem by the king of Assyria and his army, prayed: *"O LORD of hosts, God of Israel ..."* (Isaiah 37:16). Hezekiah invoked the names, *Yahveh of [armies]*, and, *God of Israel*. The result was spectacular:

> *The angel of the LORD went out, and killed in the camp of the Assyrians one hundred and eighty-five thousand; and when people arose early in the morning, there were the corpses* (Isaiah 37:36).

Israel's God — Chapter 2

The God of Israel, the God of mighty angelic armies, was called upon. The presence, attention and active intervention of the Divine character revealed in these names was guaranteed and Israel's God went against the enemies of Israel. How many people, including Christians, realize the awesome power of the God of Israel? In a moment of time 185,000 people perished. When America dropped an atomic bomb on densely populated Hiroshima in August 1945, around 100,000 people perished—roughly half the number of Assyrians killed in answer to Hezekiah's plea for help.

To SUM UP, WE HAVE FOUND that apart from only two recorded occurrences, one in the Old Testament and one in the New, the LORD (*Yahveh*) reveals Himself as Israel's God—indelibly linked by name to Israel in 255 separate Scriptures. Israel's God is the LORD of armies—mighty angelic armies, often doing battle against the enemies of Israel. Israel's God has the authority, the right, the capacity and the ability to be or to appear in whatever form His great mind can conceive. He is self-existent and pre-existent, without beginning or end, and prefers to be known as *Yahveh—the One who is, who was, and is to come.*

Israel's God is Almighty, absolute power being an attribute of His complex nature. He uses His might and power, and that of His ministering angelic servants, to accomplish His purposes and to render judgment, justice and recompense. The character, attributes and personality of Israel's God are forever unchangeable—remaining the same throughout eternity. All facets of His nature are represented in a comprehensive Name, the totality of which is the sum of His unique personality. This same personality permeates the New Testament Scriptures and pervades the world of man—charting and steering the course of history. But, let Israel's God introduce Him self—**"I AM—Yahveh of armies, the Creator, King, and Holy One of Israel—the Mighty One of Jacob."**

3

The Sovereignty of Israel's God

Israel's God has a controversy with the nations. And beginning with the flood in the time of Noah, He has often made use of the "natural" elements to judge men and nations. All the elements were created, and are not, therefore, "natural." They are part and parcel of the Creator's handiwork. Every element, including the terrifying earthquake, tornado, or hurricane is completely at the disposal of its Maker. This same Creator-God binds Himself to Israel—**He is the Maker of all things, and Israel is the tribe of His inheritance** (Jeremiah 10:16). The LORD GOD of Israel has no favorites among men or nations. The nation of Israel is not his favorite nation, it is His chosen nation. Jesus is not His favorite Son, He is His beloved Son. God shows no partiality (Deuteronomy 10:17) when administering blessing, justice or judgment—

All His ways are justice ... righteous and upright (Deuteronomy 32:4).

Consequently, His employment of the elements bless, awe, warn, terrify, or destroy according to His own particular desire:

*He makes His **sun** rise on the evil and on the good, and sends **rain** on the just and on the unjust* (Matthew 5:45).

*He makes **lightning** for the **rain**; he brings the **wind** out of His treasuries* (Psalms 135:7).

*He covers His hands with **lightning**, **and commands it to strike*** (Job 36:32).

*The treasury of **snow** ... the treasury of **hail** ... which I have **reserved for the time of trouble, for the day of battle and war*** (Job 38:22, 23).

*You will be **punished by the** LORD of hosts with **thunder** and **earthquake** and great noise, with **storm** and **tempest** and the flame of **devouring fire*** (Isaiah 29:6).

I form the light and create darkness, I bring prosperity and create disaster; I, the LORD, do all these things (Isaiah 45:7 NIV).

Israel's God, the Maker of all things, has absolute dominion over all the work of His own hands and also over every other created thing—nothing is outside of His control. He will, at leisure, *"command the **serpent**, and it shall bite"* (Amos 9:3), and He will *"command the **sword**, and it shall slay"* (Amos 9:4). For Israel's God, carrying out His desire is as simple as issuing a command to the elements, the earth, the serpent, or the sword.

MAN IS GOD'S FINEST CREATION AND God's desire is to have an intimate relationship with him. But millions have turned their backs on Him, preferring tangible materialism to spiritual contentment. Millions more spurn God, alienating themselves from Him by behavior that is abhorrent to His nature. God's love for man cannot make room for sin or self-interest, which create estrangement. Alienation from God, in turn, creates ignorance of God, and this widens the gap even further. Reverence for the Creator has been replaced by humanism and worship of things created by man's own imagination and hands.

Many leaders of our modern nations are inaugurated into office with some reference to God but it is only formal procedure, a relic from the past. These leaders often practice, condone or legislate that which God clearly hates.

The well-being of the nations lies in the hands of God, *"the Holy One of Israel."* Divine intervention is not a fable from the Dark Ages, but nevertheless, our leaders tackle their public duties with a greater belief in themselves than in the One who controls the destiny and direction of the nations. King Nebuchadnezzar of Babylon, one of the ancient world's great empires, felt much the same way as some of today's leaders do. The LORD GOD *of Israel* told him that he would:

eat grass like oxen ... until you know that the Most High rules in the kingdom of men, and gives it to whomever He chooses (Daniel 4:32).

It is clear from the number of coups, both political and military, and from the many surprise election results, that an unseen Hand is in control of all the nations.

The LORD GOD *of Israel* expresses His sovereignty over the nation of Israel:

As the clay is in the potter's hand, so are you in My hand, *O house of Israel* (Jeremiah 18:6).

The Sovereignty of Israel's God

Like a piece of clay in a potter's hand, Israel is completely at the mercy of her God, to be fashioned, shaped, blessed, or punished according to His will. So, too, are the Gentile nations:

> *He makes nations great, and destroys them; he enlarges nations, and guides them* (Job 12:23).
>
> *He removes kings and raises up kings* (Daniel 2:21).

People express astonishment that some of the most intelligent persons elected to government office often seem to make ridiculous, sometimes stupid decisions. But the hand of the God of Israel reaches deep into the affairs of man:

> *He deprives of intelligence the chiefs of the earth's people, and makes them wander in a pathless waste* Job 12:24 NAS).
>
> *The LORD foils the plans of the nations; he thwarts the purposes of the peoples* (Psalms 33:10 NIV).

God, the God of Israel, holds absolute sway over all of creation. He is *"the Possessor of heaven and earth"* (Genesis 14:22) and holds all nations in the palm of His hand. This includes total dominion over the individual:

> *A man's heart plans his way, but the LORD directs his steps*
> (Proverbs 16:9).
>
> *The lot is cast into the lap, but its every decision is from the LORD*
> (Proverbs 16:33).

Some people balk at the least mention of an omnipotent, omnipresent Being, who is in control of their personal lives, but:

> *Indeed,* **O man, who are you to reply against God?** *Will the thing formed say to him who formed it, "Why have you made me like this?"* **Does not the potter have power over the clay**, *from the same lump to make one vessel for honor and another for dishonor?*
> (Romans 9:20–21).

Like the nation of Israel, every individual is mere clay in the Potter's hand, to be fashioned into *"vessels of mercy"* (Romans 9:23), or *"vessels of wrath"* (Romans 9:22). Even our apparent free choices turn out to be God's foreordained decrees. This may sound logically absurd but it is, nevertheless, true. It should not be construed as fate, but the result of planning by an intelligence so superior to ours that we are unable to comprehend it. This Being, this Spirit, permeates and fills *"everything in heaven and earth"*

(Jeremiah 23:24). When we consider the magnitude of the heavens we should also consider that this awesome Being, the One who likes to make Himself known as the God of Israel, is of greater compass than that which He created—the *"heavens cannot contain Him"* (2Chronicles 2:6). His immensity, sovereignty, power, authority and majesty are all beyond our comprehension. He does precisely what He wants, when He wants and how He wants, without consulting anyone. His presence in the affairs of men and nations is undeniable. He is sovereign over all creation and His word is absolute and resolute. Nebuchadnezzar had a fresh understanding of the God of Israel after spending seven years living like an animal:

> *At the end of that time, I, Nebuchadnezzar, **raised my eyes toward heaven, and my sanity was restored**. Then I praised the Most High; **I honored and glorified him who lives for ever**. His dominion is an eternal dominion; his kingdom endures from generation to generation. All the peoples of the earth are regarded as nothing. **He does as he pleases with the powers of heaven and the peoples of the earth. No one can hold back his hand or say to him: "What have you done?"*** (Daniel 4:34–35 NIV).

Every leader and every inhabitant of every nation, like Nebuchadnezzar, needs to raise their eyes toward heaven and honor and glorify Him who lives forever. Then, perhaps, some sanity, которая we seem to have lost along the road of time, will be restored to us also. Scripture informs us that the LORD GOD of Israel is:

> *God of gods and LORD of Lords, the great God, mighty and awesome, who shows no partiality nor takes a bribe* (Deuteronomy 10:17).

Our nations, and particularly our leaders, need to take note of this and not simply dismiss it. What must He do to get man's attention? The possibilities are too frightening to entertain. The nations must heed Him:

> ***Listen to Me ... I am God**, and there is no other; **I am God**, and there is none like Me, declaring the end from the beginning, and from ancient times things that are not yet done, saying, "My counsel shall stand, and I will do all My pleasure," calling a bird of prey from the east, the man who executes My counsel, from a far country. Indeed I have spoken it; I will also bring it to pass. I have purposed it; I will also do it*
>
> (Isaiah 46:3, 9–11).

Putting our heads in the sand like ostriches, or telling ourselves that God is a myth and does not exist, will not make Him go away—He has nowhere

The Sovereignty of Israel's God — *Chapter 3*

to go. The whole of creation is already too small for Him. Nothing short of national repentance will cause Him to relent of the harm that He has purposed against the nations. Israel's God has no peer and holds absolute sway in heaven and earth. He controls the natural realm, the spiritual realm and the physical realm. He rules over all the kings and kingdoms and has dominion over every president and prime minister. His governing power extends over all officialdom and every citizen of every nation. And *the LORD has a controversy with the nations*.

4

Israel's Commander

When the Israelites were slaves in Egypt, serving Pharaoh, a man named Moses was called by God to lead them out from there and into the Promised Land. Moses was caring for his father-in-law's sheep in the desert when a bush burst into flame, but was not consumed by the fire. Moses approached the burning bush for closer inspection:

> *So when **the LORD** saw that he turned aside to look, God called to him from the midst of the bush and said, "Moses! Moses!" And he said, "Here I am." Then He said, "Do not draw near this place. **Take your sandals off your feet, for the place where you stand is holy ground.**" Moreover He said, "**I am the God of your father—the God of Abraham, the God of Isaac, and the God of Jacob**." And Moses hid his face for he was afraid to look upon God* (Exodus 3:4–6).

Moses stood in the presence of God. He was instructed to take his sandals off because he was standing on holy ground. There is only one other place in Scripture where a person stood in the presence of Deity and was commanded to remove his sandals because he stood on holy ground:

> *And it came to pass, when Joshua was by Jericho, that he lifted his eyes and looked, and behold, **a Man** stood opposite him with **His** sword drawn in **His** hand. And Joshua went to **Him** and said to **Him**, "Are **You** for us or for our adversaries?" So **He** said, "No, but as **Commander** of the army of the LORD I have now come." And **Joshua fell on his face to the earth and worshiped**, and said to Him, "What does my Lord say to **His** servant?" Then the **Commander** of the LORD's army said to Joshua, "**Take your sandal off your foot, for the place where you stand is holy**. "And Joshua did so* (Joshua 5:13–15).

The Bible version used here generally capitalizes names and pronouns of Deity. Joshua was in the presence of Deity, but before Whom was he standing? Nowhere in the Bible is it recorded that God's angels accepted worship from men. On the contrary, worship was forbidden to any except God Himself:

You shall worship no other god, for the LORD, whose name is Jealous, is a jealous God (Exodus 34:14).

Angels were emphatic in their refusal of worship from men. When John tried to worship angels on two occasions, he was rebuked both times: **"See that you do not do that! ... Worship God!"** (Revelation 19:10, 22:8–9). Apart from the LORD, only one heavenly Being accepts worship from men, and that is the Lord Jesus Christ. It is recorded that He knowingly accepted worship no less than six times in Matthew's gospel alone:

A leper came and **worshiped Him** (Matthew 8:2).

A ruler came and **worshiped Him** (Matthew 9:18).

Those ... in the boat ... **worshiped Him** (Matthew 14:33).

She came and **worshiped Him** (Matthew 15:25).

They came ... and **worshiped Him** (Matthew 28:9).

They saw Him, they **worshiped Him** (Matthew 28: 17).

Jesus accepts worship because He is God. Israel's God is also Israel's King:

I am the LORD, your Holy One, the Creator of Israel, **your King**

(Isaiah 43:15).

And of Israel's God and King it is written:

Behold, **your King is coming to you**; *He is just and having salvation, lowly and riding on a donkey, a colt, the foal of a donkey* (Zechariah 9:9).

There is no shadow of doubt that this refers to Jesus because He Himself fulfilled the prophecy. Kings always went at the head of their armies and the God of Israel is the LORD of armies — mighty angelic armies, often doing battle against the enemies of Israel. Is it conceivable then, that the Commander of the angelic army who met with Joshua is, as several renowned Bible expositors also maintain, the Lord Jesus? Let us consider some facts.

When Joshua, not knowing who the Man was, asked Him if He was on the side of the Israelites or on the side of the enemies of Israel, the Commander replied, **"No, but as Commander of the army of the LORD I have now come."** The Commander was neither for Israel nor against Israel, neither for the Canaanites nor against the Canaanites. He was simply there to do the will of the LORD. And most of us know of the Scripture that directly refers to the Lord Jesus and states the identical characteristic:

Behold, **I have come** — *in the volume of the book it is written of* **Me — to do Your will, O God** (Hebrews 10:7).

And we also have the words of Jesus Himself:

> *My food is to do the will of Him who sent Me* (John 4:34).

The Bible tells us that:

> *Christ Jesus ... being **in the form of** God ... made Himself of no reputation, taking **the form of** a servant ... coming in **the likeness of** men* (Philippians 2:5–7).

And on the road to Emmaus, the two disciples did not recognize the One with whom they were traveling because **He appeared in another form** (Mark 16:12). Remember, one of the names of God is *"I AM,"* which allows Him to be or become whatsoever He desires. Remember, too, that the Name of God encompasses His entire personality and that this personality is Jesus' personality. With this in mind we can better understand the passage relating to the Israelites' trek up from Egypt and their subsequent journeys through the desert:

> *Behold, I send an Angel [**Messenger**] before you to keep you in the way and to bring you into the place which I have prepared. Beware of **Him** and obey **His** voice; do not provoke **Him**, for He will not pardon your transgressions; for **My name is in Him*** (Exodus 23:20–21).

The Hebrew word *malach*, here translated as "angel," means "messenger." The use of this word is by no means limited to celestial beings with wings, but is also used to describe numerous Old Testament prophets and priests. Perhaps the best known passage containing the word *malach* is the prophecy concerning the coming of John the Baptist:

> *Behold, I send **My messenger** and he will prepare the way before **Me*** (Malachi 3:1).

A particularly significant point in our passage from the book of Exodus is that God's Name is in His **Messenger**, and, as we saw in the previous chapter, the One who carries God's Name is Jesus.

Turning to the book of Daniel we find one of the most profound and powerful Messianic passages in the Bible:

> *I was watching in the night visions, and behold, **One like the Son of Man**, coming with the clouds of heaven! **He** came to the Ancient of Days, and they brought **Him** near before Him. Then **to Him was given dominion and glory and a kingdom, that all peoples, nations, and languages should serve Him**. His dominion is an everlasting dominion, which shall not pass away, and **His** kingdom the one which shall not be destroyed* (Daniel 7:13–14).

Rabbinical scholars understand this *Son of Man* to be "King Messiah," and all of the major critical Christian Bible commentaries agree that the *Son of Man* in Daniel's vision is Jesus. *Son of Man*, of course, was Jesus' favorite term to describe Himself; His use of it is recorded 83 times in the Gospels. When Jesus used this term He was not trying to show His identification with man, He was stating who He was—the *Messiah* of God. Now let us also look briefly at the Man Daniel saw in a later vision:

> *I raised my eyes and looked, and behold,* **a Man clothed in linen, around whose waist was a girdle of the purest gold. His body was like topaz, His face was like the appearance of lightning, His eyes were like flaming torches, His arms and feet shone like the color of burnished bronze, and when He spoke His voice was like the sound of a multitude** (Daniel 10:5–6 Author's translation).

Was this heavenly Man an angel? He was certainly not an ordinary man because men do not inhabit the heavens. Compare this Man in Daniel's vision to the Man in John's vision:

> *And in the midst of the seven lamp stands* **One like the Son of Man, clothed with a garment down to the feet and girded about the chest with a golden band. His head and hair were white like wool, as white as snow, and His eyes like a flame of fire; His feet were like fine brass, as if refined in a furnace, and His voice as the sound of many waters** (Revelation 1:13–15).

There are altogether too many similarities to dismiss these two as separate Beings. We know that the One in John's vision is the Lord Jesus, not an angel; furthermore, the expression *Son of Man* ties Him to the book of Daniel. If Jesus, exhibiting almost identical features and characteristics as the Man in Daniel's vision, was not an angel, then the Man in Daniel's vision is not an angel either.

Daniel's continuing narrative tells us that he was bereft of strength in the presence of this glorious Man and fell down with his face to the ground. Notice the similarity between Daniel's reaction in the presence of the heavenly Man, and the reaction of those in the presence of Jesus—the *heavenly Man* (1Corinthians 15:48–49) and God incarnate—at the time of His arrest:

> *When He said to them, "I am He," they drew back and* **fell to the ground** (John 18:6).

This, too, was Ezekiel's reaction to his vision of the throne of God and the Man that he saw above it, and above the four-winged living creatures:

Israel's Commander — Chapter 4

And above the firmament over their heads was the likeness of a throne, in appearance like a sapphire stone; on the likeness of the throne was a likeness with the appearance of a **Man** *high above it. Also from the appearance of* **His** *waist and upward I saw, as it were, the color of amber with the appearance of fire all around within it; and from the appearance of* **His** *waist and downward I saw, as it were, the appearance of fire with brightness all around. Like the appearance of a rainbow in a cloud on a rainy day, so was the appearance of the brightness all around it. This was the appearance of* **the likeness of the glory of the L**ORD. *So when I saw it,* **I fell on my face***, and I heard a voice of* **One** *speaking*
(Ezekiel 1:26–28).

Ezekiel saw *"***the likeness of the glory of the L**ORD*"*; that likeness took the form of a Man, as did the *Son of Man* in Daniel's first vision and the heavenly Man in his second vision. Each manifestation of this supernatural Man, beginning with His appearance to Joshua, is nothing less than a manifestation of the eternal Christ Jesus, the Son of God. We should remove from our minds forever the image of a "gentle Jesus, meek and mild." He demonstrated that He is not always so gentle, meek or mild when He made a horsewhip in John 2:15, and drove buyers and sellers out of the temple along with their sheep and oxen, poured out the coins of money changers on the ground and overturned their tables. Do we imagine that there were not enough Jews sufficiently irate with Him to try to stop Him? They could not! Jesus was God thinking God's thoughts and doing what God does. He is able to love passionately and He is able to hate just as passionately everything that is selfish and evil. God's love cannot make room for sin or selfishness. Jesus displayed the fury of God and even His eyes would have flashed enough to terrify those with whom He was enraged. Here, Jesus was restricted to a body of human flesh, but the day is coming when this awesome One shall be:

revealed from heaven with His mighty angels **in flaming fire taking vengeance on those who do not know God, and on those who do not obey the gospel** (2Thessalonians 1:7–8).

The New Testament is full of warnings about the coming judgments of God. Read the words of Jesus in the Gospels. Read Peter's warnings. Read the book of Jude. Read the book of Revelation; it is full of the wrath of God that is to be poured out upon the earth.

The God of Israel is merciful and compassionate but He also administers justice with a terrifying ruthlessness that makes the earth tremble. And in the book of Revelation we see Jesus, the conquering King at the head of His armies:

> *I saw heaven opened, and behold, a white horse. And* **He** *who sat on him was called* **Faithful** *and* **True***, and in righteousness* **He** *judges and makes war.* **His** *eyes were like a* **flame of fire***, and on* **His** *head were many crowns.* **He** *had a name written that no one knew except* **Himself***.* **He** *was clothed with a robe dipped in blood, and* **His** *name is called* **The Word of God***. And the* **armies in heaven***, clothed in fine* **linen***, white and clean, followed* **Him** *on white horses. Now out of* **His** *mouth goes a* **sharp sword***, that with it* **He** *should strike the nations. And* **He Himself** *will rule them with a rod of iron.* **He Himself treads the winepress of the fierceness and wrath of Almighty God***. And* **He** *has on* **His** *robe and on* **His** *thigh a name written:* King of Kings and Lord of Lords (Revelation 19:11–16).

Jesus, Eternal Son of the Living God, is "King of Kings and Lord of Lords," and as such, He would naturally go to war at the head of His armies. The Lord God of heaven and earth, the God of Israel, *has a controversy with the nations*. He is the absolute Sovereign Possessor of heaven and earth and has enormous forces and resources with which to wage war upon the nations. He also has the unwavering allegiance of Jesus—God incarnate, warrior King and Commander of the mighty angelic armies.

5

Israel's Prince

The nation of Israel is rated today (see page 61) as the fourth most powerful fighting force in the world. The explanation for this lies not with Israel's prowess on the battlefield but with the supernatural forces aligned with Israel against her enemies. Even back in Elisha's day, when the king of Syria sent his troops to surround Dothan, Elisha spoke comfort to his alarmed servant:

> *Do not fear, for **those who are with us are more than those who are with them**. And Elisha prayed, and said, "Lord, I pray, open his eyes that he may see." Then the Lord opened the eyes of the young man, and he saw. And behold, **the mountain was full of horses and chariots of fire all around*** (2Kings 6:16–17).

As with ancient Israel, so with modern Israel. In my book, *When Day and Night Cease*, I give modern examples of supernatural intervention on Israel's battlefields that awed Israelis and struck fear into the heart of the enemy. Israel's enemies may have thousands of modern tanks but:

> **the chariots of God are tens of thousands and thousands of thousands** (Psalms 68:17 NIV).

By American calculation 1,000 x 1,000 equals one million, but here we told that *"the chariots of God"* are *"thousands of thousands,"* in other words, there are millions of chariots in the armies of God. Modern Israel's famed battle tank is called the *Merkava*, which is the same Hebrew word used for the Lord's chariots:

> *For behold, the Lord will come with fire and with His **chariots**, like a whirlwind, to render His anger with fury, and His rebuke with flames of fire* (Isaiah 66:15).

Israel is the continuity of ancient Israel—Modern Israel is the fulfillment of prophecies given to ancient Israel. And both the miraculous and the supernatural, so evident in recorded historical events associated with God's chosen nation, are increasing in frequency as Israel draws closer to her divinely appointed destiny.

THERE IS ANOTHER INTENSELY POTENT, SUPERNATURAL force allied with Israel that we have not yet considered. Consider him we must, for he possesses the incomparable power of the Almighty, and whose sole task is watching over Israel and ensuring that it fulfills its destiny. Throughout both the Old and New Testaments we have numerous references to princes, or rulers. The Old Testament Hebrew word, *sar*, and the New Testament Greek word, *archon*, have identical meanings and are applied equally to either celestial or earthly beings. Our concern here, however, is with the celestial and not with the earthly. In Isaiah 9:6 Jesus is called *sar-shalom*, the *Prince of Peace*. In John 12:31 Satan is called *archon*, the *prince* (NIV, NEB, KJV, TLB, Moffatt, etc.), or *ruler of this world*. From these two examples alone, we understand that in the spiritual realm, "prince" means one holding great power and authority.

In the tenth chapter of the book of Daniel, we have the account of how Daniel fasted, prayed and mourned for three whole weeks, and at the completion of the fast:

> *I raised my eyes and looked, and behold, a **Man** clothed in linen, around whose waist was a girdle of the purest gold. **His** body was like topaz, **His** face was like the appearance of lightning, **His** eyes were like flaming torches, **His** arms and feet shone like the color of burnished bronze, and when **He** spoke **His** voice was like the sound of a multitude*
> (Daniel 10:5–6 Author's translation)

Daniel, like John in the book of Revelation, saw the heavenly manifestation of Jesus, Son of God, Son of Man. For want of a better term and a term that is not inconsistent with Scripture, I will, refer to the One seen in Daniel's vision as the Celestial Man.

The narrative in Daniel Chapter 13 tells us that the Celestial Man was sent to inform Daniel of future events concerning Israel. Although the Celestial Man was very powerful, He was opposed for three full weeks by the ruling spiritual power over Persia, the country known today as Iran. The Celestial Man was unable to get through to Daniel until assistance was provided:

> *The prince of the kingdom of Persia withstood Me twenty-one days; and behold,* **Michael, one of the chief princes, came to help Me**
> (Daniel 10:13).

We here get a clear picture of the power of a spiritual prince. Persia's prince could successfully withstand even the Celestial Man, impeding His mission. But we are introduced now to *Michael*, one of the chief princes, who came

Israel's Prince — Chapter 5

to the aid of the Celestial Man and put an end to the resistance of the prince of Persia.

To avoid confusion, we must entirely disassociate Jesus from all "created" princes. Jesus is *Son of God* because He is eternally and essentially related to the Father, and holds the office of *Prince of Peace*—a specific title. In the passage above, *Michael* is referred to as one of the *"chief princes."* The Hebrew terminology employed means *Michael* is much more than just "one" of the great princes of the angelic beings. He is, rather, the "first in rank," or the "foremost" of the great princes. And, according to the ninth verse of Jude, he is **"Michael the archangel."** The word *"archangel"* appears only twice in Scripture and then only in the singular form. Thus, *Michael* is either the first in rank and power of a very small, select group of angels or, more probably, the only one of a kind, being the first in rank and power of the entire angelic host.

The Hebrew name Michael, literally means "Who is as God." In its treatise on the archangel, the highly respected *Keil-Delitzsch Commentary on the Old Testament* says: **"Michael is thus the angel possessing the unparalleled power of God."**

This mighty archangel, the highest in rank of all the angelic host and possessing the immense power of God, is the Guardian Prince of Israel. The Celestial Man who spoke with Daniel referred to *Michael* as, *"your prince"* (Daniel 10:21). The "your" refers not just to Daniel, but to the whole nation of Israel:

> **Michael shall stand up, the great prince who stands watch over the sons of your people** ... And at that time **your people** shall be delivered (Daniel 12:1).

Three points concerning *Michael* are substantiated here: First, *Michael* is "the great prince," as opposed to, *"a"* great prince; second, Michael stands watch, or stands guard, over the people of Israel and is, indeed, the Guardian Prince of Israel; third, when *Michael* stands up, or takes action against those opposing Israel, he prevails because of the power that he possesses. Even the combined powers of hell are no match for Israel's Prince. Possessing the power of the Almighty, *Michael* and those under his command will always triumph:

> And war broke out in heaven: **Michael and his angels fought with the dragon**; and the dragon and his angels fought, but they did not prevail, nor was a place found for them in heaven any longer
> (Revelation 12:7–8).

If we read the entire twelfth chapter of the book of Revelation from which this passage is taken, we see that the *"dragon,"* or *"Satan,"* is pursuing the woman upon whose head is *"a garland of twelve stars."* The woman, obviously, is the nation of Israel; and *Michael*, Israel's Guardian Prince, deposes *Satan* and casts him and the angels of rebellion out of heaven, because they were a threat to the purposes of God for Israel.

If we take note, also, of the kings and kingdoms mentioned throughout chapters 10 and 11 in the book of Daniel, we understand that all the world powers were aligned against Israel. The Celestial Man, when referring to the kings, kingdoms and spiritual princes, says:

> **No one upholds Me** against these, **except Michael** your prince. Also in the first year of Darius the Mede, **I, even I, stood up to confirm and strengthen him** (Daniel 10:21, 11:1).

Michael and the Celestial Man are given the task of protecting Israel and enforcing God's decrees affecting the nation. *Michael* upholds the Celestial Man—the Commander of the LORD's army of warrior angels—and lends support as He strengthens or weakens earthly kings and kingdoms, and wages war

> **against principalities, against powers, against the rulers of the darkness of this age, against spiritual hosts of wickedness in the heavenly places** (Ephesians 6: 12).

History records that Darius the Mede, whom the Celestial Man strengthened, overthrew Babylon. The destruction of the Babylonian Empire, in turn, paved the way for the return of the Jews to their own land. Thus we see a direct result of the intervention of this awesome pair.

THE DIVINE POWER AVAILABLE FOR THE defence and protection of Israel cannot be described in human terms. The King of Creation, who spoke into the darkness and brought forth whole worlds, is Israel's God. The Commander of God's army of warrior angels is the Son of Israel's God. The Guardian Prince of Israel is *Michael*, who possesses the unparalleled power of Israel's God. Considering these facts, it is not at all surprising that despite overwhelming odds, Israel has emerged victorious from each of the ten wars waged against her since the establishment of the new state in 1948 until the year 2014.

We now know that it is not the prowess of Israel, but the awesome power of her God that determines the outcome of battle—a power that is vastly greater than the largest atomic bomb that man is capable of making.

Israel's Prince — *Chapter 5*

The power of one angel is more than that of an entire army, and there are more angels than opposing forces. The power of Israel's God is colossal, the future is determined, and, *the L*ORD *has a controversy with the nations*.

PART II

Israel

6

Israel: The Nation

In the eyes of many nations Israel is an obstacle to world peace and a major problem that affects, directly or indirectly, most of mankind. Israel is the world's headache, and how the world wishes it could simply swallow an aspirin and be rid of it. But Israel cannot be gotten rid of. Many have tried to eradicate her but it keeps reappearing, and its would-be destroyers are themselves brought to ruin. It is doubtful whether anyone has the full revelation concerning Israel; but for the God-fearing, Bible-grounded, twice-born Christian, Israel proves the accuracy and reliability of God's Word, and points toward a cataclysmic end of the age and the approaching Day of Judgment.

The Jewish people have been persecuted more than any nation in world history. They were first dispossessed of their God-given land by the Assyrian and Babylonian Empires around 2,700 years ago. But God, according to His Word, brought them back to their land, re-established the nation and totally destroyed the Assyrian and Babylonian empires. Another nation, Rome, arose to dominate the world, and this mighty empire again dispossessed the vast majority of Jews people from their Divine heritage and scattered them across the world. Today, nearly 2,000 years later, Israel is once again re-established as a nation on her God given land and is heavily engaged in bringing the millions of her exiled people home. Rome, on the other hand, is a city of crumbling monuments, of ruins which tell us that the Roman empire, too, has joined the long line of historical has-beens.

The history of the Jewish people is tragic. Descendants of Abraham, a God-fearing man of faith, Israel has waxed and waned in power and influence according to her levels of reverence and obedience to her God. The pinnacle of past glory was in the days of King David, and those of his son Solomon, some 3,000 years ago. Of David, God said:

I have found David the son of Jesse, a man after my own heart

(Acts 13:22).

Of Solomon, it is written:

Solomon surpassed all the kings of the earth in riches and wisdom

(1Kings 10:23).

FOUNDED BY A GOD-FEARING MAN, Israel rose high when led by other God-fearing men. But as ungodly kings took the seat of power and ruled, the glory ebbed. The glory of Israel and the glory of her God finally departed from the land, and as a disciplinary measure, the great majority of the inhabitants also departed—sent into a 70-year exile in Babylon (Jeremiah 29:10) by the God of Israel. But true to His *Word*, He brought them back to their land at the end of the decreed period.

Israel's delivering up of the Christ to the Romans and the peoples' insistence upon His crucifixion was its ultimate act of revolt against God, bringing His wrath upon that generation. Those that survived the sword were vomited from the Promised Land, and for nearly two millennia, they and their descendants became stateless wanderers, hounded, abused and murdered, driven from country to country in fear of their lives, but still clinging to the promise that one day God would:

reach out his hand a second time to reclaim the remnant of his people ... and gather the exiles of Israel ...from the four quarters of the earth
(Isaiah 11:11–12 NIV).

And this He is doing and continues doing in our present day.

THROUGHOUT IT LONG HISTORY ISRAEL HAS misinterpreted her election to God's purposes as an election of favoritism. As a result of this spiritual blindness, her appointed destiny still awaits her. Grace and love stooped down at Calvary and said, *"Father, forgive them"* (Luke 23:34). Jesus never prayed a prayer that was not to be answered, and therefore, forgiveness has been extended to Israel by her God:

Her iniquity is pardoned; for she has received from the LORD'S hand double for all her sins (Isaiah 40:2).

Israel, God says, *"is My son, My .firstborn"* (Exodus 4:22). A son needs discipline from his Father; the Father's discipline only proves His commitment to His son. The Lord Jesus is God's *"only begotten Son"* (John 3:16), *"yet it pleased the LORD to bruise Him"* (Isaiah 53:10). If it pleased the LORD to bruise His *only begotten Son,* the One of whom He said, *"in Him I am well pleased"* (Matthew 3:17), should we think it strange that He bruises Israel whom He called *"the dearly beloved of My soul?"* (Jeremiah 12:7). If it pleased the LORD to bruise the One who is His Salvation (Luke 2:30), should we think it strange that He bruises the one through whom His Salvation comes—*"for salvation is of the Jews"* (John 4:22)? Jesus, *"though He was a Son ... learned obedience by the things which He suffered"* (Hebrews 5:8). Israel, God's *"firstborn son,"* also learns obedience by its suffering.

Israel: The Nation — Chapter 6

THERE IS A COMMON MISBELIEF IN Christian circles concerning the names Jacob and Israel. The meaning of the name Jacob (*Ya'akov*) is traditionally taught to be "supplanter," and Israel (*Yisrael*) "a prince with God." However, "supplant" in Hebrew comes from an entirely different root and that meaning can be disregarded completely. Jacob (*Ya'akov*) comes from the Hebrew word *akov*, meaning "crooked" or, "deceitful," and is related to the Hebrew word *akav*—the "heel" of his brother Esau that Jacob took hold of at birth. The meaning of Jacob is clear in Scripture:

> *Isn't he rightly named Jacob? He has deceived me these two times* (Genesis 27:36 NIV).

The word translated as "deceived" is the Hebrew word *akov*. Deceitful, crooked Jacob, however, was renamed by the LORD:

> *Your name shall no longer be called Jacob, but Israel* (Genesis 32:28).

The name Israel (*Yisrael*) is made up from two Hebrew words, *yashar*, meaning "straight," and *El*, meaning "God." The meaning of the name Israel is, therefore, "Straightened of God." Only with a right understanding of the names is it possible to see the full implication of "Jacob" and "Israel." God deliberately chose those names to demonstrate His salvation and redemption of man through rebellious Jacob—the nation of Israel.

The spiritual significance of the names Jacob and Israel is nothing short of cosmic. Rebellion is common to all men with the Adamic nature. Deceit is also the inheritance of every man:

> *the heart is deceitful above all things, and desperately wicked; who can know it?* (Jeremiah 17:9).

The deceitfulness of the human heart deceives even the man in whose breast the heart beats. And the word translated here as "deceitful" is again the Hebrew word *akov*, from which the name Jacob is derived. But the "crooked" (again the Hebrew word *akov*, from which comes Jacob), the "deceitful," shall be made "straight" (Hebrew, *yashar*) by God (Hebrew, *El*), and thus we get the name *Yisrael*—Israel. We should now be able to comprehend the import of the following:

> *Prepare the way of the LORD; make* **straight** *in the [spiritual] desert a highway for our God. Every valley shall be exalted and every mountain and hill brought low; the* **crooked** *places shall be made* **straight** *and the rough places smooth* (Isaiah 40:3–4).

The deceitful and crooked heart of man shall be changed and straightened through the Salvation provided by the LORD. Every valley (the humble person) shall be exalted and every mountain and hill (the proud people) shall be brought low; nothing shall remain the same—*"Exalt the humble, and humble the exalted"* (Ezekiel 21:26). Israel is therefore an analogy, a picture of the wonderful salvation of our God. The LORD GOD chose *"the least of all nations"* (Deuteronomy 7:7), *"perverse and crooked"* (Deuteronomy 32:5), *"stubborn and rebellious"* (Psalms 78:8) with *"hearts like flint"* (Zechariah 7:12), to make them into *"a mighty nation"* (Genesis 18:18) with *"a heart of flesh"* (Ezekiel 11:19), that the nations shall know that *"I am the LORD, the Holy One in Israel"* (Ezekiel 39:7).

THE DESTINY OF ISRAEL IS TO be the channel through which salvation comes to all mankind. Chosen vessels always suffer. Jesus, channel for God's love and redemption, suffered. The great Apostle Paul, channel for God's good news to the Gentiles, suffered (2Corinthians 11:23–27). Israel, channel for God's salvation, channel for God's Holy Prophets, channel for the Holy Scriptures, and the channel for Jesus, the Holy One of God, suffers. Both Jesus and Paul ran the race and accomplished God's purposes even though they suffered ignominious deaths in the flesh.

Israel is accomplishing God's purposes also; however, since attaining statehood again in 1948 Israel is progressively being treated as the world's scapegoat, the cause of all that ails it. During this first century of the common era's third millennium Israel will likely capture the attention of the entire world and be the target of both its inherent anti-Semitic and anti-Christ venom, but this, too, is part of its destiny. And, as the LORD manifested His power in both Jesus and Paul, so He manifests His power in Israel:

> *"For I am with you," says the LORD of hosts. "According to the word that I covenanted with you when you came out of Egypt, so My Spirit remains among you; do not fear!"* (Haggai 2:45).

Israel is not to fear. The Spirit of the LORD GOD is working in the midst of it to remove every boulder strewn in the path of the Divine plan of salvation.

God has established Israel as an independent nation for the third and final time. Modern Israel was born out of the flames of the Holocaust that claimed the lives of six million of its people. And to welcome her into the modern world of nations, the day following her declaration of statehood on May 14, 1948, she was attacked by seven hostile, but powerful, trained, well-equipped Arab nations. With supernatural help Israel won that war as she has each of the subsequent wars waged against her.

Born into a world that cares for money above life or justice, Israel has been the target of a worldwide 67-year-long economic boycott designed to strangle her economically. But despite the boycott that has robbed her of at least US$100 billion in trade, Israel, in successive years has led the entire world in economic growth—triple the growth rate of the United States or Japan. Given that Israel has a divinely appointed destiny, and given that there are enormous supernatural powers marshaled to ensure that she will fulfill that destiny, it is clear that whoever is on Israel's side is on God's side and on the winning side. Whoever is on the other side is on the losing side— they cannot win; they will surely be destroyed.

7

Israel: The Key To Prosperity

Abram, whom God later renamed Abraham, was the father of the Jewish people and of the nation of Israel. Over 4,000 years ago, when he stood alone, without offspring, the LORD identified Abraham's cause with His own. He declared Abraham to be essentially connected to His plan of salvation, and also to the prosperity and the misfortune of all who came in contact with him:

> *Now the LORD had said to Abram: "Get out of your country, from your family and from your father's house, to a land that I will show you.* ***I will make you a great nation****; I will bless you and make your name great; and* ***you shall be a blessing. I will bless those who bless you, and I will curse him who curses you; and in you all the families of the earth shall be blessed"*** (Genesis 12:1–3).

God's promise to tie the well-being of those coming in contact with Abraham to the person of Abraham, was not limited to Abraham alone. The key to every nation's and every individual's prosperity now rests upon the attitude displayed toward Israel and the Jewish people, the descendants of Abraham. We know this because of the seven instances in the above passage where the LORD uses the pronoun "you," only four are applicable to Abraham, while all seven are true of his descendants. Abraham was never a great nation. He lived a full *"one hundred and seventy-five years"* (Genesis 25:7), but is recorded as having only 18 children and grandchildren. Some 560 years later, his descendants, through Isaac, became the fledgling nation of Israel; after a further 2,000 years had passed they became a great nation.

Abraham was not personally a blessing to many—it is his descendants that have been a blessing, and it is through them that all the families of the earth are being blessed. The contribution that the Jews have made to the world is enormous. They comprise less than one quarter of one percent of the world's population, yet they have produced more than ten percent of all the world's Nobel Prize winners. They have been "blessed" with talents, gifts, and intellect far beyond the norm. The genius of the Jews in the fields of science, medicine and the arts is legendary. Through the Jewish people came the Bible and Jesus, *"the Lamb of God who takes away the sin of the world"* (John 1:29). Of course we know that Jesus was and is the *"Son of God,"* but Jesus was born into this world as a Jew, and *"Jesus Christ is the* **same yesterday, today, and forever***"* (Hebrews 13:8). Let us never forget that Jesus was and is a Jew according to the flesh.

Later, when Abraham was still without offspring, God made another promise to him:

> *I am the L*ORD*, who brought you out of Ur of the Chaldeans,* **to give you this land to inherit it** (Genesis 15:7).

Although this promise was made directly to Abraham, we know that he never personally possessed or inherited the Promised Land:

> **God gave him no inheritance in it, not even enough to set his foot on** (Acts 7:5).

It is the descendants of Abraham, through Isaac, who have possessed and inherited the land, just as it is the descendants of Abraham, through Isaac, who have brought blessing to the world. When the LORD made the promises to Abraham He was, in effect, making them to the "seed" that was in Abraham's "loins" (compare Hebrews 7:5, 9–10). This is an important point that we need to carefully grasp. It is the descendants of Abraham, through Isaac, who not only have right of possession of the land of Canaan today, from the river of Egypt to the great river, the River Euphrates (Genesis 15:18), but who are also essentially connected to the prosperity and misfortune of all who come into contact with them.

There is, however, great misunderstanding concerning the first passage of Scripture we quoted from Genesis Chapter 12. This misunderstanding will remain as long as editors of popular, English Bible versions follow "traditional" renderings, rather than stepping out of the Christian comfort zone to break new ground. The portion where the misunderstanding lies is an oft-quoted favorite of many Christians. There is nothing at all wrong in spiritualizing the passage and applying it personally to oneself or to the Church (this is called eisegesis as opposed to exegesis), but it is actually directed to the Jewish people:

> *I will bless those who bless you, and I will curse him who curses you* (Genesis 12:3).

Israel: The Key To Prosperity — Chapter 7

The blessing and cursing is dependent upon man's attitude toward Abraham and his descendants. What is done to them is as if it were done to the LORD, and thus it is written of the Jewish people:

He who harms you sticks his finger in Jehovah's eye!

(Zechariah 2:8 TLB).

To "bless" means "to honor or to bestow favor upon," and God promises to do this to those who honor and favor Israel. However, the next segment, "*I will curse him who curses you,*" misleads us by being wrongly translated in the popular English versions, which use the same translation as the NKJ above. At first glance, it would seem to be a Divine tit-for-tat statement. But in Hebrew, the two words rendered as "curse" are quite different. They are not only different but poles apart in meaning and do not even come from the same root. The first Hebrew word is *arar*, and the second is *kilel*. There are only two instances in the Bible where these two words come together in a single verse, namely, the one that we are giving attention to and the following:

*You shall not **revile** God, nor **curse** a ruler of your people*

(Exodus 22:28)

Here, the word *kilel* is translated as "revile." It is exactly the same Hebrew word used in our verse in Genesis but translated quite differently. Now let us proceed and analyze what this means to us in real terms.

It is the LORD who is speaking. It is the LORD who will "bless," and it is the LORD who will "curse." The LORD's powerful blessing causes us to rejoice:

*The **blessing of the LORD** makes one rich, and He adds no sorrow with it* (Proverbs 10:22).

*I will ... open for you the windows of heaven and pour out for you **such blessing** that there will not be room enough to receive it* (Malachi 3:10).

The LORD's powerful judgments are found in His curses:

*So the LORD GOD said to the serpent: "Because you have done this, you are **cursed** more than all cattle, and more than every beast of the field; **on your belly you shall go**, and you shall eat dust all the days of your life"* (Genesis 3:14).

That serpent, or snake, once walked upon this earth like other four-legged animals. Most people are not aware that snakes have atrophied legs tucked up inside their bodies—a perpetual, living reminder of the dreadful power of God's judicial curse.

> Then to Adam He said, "Because you have heeded the voice of your wife, and have eaten from the tree of which I commanded you, saying, You shall not eat of it: **Cursed** is the ground for your sake; **in toil you shall eat of it all the days of your life**. Both **thorns and thistles it shall bring forth** for you, and you shall eat the herb of the field"
> (Genesis 3:17–18).

Adam originally ate food that was self-perpetuated from the soil. But after the LORD cursed the ground, mankind sweated, and still sweats, to bring forth food from the earth. The thistles and thorns that wage war against farmers and gardeners, and tear our skin and clothing, are a reminder of the curse upon the earth.

We see the tragic results of the curse of the LORD concerning Jericho (uttered from the lips of Joshua but, nevertheless, the word of the LORD—see 1Kings 16:34 below):

> **Cursed** be the man before the LORD who rises up and builds this city Jericho; he shall lay **its foundation with his firstborn, and with his youngest he shall set up its gates** (Joshua 6:26).

And later we read:

> In his days Hiel of Bethel built Jericho. He laid its foundation **with Abiram his firstborn**, and **with his youngest son Segub he set up its gates**, according to the word of the LORD, which He had spoken through Joshua the son of Nun (1Kings 16:34).

Hiel thought to rebuild Jericho and his firstborn son died as he laid the foundations. When he hung the gates to the city his youngest son died also.

In all three of the above passages (there are a number of others), the word rendered "curse" is, in the original Hebrew, *arar*. It means: "to execrate," "to denounce evil against," or "something that brings great harm or trouble." In contrast to this terrible word, we look at the second Hebrew word *kilel*. The word is highlighted below in its context, and several Bible versions are used to facilitate clear understanding of its meaning:

> When she saw that she had conceived, her mistress became **despised** in her eyes (Genesis 16:4 NKJ)

> You shall not **revile** God, nor curse a ruler of your people
> (Exodus 22:28 NKJ).

> Do not **blaspheme** God or curse the ruler of your people
> (Exodus 22:28 NIV).

Israel: The Key To Prosperity — Chapter 7

*Forty blows he may give him and no more, lest ... your brother be **humiliated** in your sight* (Deuteronomy 25:3 NKJ).

*They went into the temple of their god, ate and drank, and **ridiculed** Abimelech* (Judges 9:27 NRSV).

*I am **unworthy**—how can I reply to you?* (Job 40:4 NIV).

*I am **vile**; what shall I answer You?* (Job 40:4 NKJ).

*The LORD of hosts has purposed ... to bring into **contempt** all the honorable of the earth* (Isaiah 23:9 NKJ).

We have eight passages with eight different renderings of the same word from three of the most popular English versions of the Bible published in the United States. The following definitions are taken from *Webster's Unabridged Dictionary*:

Despise: to look down upon, to have a low opinion of

Revile: to be reproachful or abusive in speech

Blaspheme: to revile or speak reproachfully

Humiliate: to lower the pride or dignity of; to humble

Ridicule: words or actions intended to express contempt and excite laughter

Unworthy: without merit or value

Vile: cheap, base, of poor quality; very inferior

Contempt: the feeling or actions of a person toward some thing he considers low, worthless, or beneath notice

These definitions give a clear understanding of what is really being said in Genesis 12:3. The LORD has promised to curse, to bring great trouble and harm to those who have a low opinion of the Jewish people. The LORD promises to curse and bring great trouble upon those who cause the dignity or personal pride of the Jewish people to suffer. The LORD promises to curse and bring great trouble upon those who subject the Jewish people to ridicule. The LORD promises to curse and bring great trouble upon those who reproach the Jewish people or subject them to abusive language. The LORD promises to curse and bring great trouble upon those who think the Jew is lacking in worth or is inferior or beneath notice. The LORD promises to curse and bring great trouble upon those who speak reproachfully of His holy people, Israel. Just as the LORD, through Joshua, issued a warning concerning Jericho, so He also issues a warning to the nations regarding the Jews.

THE LORD PROMISES TO BLESS THOSE that bless Abraham and his offspring and, conversely, to curse those who hold them lightly in esteem. He made these promises more than 4,000 years ago, and the passing of the aeons of time has not eroded the blessing nor worn down the severity of the curse. What the LORD said to Abraham still stands today and millions of people, including a multitude of Christians, are skating on extremely thin ice with regard to the curse. It behooves us to heed the warning of the LORD concerning Israel. In blessing, we shall surely be blessed, and we shall just as surely be cursed if we do not have the right attitude toward the Jews, God's chosen, covenanted people.

8

Israel: God's Superpower

In today's modern world there are around 251 nations. They range territorially from tiny to vast, with populations varying from hundreds to more than 1.4 billion people. Cultures compass the entire gamut from virtual Stone Age to hi-tech, material wealth from abject squalor to indecent luxury, and mineral wealth from nothing to exceedingly rich. Militarily, they range from the spear, to the ability to dominate and dictate policy to the entire planet. Amid this diversity of nations dwells Israel. Israel has a very small land mass—7,847 square miles (20,323 square kilometers), about the size of the state of New Jersey in America. Israel's total population—both Jewish and Arab—recently topped 8,412,000 in September 2015.

Israel has a little mineral wealth, and no more material wealth than that which it has managed to accumulate since the formation of the Jewish state in an arid and barren land 67 years ago. But what is presented in world fact books, composed, collated and edited by man, is the antithesis of what is presented in the Bible—composed, collated and edited by God's Holy Spirit.

A STUDY OF COLLECTED "FACTS" CONCERNING the nation of Israel presents a picture of an already over-populated, struggling nonentity that is opposed and criticized by most of the world's other nations—it is the nation that the world loves to hate. The Bible, on the other hand, presents Israel as the center of the world, to which everyone and everything must go "up."

Israel is the first in rank and position of all the nations—**"the chief of the nations"** (Jeremiah 31:7; Amos 6:1).

Israel is the nation that shall be the wealthiest of all the nations:

> the **abundance of the sea** shall be turned to you, the wealth of the Gentiles shall come to you ... your gates shall be open continuously; they shall not be shut day or night, that men may bring to you the wealth of the Gentiles ... you shall eat the riches of the Gentiles ... gold, silver, and apparel in great abundance
>
> (Isaiah 60:5,11, 61:6; Zechariah 14:14).

Israel has recently (2008–2010) tapped into several offshore gasfields, including one of the world's largest. At the time of writing wells are being drilled deep into the plateau on the Golan Heights and substantial reserves of oil have been found. The billions of dollars from the Gentile nations that will pour into Israel's coffers is inestimable. Almost overnight, Israel became one of the world's foremost energy powers.

Israel is the nation that shall prove to be the most militarily powerful nation this world has ever known:

> *many nations have gathered against you ...but they do not know the thoughts of the* L<small>ORD</small>*, nor do they understand His counsel; for* **He will gather them like sheaves to the threshing floor**. *Arise and thresh, O daughter of Zion; for I will make your horn iron, and I will make your hooves bronze;* **you shall beat in pieces many peoples** *... Behold, I will make you into a new threshing sledge with sharp teeth; you shall thresh the mountains and beat them small, and make the hills like chaff You shall winnow them, and the wind shall carry them away, and the whirlwind shall scatter them ...* **You are My battle-ax and weapons of war: for with you I will break the nation in pieces; with you I will destroy kingdoms** *... For the* L<small>ORD</small> *of hosts will visit His flock, the house of Judah, and will make them as His royal horse in the battle ... the one who is feeble among them in that day shall be like David, and the house of David shall be like God, like the Angel of the* L<small>ORD</small> *before them* (Micah 4:11, 12–13; Isaiah 41:15, 16; Jeremiah 51:20; Zechariah 10:3, 12:8).

The above prophecies are all post exilic and have yet to be fulfilled. And as I clearly showed in the study of prophecy presented in my book *When Day and Night Cease*, Bible teaching does not stand or fall upon "interpretation" of prophecy. Prophecies should not be "interpreted." Fulfillment of prophecy is recognized after the fulfillment, or at the actual moment of fulfillment. However, it is abundantly clear from the Scriptures that there is only one world power at the close of this age—Israel. She will be wealthy with the riches of the Gentiles and mighty with the power of God. Israel is like a capstone that fits nowhere except at the top. And until Israel finds her place at the top of the nations she will simply be a *"burdensome stone for all the peoples"* (Zechariah 12:3). Israel will prove to be the world's future "superpower." To unregenerate, obtuse intellects, this is, of course, simply ludicrous. Leaders of nations, world powers, former world powers and disintegrating world powers, will scoff at both the Bible and the picture of

Israel that it presents. And this will most likely be the root cause of their total undoing.

The United States, currently the wealthiest and most powerful nation on earth, needs to pay close attention to the demise of her former foe, the Soviet Union. The former Soviet Union was the largest country in the world—two and-a-half times that of the United States and had the largest oil and natural gas deposits in the world. Her population far exceeded that of the United States and she also possessed one of the most powerful military fighting forces in history. Soviet leaders, however, opposed Israel from every direction, persecuted the country's Jews and denied them the right to emigrate to Israel. Today, there is no Soviet Union. In its wake came economic disaster, war, turmoil, strife, poverty, privation and starvation.

For her part, Israel never lifted a finger nor fired a shot. Her God, the God of the Bible, took care of it, demonstrating to the nations of the late twentieth century and those of the new millennium, that size, position, power and material wealth is as transient as that of the nations of the ancient world.

SOME OF THE PROPHECIES GIVEN ABOVE are coming to at least a partial fulfillment today. It has already been mentioned that Israel has led the world in successive past years in industrial growth; exports are up and imports are down—the wealth of the Gentiles is beginning to come to the Jewish state. According to *Tishrei*, a Christian magazine, Israel is rated the fourth most powerful fighting force in the world, next only to the United States, Russia, and China. In January 1993, *Israel Radio* referred to an article published in *The New York Times* in which Israel was rated as the fifth world nuclear power, sharing equal place with Britain, and following the United States, Russia, China, and France.

Israel has a deliberate policy of ambiguity insofar as its nuclear capabilities are concerned, neither admitting to possessing nuclear weapons nor denying that it has stockpiled them. However, in March 2015, in what was largely missed by the mainstream media, and which can only be described as an act of revenge by US President Barack Obama against Israel's Prime Minister Binyamin Netanyahu, with whom he had cold relations, Ari Yashar and Matt Wanderman reported that the Pentagon quietly declassified a Department of Defense top-secret document detailing Israel's nuclear program.

By publishing the declassified document the US actively breached the silent agreement to keep quiet on Israel's nuclear powers. The document detailed the nuclear program in great depth.

The document notes that nuclear research laboratories in Israel were equivalent to the key American laboratories which were developing the U.S. nuclear arsenal.

The declassified document also showed that Israel, even in the late 1980s, was developing the kind of codes that would enable it to create hydrogen bombs—thermonuclear bombs considered a thousand times more powerful than atom bombs.

THE FACT THAT ISRAEL'S TINY ARMY is compared to the armies of the great nations is because she does not fight alone; she has, as we have already seen, formidable angelic help. The size of Israel's army is irrelevant. The Divine help afforded her will always be in relation to the foes opposing her on the battle-front. It has been documented by British military historian Ian V. Hogg in his book *Israeli War Machine*, that in the 1948 War of Independence, Israel fielded only around 18,000 men against seven powerful, trained and fully equipped Arab armies. Hogg shows Israel so ill-equipped that many of its men went into battle without even a weapon. Still, Israel overwhelmingly defeated the enemy and Charles Gulston writes in *Jerusalem: The Tragedy and the Triumph*:

> Although the sun did not stand still during the War of Liberation, it is said that the bees fought for Israel when the enemy was approaching Tel Aviv. Swarms of these creatures from the groves east of Petah Tikva, the oldest Jewish agricultural settlement, whose name means "door of hope," attacked the Arabs; Egyptians surrendered when they believed they were surrounded by a vast army; and sickness immobilized a combined Syrian and Lebanese force in Galilee.

The 1967 Six-Day War—in which Israel decimated five opposing armies in a lightning blitz—is written in military annals as one of the classic pieces of warfare in history. And, taken by surprise on Yom Kippur (the Day of Atonement), the holiest and most solemn day of the Jewish year—when there were no vehicles on the roads, no radio, television or newspapers, and few people would answer the telephone if it rang—Israel was attacked on two fronts by a combined force of more than 1,200,000 men from fourteen nations, and thousands of tanks and fighter-planes. Egypt and Syria were the main antagonists, and together their armies comprised more than one million of the attacking force.

Coming out of the synagogues after a five-hour service, the Israelis found themselves in their most costly war, in terms of both money and lives. It took the Israelis three days to fully mobilize their 300,000 regular and reserve soldiers and another seven to rout the enemy, inflicting terrible loss of life. The Soviet Union, which had equipped and trained the attacking armies, found its equipment was being blown to fragments by the Israelis, and was humiliated. The Kremlin sent thinly veiled threats to the White House that it would remove Israel from the world map with missiles if the U.S. did not force Israel into a cease-fire. The White House responded, forcing Israel to stop attacking the retreating armies by cutting off her military supplies and even threatening to arm Egypt and Syria if she did not cease immediately. When the cease-fire went into effect, Israeli troops were only short distances from Damascus (capital of Syria) and Cairo (capital of Egypt).

The power of man, no matter how great, is, compared with Divine power, like a toy tossed about in a tornado. Each of Israel's wars have been liberally sprinkled with supernatural manifestations that have been recorded for posterity.

WAR, UNFORTUNATELY, WILL PLAY A LARGE part in Israel's future. Christians generally abhor even the very thought of war due to their near universal pacifism. Centuries of Church teaching has bred a pacifistic mentality that has no Scriptural foundation. It is naive to think that wars will cease or even decrease before the second coming of the Lord from heaven. On the contrary, the Bible tells us that wars will increase as the Day draws nigh. Millions of Christians pray daily for the peace of Jerusalem, and have done so for nearly 2,000 years, but this has accomplished nothing, except perhaps, hastening the coming of the Lord. The results of two millennia of prayer for the city's peace contradict the teaching that God **always** answers prayer, because Jerusalem has suffered more wars, and seen more bloodshed, than any other city in the world! It has been said that if blood was indelible, Jerusalem would be red—all red. Jerusalem, the Bible informs us, is one of the greatest stumbling blocks to world peace and will be the cause, and site, of cataclysmic wars of devastation:

> *I will also gather **all nations**, and bring them down to the Valley of Jehoshaphat; and I will enter into judgment with them there on account of my people, My heritage Israel .... Their flesh shall dissolve while they stand on their feet, their eyes shall dissolve in their sockets, and their tongues shall dissolve in their mouths* (Joel 3:2; Zechariah 14:12).

That which is portrayed in Zechariah 14:12 would certainly seem to point to nuclear, biological, or chemical warfare. One particular war described by the prophet Zechariah will be of such intensity and magnitude that few from any of the nations will survive. But those that do survive will most certainly have gained a fresh understanding of Israel and a keen appreciation of the God of Israel:

> Then the **survivors** from all the nations that have attacked Jerusalem will go up year after year to worship the King, the LORD Almighty
> (Zechariah 14:16).

PRAYER, WHEN DONE ACCORDING TO THE will of God, accomplishes great things, but when done outside of His will accomplishes nothing. Thus, when Christians pray for the peace of Jerusalem, they are out of the will of the LORD because He never commanded us to do this. Yes, there is a verse in our English Bible versions, Psalms 122:6, that reads: *"Pray for the peace of Jerusalem: may they prosper who love you,"* but that is a very bad translation of the Hebrew text. In previous chapters, I have already said enough about tradition and incorrect, misleading translations of the Bible to start a holy war, and I really do not want to be caught in the crossfire by touching one of the most oft-quoted verses in the Scriptures. But *Pray for the peace of Jerusalem* is another "traditional" rendering that has little substance. It is, as they say in Yiddish, a *bubbemeiser*—a grandmother's story. But it is so much part of Church tradition that no Bible manufacturer would dare to change it even if they knew the correct way to translate it, which is doubtful. Stay with me here and I will explain: There is nothing wrong with the latter part of the verse, *"may they prosper who love you;"* it is totally kosher. But the first portion, in Hebrew, is: *"Shalu Shlom Yerushalayim."* The Hebrew word *shalu* comes from the verb *sha'al* and should never, never be translated "pray"—ever! Of the 168 occurrences in the Hebrew Scriptures, the early translators chose only this verse in Psalms 122 to translate *sha'al* as "pray;" this could only have been done through a misunderstanding of the import of the phrase. In every other instance they translated *sha'al* correctly: "ask," "inquire," "request," "salute" (greet), etc.

On the other hand, the Hebrew word for "pray" is the verb *palal*, and in each of the 83 instances where it occurs in the Hebrew Scriptures, it is translated correctly as "pray," "intercede" (in prayer) or "supplicate" (in prayer). So, what does all this mean? The answer is really quite simple: Most readers are aware that *shalom* means "peace." They are also aware that *Shalom!* is the way Israelis say "hello," and "goodbye." So, when Israelis meet, they greet others with "Peace!" And when they part, their last word to each other is "Peace!" When Jesus first appeared to the gathered disciples, He said, in Hebrew, *"Shalom alechem!"* — "Peace to you!" (Luke 24:36; John 20:19, 21, 26). After Israelis greet each other with "Peace!," they will then ask how you are by saying, *"Ma shlom cha?"*—literally, "What

Israel: God's Superpower — Chapter 8

is your peace?"—the *shlom*, as in Psalms 122:6, being the contracted pronunciation of *shalom*. Now, Psalms 120–134 are the Psalms of Ascent, that is, the Psalms that were recited, chanted, or sung, as the Israelites made the long, slow journey from their cities and villages up to Jerusalem for the appointed feasts of the Lord (see Exodus 23:14–17). Those that were traveling up to Jerusalem were cared for in the towns and villages along the way, in the homes of people who were not going up to the feast that year. As the travelers set out again on their journey, the hosts would say to the hosted, "*Shalu Shlom Yerushalayim!*"—literally, "Ask the peace of Jerusalem," but, in today's vernacular, "Say 'Hello' to Jerusalem" for me. The verse in Psalms 122 should, therefore, read: *"Greet Jerusalem: may they prosper who love you."* If the reader desires to pray for the peace of Jerusalem, the reader would be better advised to pray John's prayer at the end of Revelation: *"Even so, come, Lord Jesus!"* Peace can only come to Jerusalem after *Messiah* comes to reign in His city—*"the City of the Great King"* (Psalms 48:2). Since Jerusalem is to be the scene of judgment for many nations and must experience much, much more bloodshed before *Messiah* comes, we should pray the Lord that *"in judgment, [He] remember[s] mercy"* (Habakkuk 3:2).

As the disciples traveled to Bethany with Jesus, not realizing that He was about to ascend to the right hand of the Father, they asked Him a question that they had been anxious about for some time:

Lord, **will You at this time restore the kingdom to Israel?** (Acts 1:6).

The kingdom to which they were referring was, of course, the Kingdom of David. David's Kingdom raised Israel high above the nations, to the acme of power and influence. Its army was undefeated in battle, even when it was divided into two forces and fighting separate armies simultaneously (2Samuel 10:6–19). The military defeats and subjugation of Israel's enemies paved the way for the golden era of peace and prosperity under the rule of David's son, and people *"came from the ends of the earth to hear the wisdom of Solomon"* (Matthew 12:42). But Jesus' reply to His disciples' question is significant:

It is not for you to know times or seasons which the Father has put in His own authority (Acts 1:7).

He did not respond in the negative to the question, merely said that it was not for them to know when the kingdom would be restored to Israel. Indeed, we have an Old Testament confirmation that the kingdom of power and prosperity will return to Israel:

> *I will assemble* the lame, *I will gather* the outcast and those whom I have afflicted; *I will make* the lame a remnant, and the outcast **a strong nation**; so the LORD will reign over them in Mount Zion from now on, even forever. And you, O tower of the flock, the stronghold of the daughter of Zion, **to you shall it come, even the former dominion shall come, the kingdom of the daughter of Jerusalem**
>
> (Micah 4:6–8).

There is to be a gathering of the lame and the outcasts—the afflicted of the LORD—and this is happening today. The young, modern State of Israel is now populated with Jews who have returned from more than 140 different nations. It is this collection of outcasts that the LORD has promised to make into a strong nation, and it is to this nation that the *"dominion,"* or power, shall come—*"the kingdom of the daughter of Jerusalem."* In just a few short years, the survivors of the Holocaust and their progeny have developed into the fourth most powerful army in the world and share fifth place in the ranks of nuclear powers. But Israel is yet to develop into the most formidable military power this world will ever see. The corpses of the enemy in the war with *"Gog of the land of Magog,"* described in Ezekiel Chapters 38 and 39, will take Israel seven months to bury (Ezekiel 39:11–12). This is not at all implausible. After the Six-Day War, a correspondent wrote:

> Israeli burial squads have gone down to Sinai to inter 10,000 Egyptians killed during the headlong Israeli rush on the Suez Canal. Their bodies, putrefied and swarming with flies, have been lying for almost ten days on the blazing sands of Sinai. Of the army of 120,000, only about 3,000 have been taken prisoner.

The nations need to understand that the Almighty, the LORD of armies—God of Israel, and His mighty angelic forces—will fight for Israel with greater than atomic power, and deliver the enemy into her hands:

> *it is the* LORD GOD *of [armies], He who touches the earth and it melts*
>
> (Amos 9:5).

The Jewish people went defenseless to the slaughter during the Holocaust, but both Israel and her God have determined that it will never happen again.

The Israelis have also determined that there will never be a repetition of what happened at Masada in 73 AD. During the war against Rome, Israel was hopelessly outnumbered, and less than a thousand Jews held the mountain fortress of Masada in the Judean desert despite a two-year siege. When the Romans finally broke through the walls, they found only corpses. During the night 960 Jews had taken their own lives rather than surrender.

Israel: God's Superpower — Chapter 8

Today, many officers, recruits and graduates of Israeli military academies, take their oath of allegiance in the 2,000-year-old ruins of Masada, and swear that "Masada shall not fall again." Israel does not fight for a cause or an ideology, but for survival, and her God is lending more than a helping hand.

ONE WAY THE GOD OF ISRAEL has helped His people is by delivering enemy equipment into their hands. Some of Israel's military hardware is made up of enemy equipment. Israel strips, assesses and refurbishes captured equipment, increasing armaments and strengthening vulnerable areas, and often puts it into use against those from whom it was captured. When the Soviet Union sold its most sophisticated MiG-23 fighter-plane to Israel's enemies in 1989, Israel desperately needed to get a close look at it, to assess its capabilities and vulnerabilities so the IAF could bring it down quickly in battle. In an unprecedented incident during a training flight on October 11, 1989, a Syrian Air Force major defected to Israel with his MiG-23, the first such aircraft to reach the West. The technology provided by the plane proved invaluable for the skilled, battle-hardened Israeli pilots in aerial encounters with that type of war-plane.

In this day and age the LORD is gathering the exiles of Israel and building them into a mighty nation; and it is during the time of this ingathering that the LORD promises to bring the nations against Jerusalem (Joel 3: 1). But as has been demonstrated over and over again since the founding of the modern state, it is not a time for fear:

Behold, He who keeps Israel shall neither slumber nor sleep
(Psalms 121:4).

During the Gulf War of 1991, for example, Iraq launched 39 SCUD missiles against Israel, and 31 found their targets. (In contrast to what the media presented as the truth, the Patriot anti-missile systems were very ineffective in both Israel and Saudi-Arabia and did not bring down a single missile.) The missiles destroyed or damaged some 5,000 homes, but miraculously, only two people were killed by direct hits. Several others died from shock or shock-related heart attacks.

When wailing Tel Aviv sirens signaled the first of the missile attacks, people in the suburb of Tikva (Hope) rushed to the bomb shelter in the center of town only to find it locked and no one with the key. Having been warned that they would have only two minutes to reach the specially prepared sealed rooms in the event of a chemical attack, they quickly ran to other public shelters nearby. Seconds later the missile hit the locked shelter and exploded 13 feet (four meters) underground; the shelter was totally destroyed, and nearby buildings were damaged. There is now a monument on the site of the shelter in recognition of God's intervention—a six-winged seraphim as depicted in Isaiah Chapter 6.

MISSILE WARFARE IS NOT A NEW phenomenon. The forerunners of the modem missile were the V1 and V2 rockets introduced by the Germans during World War II. These rockets were more destructive psychologically than materially, but today, ballistic missiles are daily becoming more sophisticated, their accuracy and payload more deadly. During the Gulf War, probably for fear of an Israeli atomic reprisal, Iraq fitted only conventional warheads on the missiles fired at Israel and not the chemical warheads promised by Saddam Hussein. Chemical warfare (various types of poisonous gases) was introduced by the Germans in World War I, but because of the extremely horrific results, it was banned from use, and in 1982 the UN General Assembly imposed a further ban on the use of poison gas. Not withstanding, huge amounts of chemical weapons have been manufactured and stockpiled in the arsenals of all the major military powers and many of the Arab states. Egypt used mustard gas in Yemen during the 1960's and Syria killed 20,000 of its own people with the use of cyanide gas in 1982, and in its five-year civil war which has thus far killed in excess of 250,000 people, Syria has repeatedly used chemical weapons, both against civilians and protagonists fighting the al-Assad regime, also with horrific results.

Both sides in the Iran-Iraq war used massive quantities (1,000 tons) of nerve gas against each other, and Iraq also killed thousands of its Kurdish civilians with chemical weapons in 1988.

Biological warfare was banned in 1972, but biological weapons such as anthrax are still being manufactured by several nations. A missile fitted with an anthrax warhead has the same killing potential as an atomic or nuclear warhead but causes only a fraction of the material devastation. Anthrax can remain active and lethal for decades after its initial delivery and dispersion.

Due to the thousands of missiles being periodically fired at Israel from Gaza and Lebanon, Israel has developed a three-tier missile defense system: Iron Dome for short-range projectiles like mortars, Grad, Katyusha and other similar short-range missiles; David's Sling (also known as Magic Wand) for midrange missiles—300–1,000 miles (480–1,600 kilometers); and the supersonic Arrow for medium-range missiles 1,850–3,500 miles (3,000–5,000 kilometers) and Intercontinental Ballistic Missiles (ICBMs) which can travel above the earth's atmosphere. The Arrow is also a deterrent and

Israel: God's Superpower — Chapter 8

a means of defence against both mid-range and medium-range missiles carrying conventional, nuclear, chemical, or biological warheads. The Arrow can explode a hostile missile in the enemy's territory within seconds of its launch, dispersing the warhead's payload onto the aggressor's own civilian population. The details of the Arrow III system under development are classified, but it is known to reach an absolutely incredible velocity, climbing higher and faster than its predecessors and able to withstand accelerations of several hundred gravities.

ISRAEL ALSO PURSUES A LIMITED SPACE program designed to furnish it with intelligence on military equipment and troop movements. Hundreds of scientists, engineers, and technicians are involved in the program, including a number from the former Soviet Union. Since 1988, amid great secrecy, Israeli satellites have undergone successful launch and retrieval, and at the time of writing in 2015 Israel has six series of satellites orbiting the earth providing all forms of data. Israel is one of only six countries in the world with indigenous launch and retrieval capabilities. In November 2015 Israel formerly joined forces with NASA in a venture to put a man on Mars.

Eventually, this tiny nation, disparaged and despised, is going to be the cause of a rude awakening for many nations:

> **Multitudes, multitudes in the valley of decision! For the day of the LORD is near in the valley of decision. The sun and moon will grow dark, and the stars will diminish their brightness. The LORD also will roar from Zion, and utter His voice from Jerusalem; the heavens and earth will shake; but the LORD will be a shelter for His people, and the strength of the children of Israel** (Joel 3:14–16).

Let us not be deceived. The LORD GOD of Israel has not brought His people back to be incinerated or annihilated by hostile nations. He has brought them back to show His power through them and bring the nations to their knees—in worship. God acts first for His own glory, and then for the greatest good of the largest number of people for the longest period of time. Israel's role is extremely important in the plans of the LORD. World War I raged for four years and cost the lives of 11 million soldiers and civilians, but, within 11 days of Palestine being wrested from the grip of Islam, the war ceased. And if God was willing to allow the deaths of a further 49 million people in World War II (including six million of His chosen people by systematic murder), in order to establish the State of Israel in Palestine, what is He willing to allow in order to make His presence and salvation known to all men? Almost 3,000 years ago, *"Zerah the Ethiopian came out against [Israel] with an army of a million men and three hundred chariots"* (2Chronicles 14:9) but they could not stand against Israel. And only 22 two years ago, combined Arab armies comprising more than a million men, along with thousands of tanks—iron chariots—came against Israel; and the Arabs fared no better than did the Ethiopians. Soon, it will be the turn of other powers to confront Israel, and as David slew Goliath, so Israel will slay the giant military powers:

> *for the* L*ORD* *has a controversy with the nations; He will plead His case with all flesh. He will give those who are wicked to the sword*
> (Jeremiah 25:31).

PART III

*Judgment
Executed*

9

Judgment

After the flood, the great deluge that destroyed all the inhabitants of the earth except the eight members of Noah's family—Noah and his wife, their three sons, Shem, Ham and Japheth and their wives—the Lord swore an oath:

Never again shall all flesh be cut off by the waters of the flood; never again shall there be a flood to destroy the earth (Genesis 9:11).

The beautiful rainbow that contains all the colors of the spectrum, seen and admired by billions of this world's inhabitants, is God's confirming sign of the covenant that He made with the earth. (Today, the rainbow colors have been hijacked by sodomite and lesbian homosexuals. Much of the Western world now condones what God condemns, but God will surely have the last laugh on the Day of Judgment.) Every nation that existed prior to the flood perished. God started over again with mankind, and every nation large or small that exists today, stems from the sons of Noah. The Lord made a covenant that He would never again destroy all flesh with a flood, but He never covenanted not to destroy, punish or discipline nations individually or corporately. On the contrary, He promised **"not to leave the guilty unpunished**," and that He would punish:

the children and their children for the sin of the fathers to the third and fourth generation (Exodus 34:7 NIV).

Some will undoubtedly opine that this is unfair. But what is gained by charging God with injustice? He is *the "Habitation of Justice"* (Jeremiah 50:7) and *"the Judge of all the earth"* (Genesis 18:25). This is God's world. He makes the rules and man makes his choice. Man can choose to abide by God's rules or suffer the consequences of his rebellion.

When we study the Biblical accounts of nations that came under God's judgment throughout the millennia, we find that each of their sins are exposed for posterity. By exposing a nation's sin the Lord clearly warns other nations that to commit the same sin is to invite the same judgment. We can, therefore, from the examples provided for us, find many of the unwritten rules of God by which we must comply, or perish. We can discern the lines over which we are not to cross, and, by simple deduction, arrive at a scenario for the future, which is horrifying in the extreme. The only way to change this scenario is for nations to conduct serious soul searching, followed by genuine repentance on a national level. In a study of the judged nations we find that they had all sinned in some way against Israel, as well as committing various other sins. It is evident that sins against Israel carried some of the heaviest judgments, occasionally resulting in the total extinction of the offending nation. Besides the direct link to Israel, there are political, social, moral, and religious sins that should strike fear into the hearts of our leaders. And it is interesting to see that the most catastrophic of judgments are directly carried out by angels, giving further credence to what has been said previously regarding the function of these heavenly messengers.

Let us now look at a number of examples of judged nations, discern the sins which brought the judgments, and the degrees of severity of the judgments inflicted. God alone is the arbiter, but there are, obviously, different degrees of sinfulness attached to particular sins; otherwise all judgments would carry the same ratio of severity—which they do not. By investigating the reasons for the judgment of past nations and the degree of judgment attached to their sins, we can apply the results to the modern world. In order to keep this book from becoming overly long we must obviously limit the number of contemporary nations to which we apply our study. But, irrespective of his tribe or tongue, the reader will be able, if he is anywhere near abreast of his particular nation's political, moral, social and religious positions, to predict, with reasonable accuracy and certainty, what will befall it unless national repentance is forthcoming. The very large and very wicked city of Nineveh repented to a man, in dust and ashes, because of the preaching of one man—Jonah. Who knows what calamities might be averted if God-fearing, born-again Christians rose up and preached in their own cities a similar message to that of Jonah: *"Yet forty days, and Nineveh shall be overthrown"* (Jonah 3:4).

10

Judged

It is a universally recognized that history has a habit of repeating itself, yet man never seems to learn from the lessons of history. When we study the judgments inflicted by a righteous God upon unrighteous nations we find the cause and effect of those judgments. We find, also, that warnings are clearly spelled out for the benefit of other nations. Every Christian is a watchman—God's appointed watchman upon the walls of their city. If the watchmen fail to clearly spell out the warnings to the leaders and governments of their nations, they shall be held accountable:

> *If the watchman sees the sword coming and does not blow the trumpet, and the people are not warned, and the sword comes and takes any person from among them,* **he is taken away in his iniquity; but his blood I will require at the watchman's hand** (Ezekiel 33:6).

IT BEHOOVES US TO EVALUATE THE lessons of history. The same principles that triggered judgment 4,000 years ago triggered judgment 2,000 years ago, and will also trigger it today, and in 100 or 1,000 years time. In assessing the sins that brought judgment to the nations of the ancient world we should realize that neither the actual nation, nor its size, is important. The "superpowers" of the ancient world suffered no less than the insignificant nations—for the LORD shows *"no partiality nor takes a bribe"* (Deuteronomy 10:17). Only the nature of the sin and the judgment it brought is of any importance.

The nation of Israel, of necessity, is mentioned a number of times in the following section. I say of necessity, because 90 percent of the entire Bible, both Old and New Testaments, directly relates to the nation of Israel. The ratio of reference in this section to Israel does not mean that Israel was more wicked than any other nation, nor should it be construed that way. In the Bible the entire 4,000-year-plus history of Israel is laid bare for all to see. Most nations today would blush crimson if all their dirty laundry were to be aired in public as Israel's has been. Let us, therefore, look at the actions and their consequences, rather than at the nation.

SINS OF BIBLE NATIONS

SODOM AND GOMORRAH

The first recorded judgment upon a nation after the flood was upon the cities of Sodom and Gomorrah:

> And the LORD said, "Because **the outcry against Sodom and Gomorrah is great**, and because their sin is very grave, **I will go down now and see whether they have done altogether according to the outcry** against it that has come to Me" (Genesis 18:20–21).

From the above passage we can learn the first principles concerning God, sin and judgment. Notice, first, that a cry ascends to God when sin abounds. There are several other examples where cries for justice have reached God's ears, the first being that whenever man's blood is shed it cries out to God for justice. After Cain murdered Abel, his brother, the LORD said to Cain:

> The voice of your brother's blood **cries out to Me** from the ground (Genesis 4:10).

When the Israelites were made slaves in Egypt, *"their **cry came up to God** because of the bondage"* (Exodus 2:23–24), and *"God heard their cry"* (Exodus 3:7) and said, *"I have come down to deliver them"* (Exodus 3:8). When man is unjustly afflicted the cry of affliction calls to God for justice, and the LORD personally intervenes.

The cries of the cheated call for justice against the cheat:

> The wages of the laborers who mowed your fields, which you kept back by fraud, **cry out; and the cries** of the reapers have **reached the ears of the LORD** of Sabaoth (James 5:4).

The callous and greedy dealings of the rich and powerful, the deceitful and dishonest business transactions, all cry out to God for justice.

    Notice, too, that the LORD Himself is the One who ascertains whether the cries for justice are valid. He does not act on hearsay, nor is He moved by the petitions of the saints without investigation of the charges. All sin results in a cry for justice ascending to the LORD, and the LORD personally substantiates the truth of the cry.

The foremost sin that brought judgment to the cities of Sodom and Gomorrah was sexual perversion—"sodomy." The modern world prefers to speak of sodomy in a "nicer," more "acceptable" terms—gay, or homosexual. However, the word sodomy comes from the sin attributed to Sodom, and encompasses perverted sexual acts between males, between females, between males and animals, and also between brother and sister, father and daughter, mother and son *et al*. Trying to clean up the term for sexual perversion between humans of the same sex does not make it any the less perverted. *"**It is an abomination**"* (Leviticus 18:22), and it is described in the New Testament as *"**filthy conduct**"* (2Peter 2:7). It will bring the judgment of God upon those that commit, condone, justify, and legalize it—including the many church leaders and members who are now involved. This sin is so heinous in the eyes of God that only four people survived the wrath which was poured out upon Sodom and Gomorrah—the other inhabitants were exterminated.

The *"outcry"* that came to God was *"**against** Sodom and Gomorrah."* The inhabitants of those cities were in the habit of ill-treating strangers passing through the area and this, too, is an abomination to the Lord, who cares for the stranger as much as He does for the orphan and widow:

> **He administers justice** *for the fatherless and the widow, and loves* **the stranger** (Deuteronomy 10:18).
>
> **You shall neither mistreat a stranger nor oppress him**
> (Exodus 22:21).
>
> *If a* **stranger** *dwells with you in your land,* **you shall not mistreat him** *.... The stranger who dwells among you shall be to you as one born among you, and* **you shall love him as yourself** (Leviticus 19:33–34).

Lot, practicing the Biblical injunction to be hospitable to strangers and unaware that the travelers he met at the city's gate were destroying angels, insisted they spend the night in his home and made a great feast for them. Later, the males of Sodom came and demanded that Lot's guests be given them for gratifying their sexual lusts and perversions. Lot pleaded with the Sodomites:

> *Please, my brethren, do not do so wickedly! See now, I have two daughters who have not known a man; please, let me bring them out to you, and you may do to them as you wish; only* **do nothing to these men** (Genesis 19:7–8).

Lot was willing to give his daughters—his own flesh and blood—rather than have the men under his roof subjected to such an outrageous indignity. The angels, however, struck the people blind, and at morning light took Lot, his wife, and their two daughters from the city, and commanded them to flee for their lives and not look back. Then, they completely destroyed the entire area with fire and brimstone—its cities, villages and towns, together with all the inhabitants. Even today, vast areas of rock formation in this region are pitted and sharp, still bearing the unmistakable evidence of having been rained upon by something akin to burning sulfur pellets.

God had previously identified Abraham's cause with His own (Genesis 12:3—whoever touched Abraham touched *"the apple of His eye"* (Zechariah 2:8). Lot was Abraham's nephew. Abraham took Lot with him when he left on his journey to Canaan at the instruction of the LORD, and there was a measure of responsibility upon Abraham for Lot's welfare. Thus, when something, or someone, affected Lot, it was as if Abraham himself had been affected.

EGYPT

Egypt was the second recorded nation after the flood to come under judgment. The famous 10 plagues were judgments upon Egypt (Exodus 6:6, 7:4, 12:12). These judgments of Blood; Frogs; Lice; Flies; Diseased Livestock; Boils; Hail; Locusts; Darkness; and Death of the Firstborn destroyed the nation (Exodus 10:7) besides causing death in every Egyptian household (Exodus 12:30). Some that died would have been fathers, mothers, grandfathers, grandmothers, and aunts and uncles, not just small children. Egypt was punished primarily for her treatment of the Israelites—God's chosen people—Abraham's offspring. This sin included the oppression of the stranger in the land, and the shedding of man's blood through the murder of Israelite baby boys (Exodus 1:16,22).

AMALEK

The next nation to come under judgment was Amalek. The sin of the Amalekites was that they attacked the Israelites journeying in the desert. It was an unprovoked, cowardly attack:

> *He met you on the way and* **attacked your rear ranks, all the stragglers at your rear, when you were tired and weary*
> (Deuteronomy 25:18).

The Israelites defeated Amalek in the ensuing battle but a military defeat fell short of placating God's wrath. The God of Israel made a declaration:

> *I will utterly blot out the remembrance of Amalek from under heaven*
> (Exodus 17:14).

Judged — Chapter 10

Thus says the Lord of [armies]: **"I will punish what Amalek did to Israel** *... Now go and attack Amalek, and* **utterly destroy all that they have, and do not spare them. But kill both man and woman, infant and nursing child, ox and sheep, camel and donkey"** (1Samuel 15:2–3).

WE MUST NOT THINK THAT GOD'S judgments are always immediate. The total extermination of the Amalek race spanned 1,000 years or more. The Amalekites suffered defeat after defeat at the hands of Israel, and were finally annihilated in the great slaughter of the enemies of the Jews in the book of Esther. Haman, the arch-enemy of Mordecai, was an Amalekite (Esther 8:5) and so, apparently, were many others of those killed by the Jews when they went on the attack *"from India to Ethiopia"* — in 127 nations (Esther 1:1).

SEVEN NATIONS OF CANAAN

Some forty years after the Israelites came out of Egypt, they crossed the Jordan river and entered the Promised Land under the leadership of Joshua. They were given clear instructions for dealing with the seven nations inhabiting the land — the Hittites, the Girgashites, the Amorites, the Canaanites, the Perezites, the Hivites and the Jebusites:

When the Lord your God delivers them over to you, you shall conquer them and **utterly destroy them**. *You shall* **make no covenant with them nor show mercy to them** Deuteronomy 7:2).

Seven nations were to be completely wiped-out by Israel. Why? Simply for Israel to dwell in the land? No, never! Admittedly, the Israelites were God's **"chosen people, a special treasure"** (Deuteronomy 7:6), and the land was *"a land for which the Lord cared"* (Deuteronomy 11:12); but these nations were under judgment for sin, not because they happened to be in the way. God was ready to destroy all the nations except the Amorites in the days of Abraham, but God is patient.

The LORD told Abraham that his descendants would be afflicted in Egypt 400 years because *"the iniquity of the Amorites is not yet complete"* (Genesis 15:13–16). We deduce that the other six nations were extremely wicked, and that the moral decline of the Amorites took a further 430 years to reach the level of evil that justified obliteration. Obviously, sins of the grossest nature must have been committed to warrant the total extermination of seven entire nations. The sins that effected their demise are found in Leviticus Chapter 18 — the chapter concerning sexual morality. Here the LORD forbids sexual intercourse between brother and sister, son and mother, mother and son-in-law, father and daughter, father and daughter-in-law; the LORD forbids sexual acts between mother and daughter, father and son, male with male, female with female, or sexual acts with animals. The Lord said to Israel:

> *Do not defile yourselves with any of these things;* **for by all these the nations are defiled**, *which I am casting out before you. For* **the land is defiled; therefore I visit the punishment of its iniquity upon it, and the land vomits out its in habitants** (Leviticus 18:24–25).

Israel became the LORD'S instrument of judgment for the seven nations. Those nations committed the vilest of sins imaginable, and like Sodom and Gomorrah, were utterly destroyed because of their *"***perversion***"* (Leviticus 18:23).

ISRAEL

Israel is both fortunate, and unfortunate: fortunate, because the Jewish people are God's *chosen people, "a special treasure"* (Deuteronomy 7:6) above all the nations; unfortunate, because being God's chosen incurs stricter judgment due to the greater light experienced and enjoyed (that this principle still holds true today is shown in the New Testament: "*Let not many of you become teachers, knowing that we shall receive a stricter judgmen*t" James 3: 1); fortunate, because unlike some nations who were annihilated, the LORD promised never to treat Israel the same way:

> *I will not cast them away, nor shall I abhor them, to utterly destroy them and break my covenant with them* (Leviticus 26:44).

DUE TO SIN, FEW NATIONS IN history have been so repeatedly subjugated and subjected to such horrific slaughters of their people as Israel has been. Tens of millions of Jews have died the most terrible and barbaric deaths conceivable to the mind of fallen man. And this was not the product of the Dark Ages. Barbarism toward Jews began millennia ago and culminated in the systematic murder of six million by the Germans during World War II, an event now known to history as the Holocaust. The Jews were first beaten, hacked, or shot to death in their tens of thousands, but this proved too slow and too costly for the Germans. A precision killing machine came into operation and the Jews were killed by inexpensively produced poison gas. Their gold teeth were deftly knocked from their lifeless jaws and the tons of gold then helped finance Hitler's war machine. The hair of the women and girls was shaved off and woven into cloth, or used for stuffing mattresses. The smooth skin of the younger Jews was skinned from their bodies and made into lampshades, and the bodies of about five million were made into soap or burnt—the ash being used as fertilizer on German gardens.

ISRAEL WAS TWICE EXILED FROM ITS land after suffering terrible savagery at the hands of the LORD's instruments of judgment. Israel was judged and exiled the first time because of its rejection of the LORD:

> *My people have committed two evils: they have forsaken Me, the fountain of living waters, and hewn themselves cisterns—broken cisterns that can hold no water* (Jeremiah 2: 13).

Israel's twofold sin was to reject the Living God from Whom came their prosperity and well-being, and give attention to idols that could benefit them not at all. After decades had passed without repentance, the prophet Jeremiah, moved by the Holy Spirit, pronounced judgment:

> *O LORD, the hope of Israel, all who forsake you will be put to shame.* **Those who turn away from you will be written in the dust** *because they have forsaken the LORD, the spring of living water*
> (Jeremiah 17:13 NIV).

Only a few thousands survived the Assyrian and Babylonian swords. The Jews were *"written in the dust"*—consigned to virtual oblivion.

Some 560 years after God returned the surviving exiled Israelites, and descendants of those survivors, to their land and reestablished them, Israel soon became as deeply entrenched in the same sins as before, then added to her evils by rejecting the *Messiah*:

> *He is despised and rejected by men, a Man of sorrows and acquainted with grief.* **And we hid, as it were, our faces from Him; He was despised, and we did not esteem Him** (Isaiah 53:3).

The Spring of Living Water, in the form of *Messiah* Jesus, came to quench the thirst of the spiritually parched:

> *Whoever drinks of the water that I shall give him will never thirst. But the water that I shall give him will become in him a fountain of water springing up into everlasting life* (John 4: 14).

But instead of drinking deeply they cried out:

> **Away with Him, away with Him! Crucify Him!** (John 19:15).

Yes, the Romans did carry out the actual crucifixion, but only after the Jewish religious authorities had handed Jesus over to them and stirred up the Jewish crowds to demand His death. Thus Jesus said to Pilate, the

Roman governor, who believed he held the power of life and death over Jesus:

> You could have no power at all against Me unless it had been given you from above. Therefore **the one who delivered Me to you has the greater sin** (John 19:11).

Compounding the sin of rejecting God's Redemption was the attempt by many to stop the early, entirely Jewish Church, from spreading the Good News of God's salvation to the Gentiles. As a result, God's wrath *"came upon [Israel] to the uttermost"* (1Thessalonians 2:16).

ASSYRIA

Assyria was one of the most formidable military forces of the ancient world—cruel and terrible. The Bible informs us unequivocally that God uses powerful nations to execute His judgments in the earth. Assyria was the particular instrument used of God to bring judgment to Israel. At that time the LORD said:

> Assyria was the rod of My anger and the staff in whose hand is My indignation (Isaiah 10:5).

However, as has been said previously, it is a Biblical principal that whoever harms Israel—for whatever reason, *"sticks his finger in Jehovah's eye!"* (Zechariah 2:8 TLB). Assyria, therefore, was doomed the moment she first came against the 10 northern tribes of Israel. Assyria attacked the northern tribes first, inflicted terrible carnage and took the survivors back to Assyria as captives. Assyria then moved against the southern kingdom of Judah, destroying cities and towns until she came and besieged Jerusalem. It was here that Assyria hammered the last nail into her coffin. Even though Assyria was to have taken Jerusalem, Hezekiah, king of Judah, was encouraging the inhabitants by saying that the LORD would save them. The Assyrian officials made the mistake of blaspheming the LORD's name:

> Beware lest Hezekiah persuade you, saying, "The LORD will deliver us." **Has any one of the gods of the nations delivered its land from the hand of the king of Assyria?** (Isaiah 36:18).

The implication was that the LORD could not deliver Jerusalem from the hand of the king of Assyria—and that was blasphemy. The LORD quickly responded:

> Whom have you **reproached and blasphemed?** Against whom have you raised your voice, and lifted up your eyes on high? Against **the Holy One of Israel** (Isaiah 37:23).

Judged — Chapter 10

Naturally, Assyria did not capture Jerusalem. Furthermore:

> *the angel of the LORD went out, and killed in the camp of the Assyrians* **one hundred and eighty-five thousand;** *and when the people arose early in the morning , there were the corpses—all dead* (Isaiah 37:36).

THAT NIGHT THE LORD KILLED AROUND double the number of people that America did when it dropped its atom bomb on Hiroshima in Japan on August 6, 1945.

Following the demise of his army the king of Assyria returned to Nineveh where he was promptly assassinated by his own sons. Also, Judgment was pronounced upon Assyria:

> *the LORD will stretch out His hand against the north, destroy Assyria, and make Nineveh a desolation, as dry as the wilderness*
> (Zephaniah 2:13).

Assyria was destroyed approximately 80 years after the siege of Jerusalem, and all that remains of Nineveh is a few mounds of dirt in the suburban desert of Mosul, in modem Iraq.

BABYLON

Nebuchadnezzar, king of Babylon, came down to Israel's southern kingdom of Judah to accomplish what the king of Assyria had failed to do because of his pride and blasphemy against the LORD. The Babylonians, like the Assyrians, were the instrument to bring judgment on Judah and Jerusalem:

> *Thus says the LORD of hosts, the God of Israel: "Behold, I will send and bring* **Nebuchadnezzar the king of Babylon, My servant**, *and will set his throne above these stones"* (Jeremiah 43:10).

But, even if Nebuchadnezzar was the LORD's servant administering His justice, the Babylonians, like the Assyrians, were doomed from the first encounter with Israel:

> *Thus says the LORD of hosts, the God of Israel: "Behold, I will punish the king of Babylon and his land, as I have punished the king of Assyria" .... And* **Babylon, the glory of kingdoms, the beauty of the Chaldeans' pride, will be as when God overthrew Sodom and Gomorrah**
> (Jeremiah 50:18; Isaiah 13:19).

Approximately 60 years after Nebuchadnezzar destroyed Jerusalem, the Babylonians were conquered by the Median-Persian empire and magnificent Babylon was destroyed.

EDOM

The Edomites were the descendants of Esau, Jacob's twin brother. Edom came under judgment for four sins. She allied herself with Nebuchadnezzar when he attacked Jerusalem, and also rejoiced at Israel's destruction at the hands of Nebuchadnezzar's army:

> **As you rejoiced because of the inheritance of the house of Israel was desolate**, so I will do to you; **you shall be desolate**
> (Ezekiel 35:15)

Edom appropriated some of Israel's land for herself:

> *Thus says the LORD GOD: "Surely I have spoken in My burning jealousy against the rest of the nations and **against all Edom, who gave My land to themselves as a possession**, with whole-hearted joy and spiteful minds"* (Ezekiel 36:5).

Edom attacked Israel:

> **For your violence against your brother Jacob**, *shame shall cover you, and you shall be cut off forever* (Obadiah 1:10).

Edom suffered repeated invasions by hostile nations who inflicted great destruction. She was finally conquered by the Nabataens in the fourth century BC and Edom, as a nation, became extinct.

POLITICAL SINS

BROKEN COVENANTS

When Nebuchadnezzar first came down to Jerusalem he conquered it and took the king of Judah, his family, the officers of his army and all the men of valor, together with the leaders of the land, the rich, and the influential—thousands of captives—to Babylon (2Kings 24: 12–16). Nebuchadnezzar then took the king's uncle, Mattaniah, and made him king of Judah.

Nebuchadnezzar changed Mattaniah's name to Zedekiah, and Zedekiah swore an oath of loyalty to Nebuchadnezzar. But, Zedekiah later rebelled against Nebuchadnezzar (2Kings 24:20). Nebuchadnezzar then came back to Jerusalem, captured it again, broke down all its walls and burnt the city and Solomon's magnificent temple (2King 25:9–10).

> *Then they killed the sons of Zedekiah before his eyes, put out the eyes of Zedekiah, bound him with bronze fetters, and took him to Babylon*
> (2Kings 25:7).

Judged — Chapter 10

On the surface—through man's eyes—it appears that a terrible fate came upon Jerusalem and the king of Judah for trying to throw off the yoke of mighty Babylon. But God does not see things through human eyes! We must understand this and acknowledge the fact that God's ways are not man's ways:

> *For My thoughts are not your thoughts, nor are your ways My ways, says the* L*ORD*. *For as the heavens are higher than the earth, so are My ways higher than your ways, and My thoughts than your thoughts* (Isaiah 55:8–9).

So then, how did the God of Israel—Creator of heaven and earth and everything in it—view Zedekiah's actions? Listen:

> *"Will he who does such things escape? Can he* **break a covenant** *and still be delivered? As I live," says the* L*ORD* G*OD*, *"surely in the place where the king dwells who made him king,* **whose oath he despised and whose covenant he broke**—*with him in the midst of Babylon he shall die. Since* **he despised the oath by breaking the covenant**, *and in fact gave his hand and still did all these things, he shall not escape." Therefore thus says the* L*ORD* G*OD*: *"As I live, surely* **My oath which he despised, and My covenant which he broke**, *I will recompense on his own head* (Ezekiel 17:15,16,18–19).

ZEDEKIAH HAD SWORN ON OATH TO serve Nebuchadnezzar, but he broke his word and suffered a terrible fate—as did all the inhabitants of Jerusalem. Numerous other acts of political treachery are recorded in the Bible. A study of these reveals that God considers acts of political treachery as perpetrated against Himself personally. When an individual or a government breaks a covenant—an agreement—they have, in effect, despised and broken God's covenant—God's agreement! Perhaps we can now appreciate the Psalmist:

> L*ORD*, *who may abide in Your tabernacle? Who may dwell in Your holy hill? ... He who swears to his own hurt and does not change* (Psalms 15:1–4).

A man's word, or a government's word, must be their bond if they are to avoid the judgment of God, because ultimately, sin is only ever against Him—for example:

> *Against You, You only, have I sinned, and done this evil in Your sight— that You may be found just when You speak, and blameless when You judge* (Psalms 51:4).

Unprovoked Aggression

I have not sinned against you, but you wronged me by fighting against me. May the Lord, the Judge, render judgment this day between the children of Israel and the people of Ammon (Judges 11:27).

The Lord judged the motives of the heart, and Ammon was defeated before Israel, as will be all other aggressors.

Attacking Nations For The Purpose Of Enlarging Borders

Thus says the Lord: "For three transgressions of the people of Ammon, and for four, I will not turn away its punishment, because they ripped open the women with child in Gilead, **that they might enlarge their territory**" (Amos 1:13).

For three transgressions...and for four does not mean Ammon was guilty of only three or four sins. It means they were guilty of a far larger number but the principal one was that they attacked Israel to gain territory. For this Ammon was conquered, and her king and rulers were taken away captive.

Rejoicing At A Nation's Misfortune

I will make Rabbah a stable for camels and Ammon a resting place for flocks. Then you shall know that I am the Lord. For thus says the Lord God: **"because you clapped your hands, stamped your feet, and rejoiced in heart with all your disdain for the land of Israel**, *indeed, therefore, I will stretch out My hand against you, and give you as plunder to the nations"* (Ezekiel 25:6–7).

The modern city of Amman, capital of Jordan, is now built upon the ruins of the former Ammonite capital, Rabbah—literally meaning "the great one." Even the greatest are reduced to rubble when Israel is involved. Many nations have rejoiced at Israel's misfortunes over more than four millennia. Kings, presidents, prime ministers and many nations have passed into oblivion, but the Jews are still around after more than 4,000 years and are dwelling on the land of her Divine inheritance. In fact, the Lord makes it perfectly clear that the Jews are as eternal as night and day:

Thus says the Lord, Who gives **the sun for a light by day, the ordinances of the moon and the stars for a light by night**, *Who disturbs the sea, and its waves roar (the Lord of hosts is His name):* **"If those ordinances depart from before Me, says the Lord, then the seed of Israel shall also cease from being a nation** *before Me forever"* (Jeremiah 31:35–36).

Judged — Chapter 10

EXTREME SAVAGERY IN TIMES OF WAR OR PEACE

Thus say s the LORD: *"For three transgressions of Damascus, and for four, I will not turn away its punishment,* **because they have threshed Gilead with implements of iron**" (Amos 1:3).

The Syrians, also, were guilty of a great number of sins, but the principle one was being cruel and savage to Israelite prisoners of war. The Syrians drove over the Israelites with spiked, iron wheeled threshing machines. For this Syria was vanquished and broken up by an equally cruel conqueror — Assyria.

PRIDE IN NATIONAL SECURITY

"The pride of your heart has deceived you, you who dwell in the clefts of the rock, whose habitation is high; you who say in your heart, **'who will bring me down to the ground?'** *Though you ascend as high as the eagle, and though you set your nest among the stars, from there I will bring you down," says the* LORD (Obadiah 1:3–4).

Pride in anything except the goodness, the mercy, and the grace of the LORD will always bring destruction:

Pride goes before destruction, and a haughty spirit before a fall
(Proverbs 16:18).

Like other nations that were proud in their national security, Edom was conquered and is now extinct. Only in the fear of God is there security for any nation.

ENSNARING LESSER NATIONS

Because of the multitude of harlotries of the seductive harlot, the mistress of sorceries, who **sells nations through her harlotries, and families through her sorceries**. *"Behold, I am against you," says the* LORD *of [armies]* (Nahum 3:4–5).

The great ancient empires went "a whoring" after nations, and, by their "love-making" — their magnanimous and friendly overtures, they increased their power and influence and made the lesser nations subservient and dependent upon them. The Assyrians were the ones at fault here — they "deceived the nations with vain promises of help and protection" (*Keil-Delitzsch Commentary on the Old Testament*), and, as has been stated previously, Assyria was utterly destroyed.

NATIONAL SINS
MURDER AND PERVERSE MORALS

*The iniquity of the house of Israel and Judah is exceedingly great, and **the land is full of bloodshed, and the city full of perversity for** they say, "The LORD has forsaken the land, and the LORD does not see!" And as for Me also, My eye will neither spare, nor will I have pity, but I will recompense their deeds on their own head (Ezekiel 9:9–10).*

*By **swearing and lying, killing and stealing and committing adultery, they break all restraint, with bloodshed upon bloodshed**. Therefore the land will mourn; and everyone who dwells there will waste away with the beasts of the field and the birds of the air; even the fish of the sea will be taken away (Hosea 4:2–3).*

Murder, immoral, corrupt and perverse behavior causes an out-pouring of God's wrath that leaves a nation broken and desolate.

RELIGIOUS SINS
REFUSING TO HEAR GOD'S WORD

*They refused to heed, shrugged their shoulders, and stopped their ears so that they could not hear. Yes, **they made their hearts like flint, refusing to hear the law and the words which the LORD of [armies] had sent by His Spirit** through the former prophets. Thus great wrath came from the LORD of [armies] (Zechariah 7:11–12).*

HINDERING THE SPREAD OF THE GOSPEL

*...**forbidding us to speak to the Gentiles that they may be saved**, so as always to fill up the measure of their sins; but wrath has come upon them to the uttermost (1 Thessalonians 2:16).*

RELIGIOUS SIN CARRIES THE HEAVIER JUDGMENTS of God. "Wrath came upon them to the uttermost"—no greater outpouring of God's wrath was possible upon Israel. The Jews had been slaughtered by the millions, and banished from their land for nearly 2,000 years—hounded and driven from country to country and stripped time and time again of everything they possessed. Only the fact that God was true to His word not to utterly destroy them (Leviticus 26:44) saved Israel from extinction. To have known the Light and to have rejected it is to have rejected life itself. In the very first

Judged — Chapter 10

chapter of the Bible we have the account of creation and we are told that *"there was darkness on the face of the deep"* (Genesis 1:2). This was total, utter darkness—there had never been light. But there is a darkness greater than that of total, utter darkness—the darkness that comes from rejecting the Light.

THE OCCULT

Therefore hear this now, you who are given to pleasures, who dwell securely, who say in your heart, "I am, and there is no one else besides me; I shall not sit as a widow, nor shall I know the loss of children"; But these two things shall come to you in a moment, in one day: the loss of children, and widowhood.

They shall come upon you in their fullness because of the **multitude of your sorceries**, *for the great* **abundance of your enchantments**. *For you have trusted in your wickedness; you have said, "No one sees me"; your wisdom and your knowledge have warped you; and you have said in your heart,* **"I am, and there is no one else besides me."** *Therefore evil shall come upon you; you shall not know from where it arises. And trouble shall fall upon you; you will not be able to put it off And desolation shall come upon you suddenly, which you shall not know.*

Stand now with your **enchantments and the multitude of your sorceries**, *in which you have labored from your youth perhaps you will be able to profit, perhaps you will prevail.*

You are wearied in the multitude of your counsels; let now **the astrologers, the stargazers, and the monthly prognosticators** *stand up and save you from what shall come upon you. Behold, they shall be as stubble, the fire shall burn them; they shall not deliver themselves from the power of the flame; it shall not be a coal to be warmed by, nor a fire to sit before!* (Isaiah 47:8–14).

As man draws the curtains against the Light, his boast in God is replaced by national pride and pride in his own achievements. He turns his eyes to horoscopes, palm-readings, witchcraft and other expressions of the occult. The spread of these things within nations always heralded judgment.

Religious sin can take many forms:

Rebellion *is as the sin of* **witchcraft**, *and* **stubbornness** *is as* **iniquity** *and* **idolatry** (1Samuel 15:23).

We see from the above that witchcraft and idolatry are essentially linked together. Idolatry, too, can take different forms:

> ... *and covetousness, which is idolatry* (Colossians 3:5).

We now see that covetousness is also a form of idolatry; therefore credit card debt falls under this category. Debt comes about when we lust after things that we cannot afford. Coveting is lust and linked with witchcraft. Therefore:

> *let no one deceive you with empty words,* **because of these things the wrath of God comes** (Ephesians 5:6).

SEXUAL SINS

We saw, under the heading of "Sins of the Nations," the judgments that were inflicted because of sexual *"perversion,"* which is clearly an *"abomination"* to God. We are commanded to shun all other forms of sexual sins also:

> *Therefore put to death ...* **fornication, uncleanness, passion, evil desire** (Colossians 3:5).

THE JUDGMENT OF GOD HAS ALWAYS come upon nations that committed sexual sins. The Roman empire was a mighty empire that once had high moral values. The morality of the Romans was so high that only one couple was divorced in over 500 years, and the man's name is recorded in Roman history. But Greek morals were introduced and Rome became the scene of total depravity; this, together with the sin of touching Israel, caused the empire's collapse.

ANTI-SEMITISM

Anti-Semitism is another sin that God takes as a personal affront to Himself:

> *Now the* LORD *had said to Abram: ... I will bless you and make your name great; and you shall be a blessing.* **I will bless those who bless you, and I will curse him who holds you lightly in esteem**
> (Genesis 12:1–3 Literal translation).

We have previously studied how God identified the cause of Abraham with His own. Whoever reaches out to harm the Jews evokes a reflex reaction from the LORD GOD of Israel. The scheming of Haman, for example, led to his own execution on the gallows that he built for Mordecai (Esther 8:7). Haman's ten sons and 75,000 others died because they were ready to attack the Jews (Esther 9:16). Again, to touch the Jews is as poking a finger in God's eye (Zechariah 2:8), and to despise them is to invite His judicial cursing.

Judged — Chapter 10

WE HAVE ONLY BRIEFLY EXPOSED SINS that brought judgment, destruction or annihilation to many nations of the ancient world. There is much more to be gleaned from further study, but enough has been uncovered for application to be made to the modern world. We lose sight of God's immutability at our peril. He has not changed. Neither have His moral values or judgments. What brought His judgments yesterday, will also bring them tomorrow. But God is patient with us—His tomorrow could be months, years or decades away, or His tomorrow could literally be our tomorrow—only He knows.

We need to remember what we looked at earlier, that the LORD told Abraham his descendants would be afflicted for 400 years because *"the iniquity of the Amorites is not yet complete"* (Genesis 15:13–16). From this we learn that the LORD had already decided to destroy the Amorites, but in His patience He waited a further 430 years for their sin to reach the level which justified destruction. Just how many of today's nations has the LORD determined to destroy unless they turn to Him? Many nations in 2016 are battling the effects of "natural" disasters while struggling with economic nightmares and medical catastrophes. It is my considered opinion that all these national cataclysms are but the forerunners of what is heading our way if we do not repent. We should learn from words of Jesus:

> *There were some present at that time who told him about the Galileans whose blood Pontius Pilate had mingled with their sacrifices. And Jesus said to them, "Do you think that these Galileans were worse sinners than all the other Galileans, because they suffered in this way? I tell you no!; but unless you repent, you will all likewise perish. Or those eighteen on whom the tower in Siloam fell and killed, do you think that they were worse sinners than all other men who dwelt in Jerusalem? I tell you, no!; but unless you repent you will all likewise perish* (Luke 13:1–5).

FOLLOWING IS A LIST OF UNCOVERED sins. They are given in their groups, and with the type of judgment inflicted. Careful analysis of what is taking place among nations today and what has taken place in the past half-century or more, shows conclusively that modern nations are receiving the same judgments for committing the same sins as nations of yesteryear. We are indeed skating on very thin ice.

POLITICAL SINS

SLAVERY AND OPPRESSION: Physical catastrophes and widespread death.

DISCRIMINATING AGAINST STRANGERS (includes racial discrimination): Physical catastrophes and widespread death.

MURDER, PERVERSE AND IMMORAL BEHAVIOR: Physical catastrophes and widespread death.

BREAKING OF POLITICAL AGREEMENTS: Destruction of nation.

PRIDE IN NATIONAL SECURITY: Destruction of nation.

USING POWER AND WEALTH TO MAKE LESSER NATIONS SUBSERVIENT: Destruction of nation.

WAGING WAR AGAINST ISRAEL: Destruction of nation. Near annihilation.

ALLIES OF THOSE WAGING WAR AGAINST ISRAEL: Destruction of nation.

APPROPRIATING ISRAEL'S LAND: Destruction of nation.

REJOICING AT ANOTHER NATION'S MISFORTUNES (especially Israel's): Destruction of nation.

UNPROVOKED MILITARY AGGRESSION: Defeat with high loss of life.

MILITARY AGGRESSION TO ENLARGE TERRITORY: Destruction of nation.

EXTREME CRUELTY IN TIMES OF WAR: Nation conquered and devastated.

FRAUDULENT, DECEITFUL, AND CRAFTY BUSINESS TRANSACTIONS: Accelerated the destruction of the nation (see full Biblical accounts of the falls of Nineveh, Tyre, and Babylon).

SEXUAL SINS

HOMOSEXUALITY: Annihilation.

SODOMY, LESBIANISM (sexual perversion, including acts with animals): Annihilation.

INCEST: Annihilation.

ADULTERY, DIVORCE, AND SEXUAL LUSTS: Collapse of nation.

ANTI-SEMITISM

POLITICAL, RACIAL, OR RELIGIOUS: Judicial cursing or complete destruction of nation.

RELIGIOUS SINS

REJECTION OF GOD: Near annihilation.

REJECTION OF GOD'S SALVATION: Near annihilation.

SUPPRESSING OR HINDERING THE PREACHING OF THE GOSPEL: Near annihilation.

REFUSAL TO HEAR AND LIVE BY GOD'S WORD: Destruction of nation. Near annihilation.

PRACTICING WITCHCRAFT, HOROSCOPES, AND THE OCCULT: Near annihilation.

COVETING (form of idolatry): Physical catastrophes and widespread death.

BLASPHEMY (God cannot do something, or God will not do what He says): Destruction of nation.

PART IV

Judgment Pending

11

Prelude to Judgment

Somethings are not debatable—there is only God's side. And having the last word on any subject is also the prerogative of the LORD. Thus, when it comes to sin and judgment, the subjects are not for debate and God has the final word. There is no shadow of doubt that this world of ours is about to be shaken until the teeth of its inhabitants rattle. The rumbles of war and the smell of devastation is already in the air and is perceived by some with a prophetic call:

> *O my soul, my soul! I am pained in my very heart! My heart makes a noise in me; I cannot hold my peace, because **you have heard, O my soul, the sound of the trumpet, the alarm of war*** (Jeremiah 4:19).

It is time for the nations to prepare for war—war against the Almighty God of Israel.

Does the above statement sound too hawkish for the tender ears of modern-day Christians? Doubtless someone will say to me, "I am glad that you are not God." I can only agree. But, dear Christian, it is totally naive to think that God is not going to judge our sick, selfish, mammon-worshiping, materialistic world. Even within the Church the current best-selling books are either novels or books concerning money! All too often the prophetic voice raised within the Church itself is ignored if it does not promise a soft, rosy, comfortable future—for the Church, or for the world. But prophetic voices are being raised around the world, trumpeting a distinct sound which we ignore at our peril.

> *Surely the LORD GOD does nothing, unless He reveals His secret to His servants the prophets* (Amos 3:7).

LANCE LAMBERT, A HIGHLY RESPECTED JEWISH brother who had a vibrant international ministry (Lance went to be with the Lord in May 2015) gave the following word in Jerusalem, on November 3, 1992. Notice how clearly and completely the prophetic utterance bears out so much of what has been said in this book:

Hear this that I speak says the Lord and wait upon Me in stillness. You shall not be afraid of the turmoil that will shortly come upon all the earth, for the days of judgment have begun and I will overthrow, and overthrow and overthrow. I will not cease until the real spirit and character of fallen man manifests itself. I will allow My adversary, Satan, one last opportunity to challenge My authority, to challenge My Word, My purpose and My Messiah. For this reason I, the Lord, will cause these political, economic, religious and physical upheavals. Do not fear all of this for I am preparing the whole world for the last phase, for what those who do not know Me describe as a "new world order," but which is in fact, an old world order. It is the power and character of Babylon, energized by the spirit of darkness, the principality of Babylon. He is the spirit of Antichrist, who first manifested himself at Babel seeking to produce a one world order without Me, which attempt I foiled. But now his hour has come.

Fear not, little flock, of those who would enter My heart's purposes and desires, those whom I would train to stand with Me in these stormy times of change. It is I, the Sovereign Lord, the Almighty One, who is preparing the whole world for that man of sin to finally appear. Nothing is out of My control but all is under My authority. I am behind all the shaking, all the change and upheaval, for I am preparing the whole earth, and especially Europe and America. One superpower I have cast down, and another I am about to Judge. I will also cast down the power of Islam, for I have seen their wickedness, says the Lord. Do not ask of Me that I will defer these judgments, for I have determined to do it and will not be deflected. Stand with me that My will be done. Do not fear, nor be cast down by all these things. *My counsel shall stand and I will do all My pleasure*; all that I have purposed for My Son shall be fulfilled and all that I have intended for those whom I have redeemed, whom I have given to My Son, shall come to pass. In the midst of all these worldwide storms, I will work worldwide by My Spirit and reap a worldwide harvest. Where darkness and suffering have been the greatest, there the harvest will be the greatest. For I the Lord will prepare a people for My Glory. I will draw them from Russia and all the countries round about her, from China and all the countries round about her. I will draw them from the Islamic lands, multitudes and multitudes of the young. From the east and the west, from the north and the south, I will draw them. In all the turmoil and the confusion I will work mightily. With grace and with power will I anoint those who will be faithful, and with signs and with wonders I will attend their work. But those who shall

Prelude to Judgement — Chapter 11

be faithful to Me shall suffer. Therefore allow Me, whilst there is time, to work a deep work in you by My Spirit.

And if My heart yearns for those whom I have redeemed from the nations, that they may be as a bride to Me and share My eternal home and glory, My heart yearns with a boundless and a surpassing love for Israel and for the Jews wherever they may be. For as I am drawing the redeemed from the corners of the earth, so will I draw My Jewish people back to the land I have given them for an eternal inheritance. I solemnly pledge that I will judge every nation, and every leader that will oppose this My purpose, and I will use every means to bring them home. She, who in all her backsliding has yet carried My Name, often unknowingly, and whom My adversary has hated with a hatred as boundless as My love for her, she who has been hated, despised, afflicted and persecuted, whom the nations have cast out and trodden down under foot. I the Lord, *the Holy One of Israel*, her Savior, I the Lord, will now lead her tenderly, beaten and bloodied as she is, blind and deaf as she is, I will lead her to her place as chief of the nations. Yes I the Lord declare it, those who bloodied her and hated her, shall come bowing down to the ground before her. For in all these judgments I will save her. I the Lord will do it sovereignly in the day that I cause her to cry out to Me and will open her eyes and unlock her ears. In that day which I will make, My heart shall sing for joy and I will dance the dance of the Bridegroom. I call you therefore to intercession that will cost you everything, that this My purpose be fulfilled. *I am the Alpha and the Omega,* says the Lord God who is and who was and who is to come, the Almighty.

THROUGH MY LATE GOOD FRIEND LANCE Lambert the Lord makes it abundantly clear that it is He who is in control and it is He who causes "political, economic, religious and physical upheavals." It is so often articulated that God only "allows" calamities to occur. We would do well here to repeat a Scripture used in a previous chapter:

I make peace and **create calamity***; I, the* Lord*, do all these things*
(Isaiah 45:7).

Calamities proceed from the hand of God! The ancients certainly understood the truth of those words:

If there is **calamity** *in a city,* **will not the** Lord **have done it?**
(Amos 3:6).

Unfortunately, the ancients understood a principle which we have yet to learn.

The LORD said, through Lance Lambert, "... I am preparing the whole earth, and **especially Europe and America. One superpower I have cast down, and another I am about to Judge**." God's word tells us that:

> *by the mouth of two or three witnesses every word shall be established*
> (2Corinthians 13:1).

The following chapters of this book bear out exactly the words given through Lance—as if he had access to the notes for the manuscript! At the time of writing, the fear that is being generated throughout Europe by the hundreds of thousands of Muslim migrants gaining access into Europe, is without question a prelude to judgment upon all of Europe. With those Muslim migrants will come terror attacks, like the series of attacks that hit Paris on November 13, 2015, killing and injuring hundreds. So, too, will the millions of illegal immigrants pouring across America's porous southern border have their own part in that superpower's downfall.

The LORD will use the "turmoil and confusion" to bring souls into His kingdom, and to restore the backslidden to Himself. And He will use it to bring His Jewish people back to the land. Even at the time of writing, Jews fleeing the violence in South Africa, and from war-torn Azerbaijan, Syria, the Ukraine, and France are arriving in Israel. Russia's invasion and annexation of Crimea, and the ongoing Russian-backed hostilities in eastern Ukraine has sent thousands of Jews running to Israel. The hunters are hunting exactly as Jeremiah prophesied (Jeremiah 16:16).

God has no desire to destroy man—His finest creation. He desires only to punish the wicked, to bring correction and a change in morality, together with a heart knowledge of Himself:

> *I will shake all nations, and they shall come to **the Desire of All Nations***
> (Haggai 2:7).

The *Desire of All Nations* is the Lord Jesus. God is never in a hurry to punish a nation. Even after sentencing a nation God waits before the execution of that sentence. The only time God is shown to be in a hurry is in the parable of the prodigal son (Luke 15:20); God, depicted by the father, runs to forgive and kiss His repentant son. But God has spoken clearly and frequently in His word that He will judge the nations. There are 27 prophecies of judgment in the first 39 chapters of Isaiah alone!

> *Behold, the day of the LORD comes, cruel, with both wrath and fierce anger ... **I will punish the world for its evil** ... This is the purpose*

Prelude to Judgement — Chapter 11

*that is purposed **against the whole earth**, and this is the hand that is stretched out **over all the nations**. For the LORD of [armies] has purposed, and who will annul it?* (Isaiah 13:9,11; 14:26–27).

Furthermore, God is speaking to the nations through His prophets today! We are in the final age, and it is the era of the rise and fall of the last world powers. The LORD GOD of Israel has shown Himself repeatedly to be as utterly ruthless in performing promises of judgment as He is faithful in performing promises of blessing. He is patient but His patience must never be interpreted as weakness, only as a reluctance to destroy. And time is not a commodity that the nations can count upon. Only man dwells in a world bound by time—God does not:

with the Lord one day is as a thousand years, and a thousand years as one day (2Peter 3:8).

Many judgments cannot be averted. God has determined to carry out certain judgments and from this He will not turn aside. He alone knows the hearts of men and He knows that some nations will not repent of their wicked ways:

Can the Ethiopian change his skin or the leopard its spots? Then may you also do good who are accustomed to do evil (Jeremiah 13:23).

Nineveh, however, was an exception. A large, but wicked city, with 120,000 babies and small children (Jonah 4:11), it was told that it would be destroyed in just 40 days (Jonah 3:4), but it repented and was saved from destruction. This should offer hope for every city and nation, that, where there is true repentance there is yet hope for a tomorrow. But simply praying for judgment to be averted will accomplish nothing. A radical change of heart and lifestyle might.

ONE OF THE THEMES THAT RUNS throughout the Bible is that God will make a full end of the nations but will not suffer Israel to see the same fate—this He has pledged. And, as we have seen in the previous chapter, nations have indeed been completely destroyed, while Israel, fully deserving the same fate, has survived the calamitous punishments inflicted upon it. One particular prophecy touching the fate of Israel and that of the nations, which has yet to find its fulfillment, holds grim prospects for many nations:

*"For I am with you," says the LORD, "to save you; though **I make a full end of all nations where I have scattered you**, yet I will not make a complete end of you. But I will correct you in justice, and will not let you go altogether unpunished"* (Jeremiah 30:11).

God has declared that He will destroy **all the nations where the Jewish people were scattered** during their exiles from the Promised Land. Some of the nations involved in Israel's first exile have been totally destroyed while others have not. And during the second exile, the Jews were hounded and driven to the four corners of the earth—over one hundred nations are involved!

WE CAN SEE THAT THE CREATOR *of Israel* is determined to even the score for what happened to the Jewish people over the past 2,000 years. The God of Israel determined punishment upon Israel but the nations went too far with their savagery:

> *I am very angry with the nations that feel secure. I was only a little angry, but they added to the calamity* (Zechariah 1:15 NIV).

And one of the ways God will bring judgment upon nations is by direct military confrontation with Israel:

> *I will also* **gather all nations**, *and bring them down to the Valley of Jehoshaphat; and* **I will enter into judgment with them there** *on account of My people, My heritage Israel,* **whom they have scattered among the nations**; *they have also* **divided up My land** (Joel 3:2).

Historically it has never happened that all the nations have come against Jerusalem in battle. There is, therefore, a military conflict looming between Israel and many nations, the outcome of which is that few from among the nations survive. But those survivors will all come to know the Lord (see Zechariah 14:16).

The reasons given for such a confrontation is the treatment of the Jews in exile and the appropriation of their land—their God-given eternal inheritance—by the surrounding nations.

> *And it shall happen in that day that I will make Jerusalem a very heavy stone for all peoples; all who would heave it away will surely be cut in pieces,* **though all nations of the earth are gathered against it**
> (Zechariah 12:3).

The world knows that Israel is already a formidable military power and is continuing to build its strength. Israel is currently rated equal with Britain in nuclear weapons (without ever admitting that it even has a nuclear bomb), and continues to build up her arsenals by developing and producing weapons of mass destruction—no one really knows what secret weapons Israel has already developed, but one country, Iran, which rattles its sabers at Israel constantly was informed via a media site in Britain that Israel,

Prelude to Judgement — Chapter 11

with a single electromagnetic pulse bomb, "could send Iran back to the Stone Age." Perhaps the final conflict between Israel and the nations is that described by the Apostle Peter:

> *The heavens will be dissolved,* **being on fire, and the elements will melt with fervent heat** (2Peter 3:12).

Whatever the scenario, we know from Scripture that Israel ultimately wins and the nations are destroyed.

Many nations are so deeply stained with man's blood that only God's wrath will remove it. They, and many others, wallow in moral filth and perversion. Governments are guilty of double standards and of breaking their covenants. Politicians are corrupt—abusing their positions of power for personal and financial gain. The masses do what is right in their own eyes. It is not just an isolated nation here or there that faces destruction:

> *The faithful man has perished from the earth, and there is no one upright among men* (Micah 7:2).

No, it is many nations which face destruction today. Only in the *fear of God*—both the reverential fear, and the awesome, terrifying *fear of God*—is there safety for a nation. Repeated wars are signs of the rising tide of Divine judgment upon nations. The culmination of Divine judgment will be a cataclysmic sweep of the ungodly from the earth in the full flood of God's wrath. That God is too kind to destroy millions of people is the opiate of the masses—Christian and non-Christian alike. Hot things burn—most of us learn this law at a tender age by experience. If we disregard this law, we suffer pain. There is also a law of gravity. The refusal to believe that it exists does not alter the fact that it does. And so it is with God's laws of sin and judgment.

God's judgments are according to pattern. He first touches our blessings:

> *I will curse your blessings* (Malachi 2:2).

The accustomed blessings of rain, employment, prosperity, etc. are not available as before:

> *Your iniquities have turned these things away, and your sins have withheld good from you* (Jeremiah 5:25).

Then, He punishes with the destructive elements—wind, hail and earthquakes (i.e. Isaiah 29:6—but these punishments are designed to act as warnings of greater things to come if behavioral patterns do not change. Finally, He punishes severely *"by the* **sword***, by* **famine***, and by* **pestilence***"* (Jeremiah 44: 13).

That phrase occurs no less than 22 times in the Bible. Judgments are not restricted to any one of the three facets, nor do they automatically entail all three. A single facet, a combination of any two, or all three are used depending on the severity of the sin committed—God alone being the arbiter. It has been stated previously that simply praying for judgment to be averted, or stayed, will accomplish nothing. As an example, let us look at World War II. With the exception of communists and atheists, all sides and victims caught up in the conflict prayed. They prayed that their nations would be spared the ravages of war; that their nations would win the war; that their loved ones and themselves would be spared, etc. The war waged on for five full years, devastating nation after nation, people after people—taking 49 million lives and costing a totally incalculable amount of materials and money. Apparently, the only thing learned from that war was how to destroy an even greater amount of life and property, at a fraction of the cost and in a fraction of the time. Sin abounds far more today than it did in the 1930s. We can, therefore, expect a cataclysmic devastation of cosmic proportions within a reasonably short period of time.

WE MUST FLEE FROM THE WRATH of God. And where, you might ask, do we go to escape the wrath of God? We go to God, for it is in God that we find refuge from God! Only a liberal sprinkling of the blood of Christ can quench the flame of God's anger. The finger of *"the God of Israel"* is writing upon the walls of our nations—*"mene, mene, tekel, upharsin"* (Daniel 5:25).

God has numbered our nations, we have been weighed in the balances and found wanting.

> *"Now, therefore," says the* LORD, ***"Turn to Me with all your heart, with fasting, with weeping, and with mourning. So rend your heart, and not your garments; return to the*** LORD ***your God, for He is gracious and merciful, slow to anger, and of great kindness; and He relents from doing harm"*** *(Joel 2:12–13).*

12

Case Study:
The Soviet Union

The collapse of the Soviet Union in 1991 provides a case study in events leading to the demise of a powerful nation. We have witnessed, and are witnessing still, the consequences of national, political, religious and anti-Semitic sins—the breakup of perhaps one of history's mightiest military powers. The Soviet Union was reduced to chaos and begging for charity from its former enemies.

WHILE THE CALAMITIES EXPERIENCED BY THE Soviets are still reasonably fresh in our minds, and with current events in the region still making headlines, I have made an exception to my alphabetical list of nations in order for us to learn, at the outset, what is in store for others. Thus I have placed the former Soviet Union at the head of the list in this section.

We witnessed the judgment of a nation—not just a nation but an actual superpower—and I do not think it coincidental that it was judged severely at that time. In the list of sins in Chapter 10 we gave the judgments attached to a particular sin. The former Soviet Union committed many, almost all, of those sins. I believe that the God of Israel is clearly showing the nations what is in store—unless repentance is forthcoming.

The parallel between ancient Egypt and the former Soviet Union is remarkable. Both countries held the Jews captive. However, the children of Israel were slaves in Egypt, doing the most menial work, while those in the Soviet Union were mainly scientists, doctors, lawyers and other groups of educated intelligentsia, forming a large part of the working elite. Until the latter half of 1991, the Soviet Union had the third largest Jewish population in the world (after the U.S. and Israel). And just as Moses was sent by the LORD to Pharaoh in Egypt requesting the release of the Israelites, so world leaders (including two U.S. Presidents) and God-fearing men and women of renown went to the Kremlin, requesting the same right for the Jews of the Soviet Union—that they be allowed to emigrate. These people received the same answer that Pharaoh gave Moses—No! Soviet Jews wishing to emigrate to Israel (or anywhere else), were denied exit visas and often found themselves in prison. Applying for an exit visa automatically cost them and their families the right of employment. Denied a livelihood, existence for thousands of Soviet Jews was, to say the least, precarious and miserable.

Ten disasters (see page 78) from the hand of the Lord came upon Egypt, and the country was ruined. Today, the Soviet Union no longer exists. Newspapers and magazines from around the world told us of the awful conditions which prevailed inside Russia and other members of the Commonwealth of Independent States (C.I.S.), as the area is known today. The Chernobyl nuclear disaster in April 1986, was described in a news broadcast by *Israel Radio* in September 1992 as, "The worst peacetime nuclear disaster in world history." The news item was in honor of the 750th Jewish child arriving in Israel from the Chernobyl area suffering from the effects of radiation (the Soviets designated Jews to live around nuclear sites). The Chernobyl disaster is now estimated to have killed not just the 3,000 souls officially reported by the Soviet press, but nearer to 300,000. The area affected by radiation is still spreading. Due to drought conditions prevailing at the time, radioactive ash from spontaneous forest fires was being carried great distances by high winds. According to *U.S. News & World Report*, April 13, 1992, an earlier nuclear explosion at Chelyabinsk sent 80 tons of radioactive material into the air, forcing a Chernobyl style evacuation, but the death toll from Chelyabinsk is still a closely guarded secret even today. The same article reports that there were 270 recorded malfunctions at Soviet nuclear plants in 1991 alone! The cost in lives was enormous, but never disclosed.

Financial collapse was such that the once mighty superpower was given Third World status. As early as April 1991, Russian leaders were asking western nations—their former enemies—for "emergency credit" of billions of dollars to buy grain for the hungry masses to avoid starvation. The Ruble became virtually worthless. Due to hyperinflation, the exchange rate for the Ruble against the U.S. Dollar rose from 500 Rubles to over 1,300 in a matter of months. Vodka bought much more for the Russians than the Ruble, and also helped to dull the pain of the situation.

Vegetable crops, especially potatoes—a staple food—were continually disease ridden. They rotted in the ground, causing severe shortages and near famine conditions for the Russians. In November 1991, *USA Today* reported that most food was in such short supply that people stood in line for over four hours just to get a loaf of bread. And many times there

Case Study: *The Soviet Union* — Chapter 12 — 111

was no bread left for those at the end of the line. Fist fights and shoving-matches occurred daily in food lines that stretched for blocks. In October and November, 1990, food prices in privately owned stores rose 1,000 percent in just three weeks. A foot-long (30 centimeter) sausage cost nearly half an average month's salary. Gasoline prices sky-rocketed and cost the average Russian a week's salary just to fill the tank of his car.

THE COLLAPSE OF THE SOVIET UNION brought grave hardship on its people, especially those of Russia. Unemployment soared, and many people had no money to buy food, even if food had been available. *USA Today* reported this interview with one Russian: "'I have been faithful to my country all my life,' says a 79-year-old widow as she waits for lunch at a soup kitchen, 'and this is what I get in return? I have no money and no hope.'"

The entire world had been made aware of the judgment upon the Soviet Union. In September 1991, *The Bangkok Post* reported under the heading, "**In Soviet Union, even Santa's sack is empty**," that shops were empty of goods—there was nothing to buy. The article also quoted a typical Russian mother: "'My daughter is seven. She wants a Barbie doll,' says Marina with her voice breaking in emotion. 'I am willing to pay more than a week's salary for a Barbie, but it is impossible to buy it.'"

Catastrophic disasters had brought high and widespread loss of life. Economic collapse resulted in hyperinflation—reducing the people to paupers. High unemployment and grave shortages of all basic goods brought despair for many, while war and genocide brought total wretchedness for others. Those conditions prevailed in the areas of the former Soviet Union for more than a decade.

THE DEMISE OF THE SOVIET UNION was blazoned in banner headlines around the world on September 6, 1991; as one particular newspaper succinctly declared, "**THE SOVIET UNION IS FINISHED**." The mighty nation, the godless giant, which once enslaved a huge portion of the modern world, was reduced to nothing in a matter of months—its tentacles were cut off—and God has not yet finished. Wars between ethnic groups have taken thousands of lives—anarchy reigns among the 290 million people of the C.I.S. Lenin and Marx tried to eradicate God from the hearts and minds of the Soviet people, but, instead, it is their names, statues, and monuments that were being torn down. The commonwealth was torn apart and disintegrated. A prominent Russian physicist, Sergei Kapitza, interviewed by *U.S. News & World Report*, in April 1992, surveyed the wreckage of the society around him and summed up the situation:

Our economy is in absolute disarray, our Army is in retreat, our union is crumbled. We've had everything except a military defeat in the classical sense.

Just as the collapse of Egypt under Pharaoh brought the children of Israel out of oppression, so the collapse of the Soviet Union brought the Jews freedom from oppression also. Over 1,000,000 Jews left the boiling pot of the former Soviet Union to immediately go to Israel, and Jews still continue to arrive in Israel in 2016, from all areas of the former Soviet Union.

Some of the more obvious sins of the former Soviet Union were:

a) Slavery & Oppression
b) Discriminating against strangers
c) Pride in National Security
d) Using power and wealth to make lesser nations subservient
e) Waging war against Israel (According to a Soviet magazine, *Ekho Planety*, the Soviets took part in armed clashes between Egypt and Israel from late 1969 until early 1971, but suffered heavy casualties from Israeli bombing raids. And in the opening hours of the 1973 Yom Kippur War, Israel brought down four fighter-planes in a matter of seconds, all of which were piloted by Soviets.)
f) Allies of those waging war against Israel
g) Rejoicing at another nation's misfortunes (especially Israel's)
h) Unprovoked military aggression
i) Anti-Semitism (political, racial and religious)
j) Rejection of God
k) Rejection of God's Salvation
l) Suppressing and Hindering the preaching of the Gospel
m) Refusal to Hear and Live by God's Word
n) Blasphemy

The judgments are, therefore:

Physical catastrophes and widespread death (two times); **Destruction of nation** (seven times); **Near annihilation** (five times); **Defeat with high loss of life**; and **Judicial cursing or complete destruction of nation.**

WHEN WE CONSIDER WHAT HAPPENED TO the former Soviet Union, and what is taking place today in the areas previously under its domination, we see that the judgments were entirely accurate. We can, therefore, look at the following examples of modern nations facing judgment, and fully expect them to be sentenced, and suffer, according to their sins.

13

America

It is perhaps fortunate, that only the nation of Israel has been singled out by the LORD to have its sorry history of *"iniquity, transgression and sin"* (Exodus 34:7) recorded in such an expansive form. The world's inhabitants are able to read this historical drama in the Book of Books, the Bible, in hundreds of languages and dialects, and many who read it hold Israel up to ridicule. But, I wonder, how many of those would wish to have their own nation subjected to such intense scrutiny?

Israel has a 4,000-year-plus history—the history of many nations barely subscribe to five percent of that. Yet in their brief span of existence, the stench from their *"iniquity, transgression and sin"* reaches to the heavens.

It is fitting that America heads our alphabetical list, because without argument it is today the world leader in *"iniquity, transgression and sin"* and clearly leads all other nations in immorality and perversity, and ever seeking to widely export its home-grown depravity throughout the globe.

IN 1892 THE U.S. SUPREME COURT made a statement about America: "*This is a Christian nation.*"

In 1912 President Woodrow Wilson went as far as saying: "***America was born a Christian nation***."

In August 1947 President Harry S. Truman affirmed the 1892 Supreme Court decision by telling Pope Pius XII: "***This is a Christian nation.***"

In June 2007, abortion and same-sex marriage promoting presidential hopeful, Barack Hussein Obama said: "***We are no longer a Christian nation.***"

The early leaders made it abundantly clear that Christianity was to be the religion of America. Four times God is mentioned in the Constitution, and as a general rule only Christians were to be elected to government office. The Delaware State Constitution of 1776, was typical of that time:

> Everyone appointed to public office must say "I do profess faith in God the Father and in the Lord Jesus Christ His only Son, and in the Holy Ghost, one God, blessed for evermore. And I do acknowledge the Scriptures of the Old and New Testaments to be given by Divine inspiration."

But that was 239 years ago. Since taking office President Obama has left out the words "God" and "Jesus Christ" from some his State of the Union and other major speeches; on 2015's National Day of Prayer Obama aggressively denounced Christianity and praised Islam. He is on record as having said that the Muslim call to prayer "is the sweetest sound I know." And in September 2008, in an interview with ABC's This Week, Obama referred to "my Muslim faith." Only after ABC's host George Stephanopoulos interrupted him by saying, "You mean 'Christian faith,'" did Obama, with a smirk on his face, change his recorded words from "my Muslim faith" to "my Christian faith." Readers can draw their own conclusions about that exchange. In September 2015, a Public Policy Poll showed that only 14 percent of Republican voters believed Obama was a Christian, 54 percent believed he is Muslim. With Obama's apparent resolve to never say "Islamic terrorist" or "radical Islam, together with his reluctance to have U.S. troops engage with ISIL fighters, former House Speaker Newt Gingrich said on *Fox News* in November 2015 that:

> The President of the United States may be the most dangerous president in national security terms in American history—he lives in a fantasy world.

AMERICANS SHOULD NOT LOSE SIGHT OF the fact that Obama refuses to link Islamic terror with Islam, he always makes some excuse for the savage acts of the Islamics. Obama has allowed millions of Muslims to immigrate to America while only allowing a relative handful of persecuted Christians in who are fleeing Islamic barbarianism. And during Obama's terms in office he has already added the following staff to the White House:

> Arif Alikhan, Assistant Secretary for **Policy Development for the U.S. Department of Homeland Security**.
>
> Mohammed Elibiary, **Homeland Security Adviser**.
>
> Rashad Hussain, **Special Envoy to the Organization of the Islamic Conference** (OIC).
>
> Salam al-Marayati, **Obama adviser and founder of the Muslim Public Affairs Council** and is its current executive director.
>
> Imam Mohamed Magid, Obama's **Sharia Czar from the Islamic Society of North America**.

A staggering eighty percent of Islamic mosques and "cultural centers" in America are under the influence of the Saudi Wahabbi sect of Islam, the strictest form of Islam that promotes Sharia law, which is at odds with the Constitution. Obama is purposely filling the White House and placing the nation's security under Wahabbism. The rats are guarding the cheese!

STATE CONSTITUTIONS HAVE NOW BEEN CHANGED since the founding of the Republic and professing sodomites and lesbians, wizards and witches can, and do, get elected to public office. God is being systematically removed from the United States and being replaced by Islam. Prayer has not only been thrown out of schools, but laws have been passed to prevent pupils from assembling in groups and engaging in it privately. Bible studies are, for the most part, illegal on public-school grounds, as also is bringing a Bible onto school grounds. As Christianity in America fades away, the moral code and culture it generated recedes into total irrelevance.

U.S. government statistics show that since 1962, when prayer was abolished in schools and sequential legislation was enacted to effectively ban Bible reading, displaying the Ten Commandments, making invocations and benedictions at school functions, etc., the results have been catastrophic. David Barton writes:

> We have gone from public schools which taught moral principles and good citizenship with high scholastic achievement, to schools that have disrespect for authority, sex, drugs, anger, knives, guns, murder, no moral teachings, no mention of God and low SAT scores.

Average marks registered in the Standard Achievement Tests (SAT) have declined every year. Teenage pregnancy has risen above 550 percent and sexual diseases are at epidemic proportions and still rising; the Center for Sexually Transmitted Diseases reports a 79 percent increase for 2013 over the previous year.

The divorce rate in the U.S. has tripled each year for the past 20 years. Nationwide violent crime also rose a staggering 544 percent in 20 years from 1962, peaking in the 1990s, but even in 2013 was a staggering 450 percent higher than violent crime in the United Kingdom. In August 2015 the *New York Times* published an article in which it stated: "Cities across the nation are seeing a startling rise in murders." And in September 2015 *AFP* reported that major cities—including Washington D.C.—are seeing murder rates rising from 40.5 percent in the Capital to between 60 and 76 percent in other cities. Also, in 1992, for the first time ever, high school students graduated more illiterate than their parents. In 2014 graduating high school students had an average reading level of 12-year-olds.

There are more than 38 million teenage alcoholics today, and 1,000 teenagers attempt suicide every day. In August 1993 *TIME International* reported that over 4,000 American teenagers were shot dead in 1990, and that an estimated 100,000 students carry a gun to school. In 2014 – 2015 that figure had climbed to almost 1,000,000 high school students carrying weapons to school, and gunshot wounds are the biggest killer of teenagers. A sixteen year old white youth told *TIME*:

> If you have a gun you have power. Guns are just a part of growing up these days.

The number of murder victims of age 18 and under is up to 63 times that of other western nations! Also, the U.S. has the highest rate of incarceration in the world—more than ten times that of some other industrialized nations. As of December 31, 2013, there were over 1,570,000 inmates behind bars in America. St. Louis criminologist Richard Rosenfeld noted that "the federal prison population had spiked almost 800 percent since 1980." A report published back in 1991, in a secular U.S. magazine, claimed then that there were "more people in prison on any given Sunday than there were people in church." In April 1992, *U.S. News & World Report* carried a four page report on American crime. The report showed a direct cost to the American public during the previous 12 months of $125.8 billion. Compare that to 2010 when, according to *Forbes*, crimes involving firearms alone cost America $174 billion. Constant shootings are an indictment upon the depraved culture America offers its people. At the time of writing (December 2015) another mass shooting took place in San Bernadino, California in which 14 people were killed and 14 others injured—it was the 355th recorded mass shooting of the year, more shootings than there were days in the year.

The lowest estimates of the cost of cybercrime—crime involving the internet in which bank accounts etc. are emptied—is estimated to be $100 billion but could easily be tens of billions higher. The numbers of robberies, rapes, home invasions, *et al* are soaring. America sowed *the wind* by throwing God out of the schools and now reaps *"the whirlwind"* (Hosea 8:7).

THE TEN COMMANDMENTS EITHER HAVE TO be removed or covered up in the American courts of justice. It is not surprising, therefore, to read in the *Reader's Digest* of a judge awarding "workers compensation" to the widow of a man who fell to his death while stealing copper guttering. The judge ruled that the man was a professional thief, and as such his widow was entitled to compensation. Neither was it astonishing to read (again in the *Reader's Digest*) of an undercover agent who, within the space of six months (before his cover was blown), gathered evidence on some 80 American lawyers and judges involved in giving and taking bribes. The investigator said that the number uncovered was merely the "tip of an iceberg." Many of the verdicts handed down by American courts of law have been "bought," and the LORD says:

> "How long will you judge unjustly, and show partiality to the wicked?"
> (Psalms 82:2).

SATAN WORSHIP AND INVOLVEMENT WITH THE occult is rife throughout the country and numbers of churches of Satan have been formed. Some girls have been forced into be coming "breeders"—constantly being pregnant with child (often by their own fathers), so that the baby can be sacrificed in some demonic ritual. Girls have also been buried alive (usually by their parents) for several days as part of a satanic ritual. On May 2, 1993, a gathering of 200 witches was featured in a full-colored headline article on the front page of the *Santa Cruz Sentinel*. Various photographs were displayed of the witches burning incense and worshipping their demonic gods. In 1993 witch gatherings were being publicized locally, but in July 2015 the erection of a nine-foot-tall (2.74 meter.) statue of Satan in the city of Detroit was publicized around the world. This was partially due to the satanists demanding that the statue be placed on the same piece of ground as the monument to the Ten Commandments. Giant statues of Satan have also been erected on the capital grounds of several other U.S. states.

THE AMERICAN NEWS MEDIA WAS UNMERCIFUL in its treatment of Israel during the *intifada*—the Palestinian uprising against Israeli rule that erupted in December 1987—and published or broadcast "news" that was repeatedly described in the Israeli press as—"lies." The underlying reason for the particularly bad press given to Israel by the American media is, according to Jim Lederman's book *Battle Lines: The American Media and the Intifada*, that U.S. newsmen believe that Israel should act more civilized—more in accordance with the norms of behavior befitting a democratic country. It should be made very clear at this point that the *intifada* was actually a war, not a luncheon for foreign dignitaries at the White House. During the first five years of continuous confrontation, 1,100 Palestinians were killed—650 of them by other Palestinians and not by Israel. In America, on the other hand, some 125,000 civilian murders were committed during the same period of time—apparently this is considered by the media to be normal, civilized behavior.

It was reported by Richard Wurmbrand in the October 1987 issue of *The Voice Of The Martyrs*, that American doctors had examined prisoners held in the Romanian jail beneath President Ceausescu's palace. After the examination, the healthiest prisoners were executed—their hearts, livers, kidneys and other organs were then taken back to America by the doctors for transplant operations. Apparently, this too, is normal civilized behavior for citizens of democratic America. It is lucrative behavior, to be sure—an acquaintance of mine underwent a kidney transplant operation in 1989—even then the cost was $75,000. The *National Kidney Center* said the cost of transplantation in 2005 ranged from $210,000 upwards for a single kidney.

Around that time—before and after the year 2000—a number of American teenagers were waking up in hotel bathtubs next to a telephone with an attached note telling them to call an emergency line for help. The teens were being drugged at parties, then taken to a hotel where one of their kidneys was removed. A personal friend's 17-year-old son experienced that nightmare.

AMERICA DID NOT GET RID OF God overnight. It was simply a progression from the decay that had set in decades earlier to the rot that exists today. Slavery, racial prejudice, and a pseudo Christianity were but symptoms of the disease. The Indian reservations and black ghettos found dotted throughout the country are mute testimonies to the nation's history. On October 13, 1988, *USA Today* published an article containing an interview with a black woman whose son had been beaten, shot and lynched in 1955 for whistling at a white women. The article stated:

> lynchings would even be announced, and people would take their lunches to church because after church, they would go to the lynching.

A pseudo Christianity is rampant throughout America, and the average American "Christians" of today are:

> *lovers of pleasure rather than lovers of God, having a form of godliness, but denying its power* (2Timothy 3:5).

Gallup, and other polls taken in America reveal an alarming decline in morality among professing Christians. They show that divorce is actually higher among Christians than among the unchurched, even though God says plainly that He hates divorce (Malachi 2:16). These surveys also show that Christians steal, lie, and pilfer at the same rate as the "unchurched." Howard Hendriks mentions in his book *The 7 Laws Of The Teacher*, that research carried out by Christian youth organizations reveals that the only major difference between Christian and non-Christian youth is a verbal one: "The Christians answer 'no' when asked if they would lie, cheat, steal or go to bed with someone, while the non-Christian youth say, 'Of course, if it's to my advantage.'" The "Christian" lies about committing sin, but commits it nevertheless. This is corroborated by Dr. Bruce Wilkinson, of *Walk Thru The Bible Ministries*. While doing research for introducing a new magazine to effectively reach Christian youth in America, Dr. Wilkinson stated in October 1988, that:

> Sixty-five percent of teens attending Christian High schools in Atlanta, Georgia, were sexually active; seventy-five percent cheated regularly; thirty percent of seniors had shop-lifted within the past thirty days; forty – forty-five percent of pregnancies were aborted; ten percent have tried, or were then trying, homosexual relationships; and one hundred percent have watched "R" rated movies.

Dr. Wilkinson also quoted from research on Christian business executives, that 25 percent have had, or were currently having, an adulterous relationship, and that they watched an average of 30 – 40 hours of television each week. As far back as August 1, 1974, *Capital Voice* published the results of a recent poll:

> Fifty-one percent of the Methodist ministers in the USA do not believe in Jesus' resurrection; sixty percent do not believe in the virgin birth; sixty-two percent contest the existence of Satan; eighty-nine percent of Episcopalian [Anglican] priests do not believe the Bible to be the Word of God. They believe there is no truth.

IT IS NOT DISPUTED THAT THERE are many true, God-fearing Christians in the U.S., but a large portion of what is termed "Christianity" in America is as doomed as that which professes atheism. A pseudo Christianity inevitably involves a pseudo salvation also. It must be remembered, too, that there was always a true God-fearing remnant of people among the nation of Israel. The country was destroyed two times and neither the presence, nor the prayers, of the godly remnant in the land stopped the destruction. No doubt this may have been partially due to their general lack of effort in combating the prevailing godlessness.

It is a well known fact that American people are usually very generous. It is not so well known that of all the collective moneys given to the Church worldwide in 1990, 96 percent came from the pockets of American Christians. This is very commendable and worthy of recognition. What is not commendable, however, is that 94 percent of this money was spent inside America—on church buildings and administration—only six percent went toward missions.

As we approached the new millennium, prominent Christians in America proclaimed that, at the then current rate of church growth, nearly all the world would be Christian by the end of the decade (2000). It would be laughable if it were not so sad. And throughout America great claims are still being made today of revival and tremendous increase in church congregations. The following statement from the *Barnea Research Group*, says it all:

> Eighty percent of all U.S. church growth is "transfer growth"—people moving from one church to another, instead of the unchurched people coming into church.

Thomas Macaulay, the British historian who died in 1861 on the eve of the American Civil War, wrote of the United States:

> Your republic will be fearfully plundered and laid waste by barbarians in the twentieth century as the Roman Empire was in the fifth, with this difference: that the Huns and Vandals will have been engendered within your own country, by your own institutions.

When we consider the above facts and figures, and those which are to follow, we see the truth of Macaulay's prediction. The generic American barbarians did indeed rise up in the twentieth century, but they are absolutely running amok in the twenty-first century.

The American publishing empires that market pornographic magazines such as *Playboy* and *Penthouse*, as well as the giant pornographic film industry, have spread their filth all over the world, corrupting the morals of old and young, male and female alike. All an American (or visitor to the U.S.) needs is a telephone and credit card to get "live" filth pumped into his ears any time of the day or night. The movie industry also feels that it must have naked bodies, sex, and foul language to attract audiences. Films such as *The Last Temptation of Christ* go well beyond the definition of blasphemy.

IN NEW YORK IN 1990, HOMOSEXUALS marched through the city and the Empire State Building was lit up in lavender in their honor. The sodomites had signs saying, "We want your boys; God is gay." On 26 June 2015 the U.S. Supreme Court ruled that same-sex homosexual marriage was every person's right. President Barack Obama then had the White House lit up in the colors of the rainbow to celebrate the Supreme Court's disgraceful ruling which legalized homosexual marriage nationwide. However, the LORD has something to say on the subject:

Sodom and Gomorrah, and the cities about them in like manner, giving themselves over to fornication, and going after strange flesh, are set forth for an example, suffering the vengeance of eternal fire (Jude 7).

ABORTION IS NEVER SPECIFICALLY MENTIONED IN the Bible. The crime is so heinous that none in the ancient world needed to be admonished against it. About the closest we can get Biblically to something akin to abortion is found in examples where pregnant women were ripped open in times of war, about which the LORD was furious:

*Thus says the LORD: "For three transgressions of the people of Ammon, and for four, I will not turn away its punishment, **because they ripped open the women with child** in Gilead* (Amos 1:13).

Preventing a woman from conceiving also brought its own share of dire consequences from the LORD:

*Er, Judah's firstborn, was wicked in the sight of the LORD, and the LORD killed him. And Judah said to Onan, "Go in to your brother's wife and marry her, and raise up an heir to your brother." But Onan knew that the heir would not be his; and it came to pass, when he went in to his brother's wife, that **he emitted on the ground, lest he should give an heir to his brother**. And the thing which he did displeased the LORD; therefore He killed him also* (Genesis 38:7–10).

The sacrifice of children to the gods, also brought strong reaction from the LORD. He considered the children as His own—

you have slain My children ... "Woe, woe to you!" *says the LORD GOD* (Ezekiel 16:21, 23).

Abortion is nothing less than the sacrifice of children to the god of sex—the horrendous modem immolation of millions of fetuses on the altar of sexual gratification.

According to the book *Abortion: Questions & Answers*, by Dr. & Mrs. J.C. Willke, 1,600,000 abortions take place in America each year, which simply means 1,600,000 American mothers-to-be murder their babies every year. The Guttmacher Institute which documents abortions, states: "From 1973 through 2011, nearly 53 million legal abortions occurred in America." We should notice here that it is "legal" abortions mentioned—it does not include the multitudes of illegal abortions carried out each year. *Planned Parenthood*, a giant federal-funded ($528.4 million in 2014) nationwide series of abortion clinics was responsible for 327,653 of the abortions performed in 2014.

CNSNews.com reported on July 31, 2015, that White House records show that Cecile Richards, *Planned Parenthood's* president, had made 39 visits to the White House since President Barack Obama took office.

Addressing the *Planned Parenthood* Conference in April 2013 at the Marriott Wardman Park Hotel in Washington, D.C., President Obama extolled the virtues of *Planned Parenthood*, declared it essential to the "health" of American women and in fifteen minutes never once mentioned "abortion." Instead, he used euphemisms like "health care," "choice," and "contraceptive care," when in fact the mammoth abortion provider is guilty of infanticide. Obama ended his address by saying:

> I want you to know that **you've got a president who's going to be right there with you, fighting every step of the way**—thank you, Planned Parenthood. **God bless you**."

PRESIDENT OBAMA, MORE OF MUSLIM THAN a Protestant liberal-humanist Democrat, has full support from his Democrat Congressmen. However, *CNSNews.com* reports that Cardinal Raymond Burke, head of the highest court at the Vatican, said that House Minority Leader Nancy Pelosi, a Catholic,

> must be denied Communion under the law of the Catholic Church because of her longstanding support for abortion.

Regarding Pelosi, Cardinal Burke further said:

> This is a prime example of what Blessed John Paul II referred to as the situation of Catholics who have divorced their faith from their public life and therefore are not serving their brothers and sisters in the way that they must—in safeguarding and promoting the life of the innocent and defenseless unborn.

ABORTED BABIES' TINY BODIES ARE USED for experiments—often while they are still living, and according to both *Prophecy Today* and the *Lydia Information Bureau*, tens of thousands are reduced to ingredients for face cream that American women use to retard the aging process.

Planned Parenthood goes one step further: secret videos released in July and August 2015 by the *Center for Medical Progress* shows *Planned Parenthood's* "doctors" and "administrators" selling baby parts—hearts, livers, lungs, brains, and assorted tissues—on a price "per item" basis. *Planned Parenthood* officials discussed altering the abortion process to get "intact, fetal cadavers," and to help identify body parts from aborted twins, including intestines, brain, lung, arm and "orbits" (eyeballs). It was admitted that baby parts were being transported across state borders contrary to federal law, but they said *Planned Parenthood* had to be careful with this.

The same people who say that an unborn human fetus is "a meaningless clump of cells" are harvesting "livers and lungs and kidneys." On one of the videos it was alluded that undamaged, intact babies could be supplied whole. When pressed by the undercover reporter, posing as a buyer, how a live baby would be killed, the staff of *Planned Parenthood* declined to answer the question. However, in the 11th video secretly filmed in Planned Parenthood in Austin, Texas, and released in late October 2015, Dr. Amna Dermish, the abortion "doctor," describes what she does to get undamaged baby organs—an illegal partial-birth abortion.

She uses a sonogram so she can move the child into a breach (feet first) position, pulls the child out feet first, when she gets to the neck she snips the spinal cord killing the baby. In other words, she is performing an illegal partial-birth abortion, killing a live-born baby in order to harvest its organs. According to the video, she especially hopes this procedure yields intact fetal heads for brain harvesting

Her method would be very similar to the method used by an abortionist in a legal case that took place in January 2011, in West Philadelphia. The abortion "doctor," working in a "filthy, foul-smelling house of horrors," was charged with murder following the death of a woman who suffered an overdose of painkillers while awaiting an abortion. The abortionist was also charged with delivering seven babies alive and then using scissors to kill them.

District Attorney Seth Williams said the abortionist "induced labor, forced the live birth of viable babies in the sixth, seventh, eighth month of pregnancy and then killed those babies by cutting into the back of the neck with scissors and severing their spinal cord." A method referred to it as "snipping," prosecutors said, which is the same as that described by the government funded Planned Parenthood. Prosecutors estimated the abortionist ended hundreds of pregnancies by cutting the spinal cords, but they said they couldn't prosecute more cases because he destroyed files. "These killings became so routine that no one could put an exact number on them," the grand jury report said. "They were considered 'standard procedure." And the same president that had the White House lit up in rainbow colors to celebrate the obscene Supreme Court ruling on homosexual marriages asked for God's blessing on America's largest abortion provider. America—One nation under God? Never, it is: America—One nation under judgment.

In a sixth video released by the *Center for Medical Progress*, Whistle-blower Holly O'Donnell, a who worked at one of *Planned Parenthood's* clinics as a former Blood and Tissue Procurement Technician for *StemExpress*, a biotech company that partners with *Planned Parenthood* clinics to purchase their aborted fetus parts and resell them. O'Donnell said there was wanton disregard for either human life or the need to get a mother's consent to sell her aborted baby's parts.

Federal laws on the procurement and use of human fetal tissue require that patients consent to the tissue donation subsequent to consenting to the abortion procedure. As a procurement technician O'Donnell's job was to identify pregnant patients matching the specifications of *StemExpress* customers and to harvest the fetal body parts from their abortions. "It's not an option, it's a demand," O'Donnell said, adding:

> If there was a higher gestation, and the technicians needed it, there were times when they would just take what they wanted. And these mothers don't know.

In July 2015, *CNSNews.com* reported that Catholic Bishop Thomas Paprocki, head of the Roman Catholic Diocese of Springfield, Illinois, said:

> the moral decadence of our twenty-first century Western world now rivals the decline and fall of the Roman Empire. Historians tell us that abortion and infanticide were widespread, commonplace, and for the most part legal in the classical world of the Greeks and Romans. Perhaps if they had the technology at the time, they would have sold fetal body parts for profit.

Bishop Paprocki went on to say:

> It should not surprise us that the nationwide abortion provider *Planned Parenthood* has been exposed for trafficking and selling the body parts of aborted babies. I say we should not be surprised, but we still should be shocked and appalled at this moral depravity.

Paprocki pointed out that:

> the sale or purchase of human fetal tissue is a federal felony punishable by up to 10 years in prison and a fine of up to $500,000 .... Unborn babies are absolutely unable to consent to donating their organs, and the harvesting of their organs involves the premeditated killing of these babies.

Woe unto them! for they have gone in the way of Cain, and ran greedily after the error of Balaam for reward (Jude 11).

America — Chapter 13

AMERICAN TELEVISION IS BY FAR THE most universal, morally corrupting medium available. And by its carefully presented news stories, often flagrantly false, it influences American foreign policy and dictates its own predetermined ideas to the masses. It is a fact of history that whoever controls your information controls your judgment, and will, ultimately, control your actions.

The predominance of violence and sex in programs screened 24 hours day and night, is the major contributing factor for the accelerated breakdown of morality in America. According to an advertisement for *TV, etc.*, in the August 1990 edition of *Christianity Today*:

> ... the typical American child watches three and a half hours of television each day. By the end of high school he or she will have spent 22,000 hours in front of the television set!

That was 1990. Fast forward 25 years and the latest figures tell us that children in the U.S. still watch an average of three to four hours of television a day. By the time of high school graduation, they will have spent more time watching television than they have in the classroom. So, nothing has changed except the television content.

Thousands of studies conducted since the 1950s have asked whether there is a link between exposure to media violence and violent behavior. All but 18 of the studies have answered, "Yes." The evidence from the research is overwhelming:

> Extensive research evidence indicates that media violence contributes to aggressive behavior, desensitization to violence, nightmares, and fear of being harmed. Watching violent shows is also linked with having less empathy toward others. Violence, sexuality, race and gender stereotypes, drug and alcohol abuse are common themes of television programs.
>
> An average American child will see 200,000 violent acts and 16,000 murders on TV by age 18. Two-thirds of all programming contains violence. Programs designed for children often contain more violence than adult TV.

The stark reality of watching 22,000 hours of television, is that it equals the amount of time spent working an eight hour, five-day week—for ten years. This means that by the time the "typical American child" finishes High School he or she is brain-washed— politically and morally. There are some good, wholesome programs, but they do not appeal to the American majority.

Television is also the principal contributor to the covetous nature of the American populace. A continual bombardment of commercials imploring the battered viewer to "Buy!" "Buy!" "Buy!," is only interrupted for the space of a few brief minutes to return to the program. Americans live way beyond their means and prop up their life styles by being constantly, and deeply, in debt. The debt accrues because people must have what they cannot afford, and they load themselves with monthly payments on houses, cars, appliances, clothing, holidays, dental bills, etc. The purchaser often pays two to three times the actual worth of each individual item due to the high interest attached to the debts. The Bible calls this manner of living *"covetousness, which is idolatry"* (Colossians 3:5). The things which we possess often possess us and lead us further away from God:

> *They were filled and their heart was exalted; therefore they forgot Me*
> (Hosea 13:6).

THE GREAT AMERICAN DREAM HAS FADED away for many Americans. Imports are soaring while manufacturing and export figures are falling or remain almost static. Unemployment figures continue to climb and the official 2014 – 2015 figures are fudged and do not take into account the millions who have given up hope of ever finding a job. Americans not in the workforce in July 2015 reached a 38-year high of 93.8 million. Once unemployment benefits cease a person is no longer counted among the unemployed, which is where the government obtains its unemployment figures. The United States has moved from being the biggest creditor nation to the biggest debtor nation. The national debt in 1990 was $3.8 trillion and the forecasted debt by the U.S. Department of the Treasury for 1995 was fractionally less than $10 trillion. In August 2015 the national debt stood at $18.15 trillion and passed 103 percent of the GDP (Gross Domestic Product—the net sum minus taxes on all products and services in the nation); however the GDP for 2013 was $16.77 trillion and 2014's GDP was $17.42 trillion so 2015's national debt has already passed well beyond the year's GDP figure. The Congressional Budget Office (CBO) predicts that when President Obama leaves office the nationals debt will have risen from $10.6 trillion to $19.1 trillion, close to a doubling of the debt under his leadership.

This debt must be repaid at some future date if the economy is not to collapse entirely. To repay the national debt in 1995 would have meant that every man, woman and child would have had to pay $40,000 to the U.S. government—in cash. In 2015 every man, woman, and child in America currently owes $59,743 for their share of the U.S. public debt. The entire financial structure of the U.S. is like a house of cards. Larry Burkett, in *The*

America — Chapter 13

Coming Economic Earthquake, records that personal bankruptcies jumped from less than 100,000 in 1970 to nearly 700,000 in 1990. However, in 2010 filings reached 1.53 million but dropped again to 988,000 in 2014 but are expected to rise once more in 2015.

AMERICAN BANKS HAVE BEEN FAILING AT an alarming rate of about 13 each month for years. In just the first ten months of 1991, 117 U.S. banks failed. The U.S. subprime mortgage scandal—officially called a "crisis," but factually it was a scandal—enriched Wall Street tycoons but toppled the entire world's economy. It crashed the U.S. housing market and created a national banking emergency with banks toppling like dominoes. In an e-letter from the *Personal Liberty Digest* on 6 August 2015 it was stated that nineteen major banks would likely shut down soon, which was a "terrifying" prospect and could cause "mass panic." America has yet to recover from the Great Recession which was entirely of its own making.

AMERICAN DIPLOMATIC SUCCESSES ARE NOTHING TO boast about either. President Truman was indeed the first head of state to recognize the new State of Israel in 1948—11 minutes after its declaration. But he did so in direct opposition to the U.S. State Department, which had used every conceivable device to stop the state of Israel from being born. Abba Eban, in his book *Personal Witness*, writes that the language of George Marshall, the Secretary of State, was "virulent" when admonishing Truman for wanting to recognize Israel:

> They don't deserve a state, they have stolen that country. If you give this recognition, Mr President, I may not vote for you in the next election.

And George Kennan, the head of the State Department planning staff, wrote:

> U.S. prestige in the Muslim world has suffered a severe blow, and U.S. strategic interests in the Mediterranean and the Near East have been seriously prejudiced.

CONCERNS FOR "U.S. PRESTIGE IN THE Muslim world," and for its "strategic interests" in the region is what guides the State Department's relationship with Israel—a prescribed policy of double standards. The United States has been a "friend" to Israel only insofar as it has suited it to be. Much is made about the $3 billion aid package that Israel receives from the U.S., but how many people realize that from this package Israel must pay the U.S. $800 million in interest and $400 million in loan repayments—constituting 40 percent of the entire package? Of the remaining $1.8 billion, Israel receives

$400 million in cash, while $1.4 billion must be spent in the U.S. Thus it costs the U.S. government $400 million to keep Israel dangling like a puppet on a string. Other nations, Egypt for example, are forgiven their multi-billion dollar debts, but Israel is "given" aid in order to repay the enormous amounts of interest charged on its loans.

An example of American control of Israeli domestic affairs was the forced cancellation of the *Lavi* fighter-plane. Israel had spent years and millions of dollars developing the Lavi, and it was being constructed according to Israel's wide operational experience in the theatre of war. Three prototypes were operational by 1988 and the plane was said to be the best war-plane being produced anywhere in the world. The U.S. government threatened Israel with penalties if it did not stop production of the Lavi. Apparently it constituted a threat to the sales of the American F-16 fighter-jet. Israel complied.

The United States has been the only major weapons supplier to sell arms to Israel since the 1967 Six-Day War. Britain, France, China and the former Soviet Union refuse to sell to Israel—instead they supply the Arab nations who are in a declared state of war with Israel. Less publicized is the fact that the United States also sells tens of billions of dollars worth of arms to the Arab states—ostensibly to keep a "military balance." The Tel Aviv *Nativ Center for Political Research*, in the June 21, 1993 issue of its *Middle East Intelligence Digest*, said the staggering sum of almost $1 trillion had been spent on arms in the Middle East since 1973. Other reports show that of this huge amount, Israel procured only 15 percent. Nearly six times the amount of arms sold to the Jewish state was sold to the Arabs. Who is kidding whom with statements about keeping a military balance? What type of balance is 85 to 15? Almost the whole world knows that American interests lie more with Arab oil and arms sales than with Israel. Little has changed in U.S. policies since 1993—Britain, France, Russia, and China still sell weapons to the Muslim states and refuse to sell weapons to Israel, while the U.S. maintains its bank balances by arming both Israel and the Muslim nations in a state of war with Israel. On July 16, 2014 *CNSNews.com* reported:

> At a time when Hamas continues to fire salvos of rockets into Israel while rejecting a ceasefire proposal, the United States has finalized a deal to provide the Palestinian terrorist group's leading supporter, Qatar, with weaponry worth $11 billion.

Some months after the first Gulf War the *Jerusalem Post* carried an article in which an American working in Kuwait was asked by a Kuwaiti, "***If we grew carrots, do you think you would save us?***"

America — *Chapter 13*

After the Gulf War, calls were made by all the major powers for arms control. In March 1993, the Christian Friends of Israel *Watchman's Prayer Letter* told us:

> Two years after the Gulf War, the Middle East arms race is in full swing again as if nothing happened. Calls for arms control have vanished. France, Britain and the United States were locked this month against one another, in the battle for a $4 billion arms contract with the United Arab Emirates ... Along with this move by these three countries, more than 350 weapons manufacturers from 34 countries turned up for the opening of the Gulf region's largest "arms bazaar" held in Abu Dhabi.

America, like all the rest, sells arms—weapons of death—simply out of greed. The deaths, the mutilations, the injuries and the misery inflicted as a result are of no consequence when mammon reigns supreme. The word, "righteousness," has been dropped in favor of "advantageous." A report in the 1992, 4th Quarter issue of the *Dispatch From Jerusalem*, says:

> Israeli officials are outraged over the proposed sale of an American super-secret spy satellite to the United Arab Emirates. For years Israel has begged the Americans, without success, to receive detailed satellite pictures of the region. The Israelis were even refused this information when Iraqi SCUD missiles were raining down on Tel Aviv. America has also denied help to the Israelis as they attempted to build a satellite of their own.

It has been the double-dealing by America that forced Israel into developing its own satellite systems (mentioned on page 69), now Israel often shares intelligence data gathered by its satellites with the U.S. And the "Yes," "No," "Maybe" approach to being able to purchase defensive weapons and military hardware pushed Israel into developing many of its own weapons and military hardware. Israel is today the eighth largest exporter of arms in the world, the proceeds of which are fed straight back into its weapons research and development program.

Shmuel Katz, writing in the *Jerusalem Post* on April 6, 1993, points out that in August 1975 the U.S. applied pressure to Israel to give up territory gained from Egypt in the 1973 Yom Kippur war. This territory was considered vital to Israel's security and also contained the Abu Rodeis oil-field. Loss of the oil-field compelled Israel to spend billions each year on oil. The reward for complying to the dictates of the U.S. government was:

> ... a major pledge to supply Israel with the upcoming F15s. When, three years later, the planes reached production, this pledge, be it

remembered, was violated by the new president, Carter, who refused to supply the planes unless Congress authorized him to sell F15s also to Saudi Arabia; and the pledge was violated further, in 1981, by the Reagan administration when it supplied the Saudis with enhanced-offensive equipment for the F15—thus stultifying completely the original "concession" to Israel.

THE HABIT OF MAKING POLITICAL COVENANTS and breaking them has been a norm in the way the U.S. has related to Israel. In June 1967, just prior to the Six-Day War, president Johnson "could not find" the 1957 document which recorded the pledge to aid Israel if Egypt closed the Tiran Straits, which it had done on May 23. The editor of the *Middle East Intelligence Digest* comments in the June 12, 1992, issue:

> Making promises, getting Israel to make decisions based on these promises, and then breaking them; this has apparently been a center-pin of US diplomacy in the Middle East.

The H.W. Bush administration was repeatedly described in Israel as "the most unfriendly U.S. administration in Israel's history." The *Jerusalem Post International Edition*, March 21, 1992, quotes James Baker, Bush's Secretary of State, as saying, "the Jews can go to hell;" however, John Loftus and Mark Aarons in their book *The Secret War Against the Jews* say Baker actually said: "Fuck the Jews, they won't vote for us anyway."

An article headed: "Baker promised Husseini a state," in the *Jerusalem Post International Edition*, February 13, 1993, reports: "Palestinian leaders here told their followers they were assured by former U.S. Secretary of State James Baker that they would see an independent Palestinian state." Under the guise of being an "honest broker" between Israel and the Arab nations, America had already sold Israel out. George Habash, a PLO terrorist leader said on June 9, 1989, over the Lebanese *Voice of the Mountain Radio*:

> The establishment of a Palestinian state in the West Bank and Gaza will be the beginning of the downfall of the Zionist enterprise. We will be able to rely on this defeat in order to complete the struggle to realize our entire goal.

The establishment of a Palestinian state is lauded as a defeat for Israel. A Palestinian state is publicly claimed to be a launching pad for a war aimed at totally destroying Israel, and the American State Department knowingly promotes it right up to this present day.

After Iraq invaded Kuwait in August 1990, the United States pledged to protect Israel from Iraqi aggression. An Israeli general interviewed on *Israel Radio*, commented:

America — Chapter 13

> If we were to rely upon the promises of the U.S. we would be at the bottom of the sea.

BRUCE BRILL, A MIDEAST INTELLIGENCE ANALYST, who served in the U.S. Army Security Agency at the U.S. National Security Agency at Fort Meade, Maryland, from 1971 to 1974, told Israel of the deliberate withholding of vital information by America. The following extract is from an article written by Brill and published in the *Jerusalem Post* on Friday, October 23, 1992:

> The traditional antagonism of the US State Department toward Israel is mirrored in the US intelligence community. For example ... While working at the Agency as an Arabic and "Special Arabic" traffic analyst in the early 1970s, I learned of the planned October 6, 1973, invasion of Israel by Syria and Egypt — 30 hours before the US notified Israel.
>
> Upper-echelon Agency personnel knew of the planned attack hours, if not days, prior to that. Not passing this vital information along in time resulted in the unnecessary deaths and maiming of thousands of young Israelis.
>
> The US intelligence community's anti-Israel policy has until now been successfully kept secret, even at the Agency itself, since "the need to know" rule governing such policies is strictly applied only to select non-Jews ... I naturally assumed that Israel, America's publicly declared friend, would have been notified immediately through the proper channels about the imminent attack on October 6, 1973. Now I live haunted by the possibility that, somehow, I could have discovered that the intelligence was not being forwarded, gotten it to the Israelis and thereby saved some measure of the anguish that became known as the Yom Kippur War.
>
> Yet I didn't, and I agonize over it each Yom Kippur. I was a loyal American military intelligence analyst who **contributed toward Israel's planned demise**.

Apparently, U.S. administrations were surprised that Israel had continued to exist in the face of such powerful opposition. Some years ago, Professor Eugene Rostow, a former under-secretary of state, told how shocked he was when, at a cocktail party during an international conference in Brussels, he heard an American diplomat describe Israel as a "passing phenomenon."

THE DOUBLE STANDARDS EMPLOYED BY THE U.S. against Israel are appalling. Israel has been placed under microscopes by both the government and the media. Every action is both analyzed and criticized. Wherever an Israeli might travel, the voice of Uncle Sam condemns him in newspaper headlines. Some of those headlines read: **US joins UN criticism of Israeli plan** (*Bangkok Post*, December 22, 1990); **US troops fly home as Bush warns Israel** (*The Hong Kong Standard*, March 8, 1991); **Baker blames Israel for lack of progress** (*The Cedar Rapids Gazette*, April 27, 1991); **Bush Bashes Israel** (*Newsweek*, March 9, 1992). Thousands of such headlines reporting U.S. condemnation of Israel still appear all over the world. But when the Bush administration wooed Syria into joining the coalition against Iraq for the 1991 Gulf War, it, and the entire American media, turned a blind eye to the Syrian invasion of the Christian enclave in Beirut and completely ignored the carnage. Some 40,000 Syrian troops, backed by 2,000 tanks wiped out thousands of Christian soldiers. Gruesome pictures of 600 Christian officers, bound hand and foot—and shot through the back of the head—were published in Israeli papers and broadcast on local television. The American media ignored the whole thing—it was simply not "advantageous" to American interests. Will God forget such hypocrisy? Indeed He will not.

AFTER TAKING OFFICE IN 2008 PRESIDENT Barack Obama steadily manufactured a "full-blown" crisis in U.S.-Israel relations because Israeli Prime Minister Binyamin Netanyahu did not bow before him like other international political sycophants were doing. The 2015 relationship between the two countries is the worst in two decades. Prime Minister Netanyahu believes President Obama is hopelessly naive about the Middle East and he has not only been disrespected by Obama, but has also been deliberately misled by him on matters concerning Iran's nuclear program.

In September 2009, then U.S. Secretary of State Hillary Clinton, with reference to Prime Minister Netanyahu, was advised to:

> find the ground from which you can make his politics uneasy— I think you can do that even with current concerns in Israel about U.S. posture.

A number (most) of U.S. presidents have sought to bring down Israeli prime ministers whose policies have differed from those of the U.S. Sometimes they have been successful like President H.W. Bush bringing down Prime Minister Yitzhak Shamir, and President Bill Clinton bringing down Prime Minister Netanyahu in his first term. Clinton sent his top campaign people to set up an office in Jerusalem to specifically get Ehud Barak elected as prime minister, and they succeeded.

President Obama had some of his electioneering people working to oust Netanyahu in March 2015 and, according to a U.S. investigation launched after the elections, Obama even used federal funds to strengthen Netanyahu's opposition. However, Obama did not succeed in pulling down Netanyahu.

Instead, Netanyahu handed his opposition a humiliating landslide defeat. The Chief Editor of the *Times of Israel* reported the following morning:

> King Bibi had not merely managed to hold onto his crown. He had cemented his rule.

AT THE HEIGHT OF THE OBAMA anti-Netanyahu crisis, which is ongoing at this time, Iran was, and is still, hell-bent on producing nuclear weapons and repeatedly makes threats to annihilate Israel. Most of the world ignores Iran's threats against Israel because most of the world is inherently anti-Semitic. However, Israel made plans to attack and destroy Iran's nuclear facilities seeing it as an existential threat to the nation.

Israel coordinates closely with America on its military activities and it was no different when it came to planning a sophisticated attack against some fifteen or more nuclear sites in Iran. Israel would have up to 150 fighter-jets in the air practicing at one time, but when Netanyahu notified Obama of Israel's intention to strike Iran, Obama would have the information "leaked" to the world's media. Obama also placed other countries in grave danger when he divulged which airstrips in which country Israel would use. Israel, of course, kept shelving its plans. According to an October 2015 *Wall Street Journal* report, "'Nerves frayed at the White House' when the US discovered Israeli air activity over Iran in 2012, and Washington dispatched an aircraft carrier to the Mideast and also prepared attack aircraft." Obama's "leaks" to the media at the time made an attack too risky for Israel to undertake, but 2012 had not been the only time Israel penetrated Iran's air defenses.

When it was considered to be too late for an attack on Iran's nuclear facilities, that the "window of opportunity" had closed, a senior Obama administration official—said to have been Obama himself—called Netanyahu "chicken-shit" for not attacking Iran.

IN WHAT WAS LARGELY MISSED BY the mainstream media and which can only be described as an unprecedented act of revenge, no doubt emanating from President Obama's intense dislike of Prime Minister Netanyahu, the Pentagon, in March 2015, quietly declassified a Department of Defense top-secret document detailing Israel's nuclear program. Israel's nuclear program, a highly covert topic that Israel has never formally acknowledged and which the U.S. up until that time had respected by remaining silent.

By publishing the declassified document the U.S. actively breached the silent agreement to keep quiet on Israel's nuclear powers. The document detailed the nuclear program in great depth.

A highly suspicious aspect of the document is that while Obama saw fit to declassify sections on Israel's sensitive nuclear program, he kept sections on Italy, France, West Germany and other NATO countries classified, with those sections blocked out in the document.

The document noted that research laboratories in Israel were equivalent to key U.S. laboratories developing America's nuclear arsenal. The declassified document informed the world that Israel was developing the kind of codes which would enable it to make hydrogen bombs—codes which detail fission and fusion processes showing that in the late 1980s Israel already had the ability to create bombs considered a thousand times more powerful than atom bombs.

AT THE TIME OF WRITING THE U.S. Congress was facing a September 17, 2015 deadline to accept or reject a negotiated deal slowing Iran's ability to produce nuclear weapons. President Obama used lies and innuendoes in order to prevent Congress from rejecting the deal, which has a number of very serious flaws. Obama's Democrats prevented the deal from even coming to a vote at all, which went against Congressional law. Obama called the action "democratic." It was unfettered fawning on the part of the Democrat members of Congress. And at the end of November 2015 the U.S. State Department wrote in a letter to Representative Mike Pompeo (R-Kansas) that:

> President Obama's nuclear deal with Iran is not a "legally binding or signed" agreement, but rather a reflection of "political commitments."

With Obama wanting to establish a legacy for himself, and Netanyahu wanting to preserve Israel's existence, the pair continually butted heads over the nuclear deal. With Obama being so politically powerful there were bound to be severe negative repercussions for Israel. Israel, however, does not plan to absorb an Iranian nuclear attack in order to maintain a quasi relationship with Obama.

ALL THE SIGNS OF DIVINE JUDGMENT can be observed throughout the U.S. today. The government debt is the largest debt recorded in world history, and total economic collapse appears more and more likely. AIDS and other sexually transmitted diseases, together with cholera, malaria, typhoid, tuberculosis, etc., are increasing every year. Physical catastrophes, which cause many deaths and widespread destruction, cost billions in damages—$15.3 billion in 2014—and are becoming more frequent.

In August 2005 Hurricane Katrina blew into New Orleans, creating America's all-time costliest disaster at $108 billion. At the time of writing California is gripped in a devastating years-long drought which threatens to turn it into a dustbowl. Stealing other people's water has become the preferred occupation for many residents and is the state's most lucrative and fastest expanding business. Wildfires in California and elsewhere are destroying thousands of homes, and at the time of writing, more than 9.3 million acres have gone up in smoke in 2015.

On April 24, 2015, the *Express* reported that Scientific experts at the European Science Foundation said "volcanoes, especially super-volcanoes like the one at Yellowstone National Park, Wyoming, which has a caldera measuring 34 by 45 miles (55 by 72 kilometers), pose more threat to Earth and the survival of the human race than asteroids, earthquakes, nuclear war, and global warming." They say Yellowstone is "one of the world's most dangerous active volcanoes—a ticking time bomb," which they conclude may well to go off sometime within the next 70 – 80 years and could "wipe out the western USA and affect the course of global history."

AMERICA SUFFERED A HUMILIATING AND COSTLY defeat in Vietnam. It was also forced to withdraw from Lebanon in 1983—"a major American diplomatic and military fiasco," according to Howard M. Sacher in *A History of Israel*. Volume II. The Gulf War, however, restored some American credibility in the eyes of the world. This was not so much of a war between nations but more of a war between gods. It was a conflict between Iraq and a coalition of 39 nations including the U.S., Britain, Egypt, France, and Saudi Arabia; 28 nations contributed troops. And although the LORD GOD of Israel won the war hands down against Allah, god of Islam, America took all the credit for it and General Norman Swartzkopf made millions by writing a book.

There were few, if any, real battles between the opposing armies in the Gulf War. The Iraqis retreated so rapidly that American armored vehicles got too far ahead of the supply lines and ran out of fuel chasing them. A member of the 101st Airborne based at Fort Campbell told me that when they parachuted into the war zone, their feet went down on the ground and Iraqi hands went up in the air. This professional soldier said that he did not fire a single shot during the entire war.

According to *Israel Radio* on June 26, 1992, Swartzkopf misled the world's masses when he showed them a destroyed SCUD missile launcher when in fact it was a fuel tank. And in an interview with Israel *Air Force Magazine*, and reprinted in the *Jerusalem Post* on January 11, 1992, the head of the IAF intelligence said, "Israel has no proof that even one Iraqi mobile SCUD launcher has actually been destroyed." Israel was anxious to see every SCUD launcher destroyed and wanted the air force to take them out personally. But she did not get involved in the war and American author Jim Lederman, in his book *Battle Lines*, tells why:

... both print and television bought into and blandly accepted the story line promoted by the [U.S.] administration praising Israel for its "restraint" in not retaliating after SCUD ground-to-ground missiles hit Tel Aviv. In fact, the United States had the Israelis by the political and military jugular throughout the crisis period. They refused to give the Israelis the International Friend or Foe (IFF) codes used by allied air craft over Iraq. Had the Israelis tried to retaliate from the air, they might not only have seen their own planes shot down but, more important, they might have shot down an allied plane.

The successes claimed during the Gulf War turned out to be patently false. It has been conclusively proven that the "hero" of the war—the *Patriot* anti-missile missile—although conceptually good, was highly ineffective. Thirty-one of the 39 SCUD missiles fired at Israel were not brought down and these damaged or destroyed some 5,000 Israeli homes. The SCUD missile that slammed into a U.S. barracks in Riyadh caused most of the American fatalities of the war.

According to the *Nashville Banner* of April 10, 1992, both the Stealth Fighter and the Tomahawk missile were only 50 percent accurate, and the laser guided bombs (i.e. "smart bombs") only chalked up 60 percent. The *Banner* also said that the declared number of destroyed armored vehicles was inflated by more than 70 percent. Jim Lederman, in *Battle Lines* says:

> ... the laser guided bombs, for example, were always shown to have worked perfectly ... All American television networks ended up running patently absurd stories blaming those deaths of allied soldiers from friendly fire entirely on human error, not on the prized and precious equipment.

The number of opposing Iraqi troops was constantly given as more than 500,000. But according to a Washington report published in *The Courier Journal*, April 22, 1992:

> The United States and its allies faced a demoralized Iraqi military of 183,000 troops, less than half estimated by the Pentagon ... U.S. and allied troops held an overwhelming 5-to-1 advantage at the start of the ground war on February 23, 1991.

Ze'ev Eitan, senior research associate at the *Jaffee Center for Strategic Studies* in Tel Aviv, also states:

> Claims made immediately after the Gulf War had Iraq suffering 100,000 fatalities. Another figure cited was 150,000 .... The numbers accepted now vary from 8,000 to 20,000.

America — Chapter 13

The success of the Persian Gulf War was plainly not all that it was made out to be: the performance of U.S. weaponry was exaggerated; the number of casualties and extent of damage to enemy equipment was greatly distorted; and the number of enemy troops was half of what was reported. These facts do not appear to be widely known. Saddam Hussein was not forced from power and he lived to cause more turmoil. But after the defeats in Vietnam and Lebanon, the huge successes claimed in the Gulf War has restored the lost pride of the fiercely patriotic American people. However, the U.S. and Britain was forced to declare war upon Iraq again in 2003 and this time Saddam Hussein was forced from power and subsequently hung for crimes against humanity (see Chapter 20—Iraq).

It is my firm opinion that the God of Israel was the architect of the Gulf Wars, and that He orchestrated them with a particular purpose in mind. There is no doubt that the eight-year-long Second Gulf War, humiliated Iraq, but it did not destroy it. The U.S. lost 36,700 of its troops to death or injury, but in 2015, the U.S. itself is being humiliated in Iraq because of the rise of Islamic jihadists fighters, led by Saddam Hussein's former army officers. ISIL has taken over large areas of the country, defeating hands-down the Iraqi troops "trained" to replace American troops when they pulled out.

The U.S. is also being humiliated by the Muslim Taliban in Afghanistan, a country which the U.S. invaded following the horrific destruction of New York's Twin Towers and the death of some 3,000 American civilians by al-Qaeda terrorists in September 2001. Following 14 years of warfare, which has thus far cost America 21,000 dead and wounded, the U.S. is carrying out a staged withdrawal—with its tail between its legs. All the boasting about a "New World Order" and a "thousand points of light" by President H.W. Bush made the U.S. overly confident in its military strength and capabilities—a number of coalition members withdrew their troops and support for the war in Afghanistan, rightly judging it to be a lose-lose conflict for the West.

Due to U.S. meddling and muddling in the Middle East the whole region is aflame today, it is a powder keg waiting to explode into a full blown Word War III. Murder and mayhem now rules supreme in the Middle East and it is being exported back to Western nations—the jihadi chickens are coming home to roost. The Twin Towers disaster was but an Islamic appetizer, the main course is still cooking. America will get a taste of what Israel has been fed for its 67-year modern history. The die has been cast; the LORD will use the Middle East mayhem to entice the "New World Order" into a confrontation with Israel sometime in the not-too-distant future, and that means judgment. Indeed, judgment has already begun for America. Its sins are very many and we have merely looked at a few on the top of the pile. Looking at America, once the most powerful nation on earth, we see it disintegrating before our very eyes. Before his death in 1975 at age 86, historian Arnold J. Toynbee said:

> Of the twenty-two civilizations that have appeared in history, nineteen of them collapsed when they reached the moral state the United States is in now.

That was 40 years ago. The moral state of the U.S. has since degenerated into total perversity and joyful heathenism. Toynbee also said:

> "Civilizations die from suicide, not by murder."

The once great United States has committed suicide and is in its death throes. Their is a large chorus of historians and Christian clergy saying that America now rivals the decline and fall of the Roman Empire. However, the LORD says:

> *If My people who are called by My name will humble themselves, and pray and seek My face, and turn from their wicked ways, then I will hear from heaven, and will forgive their sin and heal their land*
> (2Chronicles 7:14).

American Christians need to deal with their sin of spiritual apathy, repent of it and bring forth fruits worthy of repentance. Then they must cry out to the Lord for mercy on behalf of their nation.

Sins briefly touched upon in this chapter are:

a) Rejection of God
b) Rejection of God's Salvation
c) Suppressing or Hindering the preaching of the Gospel
d) Refusal to hear and live by God's Word
e) Practicing witchcraft, horoscopes and the occult
f) **Coveting** (form of idolatry)
g) Blasphemy
h) Slavery and Oppression
i) **Discriminating against strangers** (includes racial discrimination)
j) Murder, perverse and immoral behavior
k) Breaking political agreements
l) Pride in National Security
m) Using power and wealth to make lesser nations subservient
n) Allies of those waging war against Israel
o) Homosexuality

America — Chapter 13

p) **Sodomy** (sexual perversion, including acts with animals)
q) **Incest**
r) **Adultery, divorce and sexual lusts**

The judgments are, therefore: **Near annihilation** (eight times); **Physical catastrophes and widespread death** (five times); **Destruction of nation** (eight times); **Annihilation** (three times); and **Collapse of nation**. Unless sincere repentance is soon forthcoming, America has a clear indication of what to expect from the hand of the LORD. Without repentance America has no hope—it is being sucked into the vortex of God's wrath—*for the LORD has a controversy with* America.

14

Britain

Britain is another dying empire. Its great decline is a forewarning of the cataclysm that is yet to come. Those with a sense of nostalgia call it "Great Britain," but it is no longer "great"—it is now a part of Europe and may soon be back to being just an island again. Some call the whole of the British Isles the "United Kingdom," but Northern Ireland fought against British rule for more than a 100 years, and Scotland holds referendums, hoping to secede from what was placed upon them by force via the ballot box.

Britain was a mighty power that reached to the ends of the earth, but it made the same mistake that so many other great world powers had made before her—she touched *"the apple of* God's eye" (Zechariah 2:8).

DURING WORLD WAR I, BRITAIN RAN out of acetone, a chemical imported from Germany and from which cordite, an essential component of gunpowder, was made. Britain, unable to manufacture high explosives, was in dire straits. Defeat by her enemies was inevitable if a synthetic cordite was not produced. A brilliant Jewish chemist, Chaim Weizmann, was summoned to the British War Office by the First Lord of the Admiralty, Winston Churchill, and asked to produce 30,000 tons of synthetic cordite. Weizmann, with every available government facility at his disposal, manufactured a synthetic cordite which actually produced a higher explosive than cordite from acetone.

During the time Weizmann was busy producing cordite, British forces, led by General Edmund Allenby, were fighting the Turks for control of Palestine. After Weizmann had produced the requested amount of cordite he was asked what he wanted as recompense. He replied:

> If Britain wins the battle for Palestine, I ask for a national home for my people in their ancient land.

To this Britain agreed. Shortly afterward, on November 2, 1917, the British Foreign Minister Arthur James Balfour, on behalf of the government, issued the following statement which had been submitted to, and approved by, the Cabinet:

> His Majesty's Government views with favour the establishment in Palestine of a national home for the Jewish people, and will use their best endeavours to facilitate the achievement of this object, it being clearly understood that nothing shall be done which may prejudice the civil and religious rights of existing non-Jewish communities in Palestine, or the rights and political status enjoyed by Jews in any other country.

The following month, on December 11, General Allenby formally took possession of the city of Jerusalem. On October 28, 1918, the last engagement was fought with the Turks, and three days later, on October 31, an armistice was signed. For Turkey, the war was over, and Palestine was completely in British hands (as was most all of the Arab world).

But just as the Pharaohs of old forgot the good that Joseph had done for Egypt, so too did succeeding British prime ministers ignore the good that Weizmann had done for Britain. Huge reserves of oil were being systematically uncovered: in Iraq (1923); Bahrain (1932); Saudi Arabia (1937); Kuwait (1938); and Qatar (1940). The Arabs were soon to possess 60 percent of the world's known oil reserves and Britain began dreaming of a vast, incredibly wealthy overland empire stretching from South Africa to India. Palestine itself was the land bridge between Cairo, Damascus, and Baghdad, and now the Jews had become the proverbial fly in the ointment.

British opposition to the Jewish National Home grew, and expressed itself in violent hatred of the Jews. The British were swept up in "an unprecedented epidemic of anti-Semitism," wrote Vladimir Jabotinsky, one of the early Zionist leaders.

> Not in Russia, nor in Poland had there been such an intense and widespread atmosphere of hatred as prevailed in the British army in Palestine in 1919 and 1920.

Colonel Richard Meinertzhagen, the British Chief of Intelligence in the Middle East at the time, says the British army actually instigated the riots against the Jewish presence in Palestine. In *Middle East Diary, 1917 – 1956*, Meinertzhagen writes about a meeting between the Jerusalem military governor's chief of staff, Richard Waters-Taylor, and Haj Amin al-Husseini — an evil, unscrupulous Arab leader in Palestine:

> Waters-Taylor saw Haj al-Amin on the Wednesday before Easter [1920] and told him that he had a great opportunity to show the world that **... if disturbances of sufficient violence occurred in Jerusalem at Easter ... General Allenby would advocate the abandonment of the Jewish National Home.**

Britain — Chapter 14

The first riot took the lives of six Jews and wounded 211 others. Jewish police had been taken off duty and the security forces were nowhere to be found. On the day of the rioting Meinertzhagen records that Jerusalem was covered with posters reading: "***The Government is with us, Allenby is with us, kill the Jews; there is no punishment for killing Jews***." Arab riots, under the watchful eyes of the British authorities, were soon to take hundreds of Jewish lives and cause thousands of casualties.

The British High Commissioner even appointed Husseini, the perpetrator of the riots, as Grand Mufti (Muslim spiritual leader) of Jerusalem. Meinertzhagen says of Haj Amin:

> He hates both Jews and British ... his appointment is sheer madness.

Haj al-Amin was the leader of both anti-Jewish and anti-British activity, and later became a confident and helper of Adolf Hitler—active in pressuring Hitler to formulate a plan to exterminate Europe's Jews rather than deporting them to Palestine.

Neville Chamberlain's administration committed political treachery in 1939 by introducing on May 17, what came to be known as the White Paper. The infamous document stated that:

a) An independent Arab State was to be set up in Palestine within ten years;

b) A total of 75,000 Jews were to be admitted to Palestine during the next five years, and after five years there would be no further Jewish immigration without the consent of the Arabs;

c) Land restrictions were to be imposed, and only small parcels of land in restricted areas would be available to Jews.

THIS ABOUT-FACE IN BRITISH POLICY was intended to win the Arabs to the British cause. Britain considered it more advantageous to appease them than the Jews. Winston Churchill denounced the White Paper as a betrayal akin to the Munich treaty (on September 30, 1938, Chamberlain met with Adolf Hitler in Munich, where he betrayed Czechoslovakia, and came back to London announcing "peace for our time"—49 million lives were to be lost during the next seven years). Chamberlain and his Foreign Secretary, Lord Halifax, are recorded by Abba Eban in *Personal Witness*, as saying:

> When war comes, the Jews will have to support us because the enemy is Hitler. The Arabs will have a choice. Support of Hitler is a viable option for them. Therefore, **we must support the hostile Arabs and distance ourselves from the cooperative Jews**.

JEWS HAD ALWAYS MAINTAINED A PRESENCE in their homeland even after the wars with the Romans in the first and second centuries, and despite the persecution suffered at the hands of both Muslims and Christians. David Dolan says in *Holy War for the Promised Land*:

> Official records listed 43 Jewish communities in the sixth century: 12 along the coast, in the Negev Desert and east of the Jordan River; and 31 in the Galilee and Jordan Valley.

A GREAT DEAL OF ATTENTION IS given in the anti-Israel world press to the claims made by Muslim Arabs, namely that the Arabs were always the great majority in Palestine, and that Israel stole their land. When we consider the official record of 43 Jewish communities, together with the writings of famous authors, we find a huge discrepancy between fact and Arab fantasy. For instance, in 1866, W.M. Thompson wrote in his book *The Land and the Book*:

> How melancholy is this utter desolation! **Not a house, not a trace of inhabitants, not even shepherds**.

Mark Twain toured the Holy Land the following year—in 1867, and in *The Innocents Abroad*, wrote:

> The hallowed spot where the shepherds watched their flocks by night, and where the angels sang, '*Peace on earth, goodwill to men*,' is **untenanted by any living creature** and the desert places around them sleep in the hush of a solitude that is inhabited only by birds of prey and skulking foxes ...
>
> ... a desolate country whose soil is rich enough, but is given wholly to weeds—a silent mournful expanse. **We never saw a human being on the whole route**.

Forty-three Jewish communities: along the coast or given to studying Holy Scripture in Jerusalem or in the Galilee, but no trace of Arabs. Where, then, were all the millions of Muslims that were claimed to have been living in the land? They were obviously not keeping flocks of sheep and goats in open fields. Perhaps they were in Jerusalem—the city that housed the largest population in Palestine? The American newspaper *Pittsburgh Dispatch* of July 15, 1889, explodes that myth also:

> **Thirty thousand** out of 40,000 people in Jerusalem are Jews.

And most of the 10,000 non-Jews were Christians, not Muslims.

Britain — Chapter 14

The truth of the matter is that the majority of Palestinian Arabs came in the twentieth-century to take advantage of the improved conditions and jobs created by the Jews. After the Balfour Declaration that promised a Jewish national home in Palestine, Jews began to make their way to the land in ever increasing numbers. Agriculture and manufacturing flourished with their determined efforts and Arabs were attracted to Palestine like bees to a honey pot. Chaim Weizmann, in his autobiography, *Trial and Error*, printed a letter from Emir Feisal, the leader of that part of the Arab world. The letter was addressed to Felix Frankfurter (later Justice Frankfurter of the U.S. Supreme Court) who represented the Jews in negotiations with the Arab delegation on February 6, 1919, at a conference in Versailles, Paris:

> Hedjaz Delegation
> Paris
> March 3, 1919.
>
> Dear Mr. Frankfurter:
>
> I want to take this opportunity of my first contact with American Zionists, to tell you what I have often been able to say to Dr. Weizmann in Arabia and Europe.
>
> We feel that the Arabs and Jews are cousins in race, suffering similar oppressions at the hands of powers stronger than themselves, and by happy coincidence have been able to take the first step toward the attainment of their national ideals together.
>
> We Arabs, especially the educated among us, *look with the deepest sympathy on the Zionist movement*. Our deputation here in Paris is fully acquainted with the proposals submitted by the Zionist Organization to the Peace Conference, and *we regard them as moderate and proper. We will do our best, in so far as we are concerned, to help them through; we will wish the Jews a most hearty welcome home.*
>
> With the chiefs of your movement, especially with Dr. Weizmann, we have had, and continue to have, the closest relations. He has been a great helper of our cause, and *I hope the Arabs may soon be in a position to make the Jews some return for their kindness.*
>
> Yours sincerely,
> (*Sgd*.) Feisal

THE LEADER OF THAT PART OF the Arab world (the emir later became King Feisal of Iraq, and his brother Abdullah became king of Trans-Jordan) welcomed the Jews home to their ancient land. He acknowledged their expertise and welcomed it for the benefits it would bring to his people. Not only did Feisal welcome the Jews home, but article IV of the Arab-Jewish Agreement that he had signed at the Versailles conference said:

> *All necessary measures shall be taken to encourage and stimulate immigration of Jews into Palestine on a large scale, and as quickly as possible.*

The British leaders knew this only too well, but a Jewish National Home in Palestine no longer suited their purposes. It was more advantageous to placate the minority extremist element due to the possibility of war and the Arab capability to supply oil.

The Jews reacted bitterly and with anger to the White Paper. They declared their total rejection of it and announced a policy of non-cooperation with the mandatory authorities. They would continue to bring immigrants into Palestine legally, or illegally. They declared the White Paper illegal and, therefore, non binding, and that they would fight it to the bitter end. The first demonstrations were peaceful, but after the British troops leveled their rifles at demonstrators in Jerusalem, a riot broke out and tensions and confrontations escalated daily. The White Paper also served to accelerate the rate in which Jews developed new communities in Palestine.

THE WAR YEARS PUT THE GOVERNMENTAL issue of a Jewish National Home on hold, but Jewish anger intensified as Britain denied them entry to their ancient land at the time of their greatest need. Fleeing Jews became trapped in Europe having nowhere to run from the Nazi murder machine. Tens of thousands of Jews needlessly perished because Britain would not allow them into Palestine. William L. Hull, in *The Fall and Rise of Israel*, writes of the Jews who fled from the Nazis, trying to reach Palestine:

> The White Paper regulations, that which has been described as "the bastard child of Chamberlain's appeasement program," refused them an entry to their ancient land and to life. And so they died, in Europe, in the Black Sea, in the Dardanelles, in the Mediterranean, in a Palestine harbor, in *kibbutzim*, in Mauritius, on Cyprus. They died because cruelty and evil and anti-Semitism are not confined to one race or nation but are found everywhere. They died because men used administrative laws (in themselves illegal) as clubs, rifles, as weapons to kill them.

History books such as *The Holocaust* by Martin Gilbert and *Personal Witness* by Abba Eban, have numerous references to the British government's first-hand knowledge of the Jews' fate at the hands of the Nazis. Arab

Britain — Chapter 14

cooperation and Arab oil, however, were always more important than the welfare of the Jews. Abba Eban says:

> Churchill had been virulently opposed by his generals and by his foreign secretary, Anthony Eden, whenever he made a proposal to alleviate the grief and humiliation of the Jews.

The British navy patrolled the seas and intercepted ships full of Jews escaping the Nazis. Most ships were turned away under the threat of British guns—a number sank, sometimes with the loss of all on board. Some were escorted to Cyprus where the Jews were interned, and one was even escorted back to Germany of all places. British troops did not hesitate to use rubber truncheons or rifle butts to beat unarmed, desperate Jews into submission or unconsciousness. Eban continues:

> If anyone had ever wanted to know what Churchill meant by a "squalid war" he would have found out by watching British soldiers using rifle butts, hose pipes and tear gas against the survivors of the death camps. Men, women and children were forcibly taken off to other ships, locked in cages, and sent out of Palestine waters.

As Hull puts it in *The Fall and Rise of Israel*:

> There was no mercy in the hearts of those who led Britain in those days.

He adds:

> When negotiations were conducted with Hungary the next year [1944] to rescue a million Jews from the gas chambers by the paying of two million dollars, the reaction of a high British official was, "But what will we do with them?" The deal was not consummated; the gas chamber claimed its own.

Broken British promises sentenced a million Hungarian Jews to death. Denied both mercy and the right to return to their land, they were driven into Nazi gas chambers and murdered in the most bestial fashion (see pages 176 – 178). Winston Churchill, the British Prime minister who led Britain to victory during World War II, had vigorously opposed the White Paper of the Chamberlain era, and a member of his cabinet called the successive broken promises to the Jews a "cynical breach of pledges." Before Churchill could act in favor of establishing a Jewish National Home in accordance with the Balfour Declaration, the British public removed him from office in postwar elections. He was succeeded by Clement Atlee and Ernest Bevin, of whom the latter, as Foreign Secretary, showed far more prejudice than pragmatism toward the Palestine question.

IT WAS AT THIS POINT IN history that the British empire began to decline. On the verge of bankruptcy, Britain began to pull out from India, Cyprus, Malta, Greece, Turkey, etc. In Palestine, Jewish resistance to British rule grew, and railways and bridges were blown up to frustrate British movements. One hundred thousand British troops were kept in Palestine after the end of World War II to deal with the problem. The British public was becoming increasingly angry because their men had not come home from six years of war, and now they were dying in skirmishes with Jews in Palestine. Anti-Semitism became more and more overt, and Abba Eban describes himself as being "filled with hot rage" when he saw the following order pinned to the notice board of his place of employment in Jerusalem:

> No British soldier is to have any social intercourse with any Jew and any intercourse in the way of duty should be as brief as possible and kept strictly to business in hand. I appreciate that these measures will inflict some hardship on the troops but I am certain that if my reasons are fully explained to them they will understand their propriety and **will be punishing the Jews in a way that the race dislikes as any by striking at their pockets and showing our contempt for them**.

This "scurrilous document," as Eban called it, was the work of General Evelyn Barker, commander of the British forces in Palestine. Britain, the only country that waged six long years of war against Hitler, had absolutely y no compassion for the surviving remnant of Hitler's plan to eradicate European Jewry. A firm and faithful supporter of Ernest Bevin, Christopher Mayhew, made the following entry into his diary on May 16, 1948:

> I must make a note about Ernest's anti-Semitism.... **There is no doubt to my mind that Ernest detests Jews**. He makes the odd wisecrack about the "chosen people" ... declares that the Old Testament is the most immoral book ever written and declares publicly: "We must also remember the Arab's side of the case. There are, after all, no Arabs in this House (loud cheers)" [a snide reference to Jews having been elected to Parliament, but no Arabs]. I tell him afterwards that this remark is going too far and we have a general talk about the Jews. **He says they taught Hitler the technique of terror and were even now paralleling the Nazis in Palestine**. They were preachers of violence and war. "What could you expect when people are brought up from the cradle on the Old Testament?" I starkly deny most of it and tell him that anyway, true or false, what he says in public on this subject only gives his enemies a handle against him. He smiles sardonically. I allow him only one point, that in giving voice to his irrational and indefensible prejudices, **he is speaking for millions of British people**.

Britain — Chapter 14

Even though the Arabs were opposed to British rule and fought against it equally as fiercely as the Jews, the British had two sets of rules—one for Arabs, and one for Jews. Arab homes and buildings were not searched for arms, but Jewish homes were. Arabs were not body searched for weapons, but Jews were. The British however, were gentlemen when it came to searching females, and for this reason Jewish weapons were mainly moved around by being hidden under women's clothing. The penalties for Jews being found in possession of a weapon or a cache of arms was severe. Hull, in *The Fall and Rise of Israel* records:

> One man who was arrested had a revolver and thirteen rounds of ammunition. He produced a license which permitted him to carry a revolver and twelve rounds of ammunition. For the **one extra round** he was convicted and sentenced by a military court to **seven years imprisonment**.

Jewish resistance became stronger and more effective. The Jews were determined to drive the British out of Palestine. They humiliated the British Imperial Lion by stomping heavily on its tail. In an attempt to stop the Jewish resistance to their rule in Palestine and to stem the flood of Jews being smuggled in, the British began using the gallows and hung some of the leaders of the growing resistance movement. The Jews responded in kind by hanging a higher ranking British officer for each of their own that were executed—this caused hangings to cease. The British flogged Jews for various offenses, until the Jews again retaliated in kind. A front page article in the *Palestine Post* of December 31, 1946, quotes the British newspaper, the *Daily Telegraph*, in its condemnation of a Jewish flogging of a British officer:

> There is no parallel between the flogging by illegal terrorist action of a gallant officer carrying out the discipline of his country, and the flogging of a youth judicially carried out, who has broken the discipline of his country. Terrorists can have no idea of the rancor let loose by this attack on the honor of the army.

Humbling followed humbling for the British in Palestine. The Jews dynamited British headquarters in Jerusalem's famous King David Hotel, killing 80 British officers and wounding 70 others. The headquarters was a veritable fortress—surrounded by barbed wire and well guarded at the entrances. Hull records that a warning was given by the Jews from between 15 to 20 minutes prior to the explosion, but that the Government official who received the warning said

We are not here to take orders from the Jews. We give them orders.

A serious wound had been inflicted on British pride, and, as they licked that wound, the *New Statesman* reflected the mood of the nation by publishing a full front page editorial entitled, "**War for the White Paper?**" Portions of the editorial were reprinted on the front page of the *Palestine Post* (a copy of which hangs on my office wall), Sunday, June 23, 1946, and the following is from a segment subtitled, "**Atrocity Stories**":

> After alluding to the secret raid plan of the authorities for a campaign against the Jews the article said that in fighting the Jews, the Government had the help of the BBC and probably of most of the widely-read papers, and there would be **a flood of anti-Jewish "atrocity" stories and editorials on the righteousness of liquidating the obstinate survivors of Hitler's gas chambers**. Public opinion, which was already unsympathetic, might not actively oppose the Cabinet until it discovered that an Anglo-Jewish war demanded larger reinforcements and more costly operations ... .
>
> ... the present [British] blindness was **due to determination to conclude a settlement with the Arab princes, which had been in preparation since Mr. Chamberlain's White Paper. Mr Atlee and Mr. Bevan regarded the Jews as a nuisance and an obstacle in the way of Anglo-Arab unity**.

MORE THAN ANYTHING ELSE, THE RECIPROCAL hanging and flogging of British officers drove the British to finally relinquish their mandate of Palestine to the United Nations on May 14, 1948. Britain relinquished her mandate to the United Nations, and her police fortresses and other strong points to the Arabs. She also encouraged the Arab nations to go to war, and trained, supplied, and directed the strategy of the seven Arab armies that invaded the new Jewish state on the day following the expiration of the mandate. The British sponsored the invasion, took a limited part in the fighting, and suffered the embarrassment of having some of their officers taken prisoner. Hull records that they were subjected to further humiliations when, for example, the poorly equipped Jews broke through the British defence of Jaffa—"a solid wall of British tanks and seventy-five pounder cannon"—and captured the city. The British commander had orders, says Hull, "**to save the city for the Arabs at all costs**." And on January 7, 1949, Israeli fighters shot down five British planes—four Spitfires and a Mosquito—which were carrying out flights over Israeli positions. The old, secondhand Israeli planes hardly constituted an air force, but they humiliated the RAF which had so decisively beaten the German Luftwaffe in the Battle of Britain.

Britain — Chapter 14

WHEN WE TRACE THE CURRENT, ONGOING Arab-Israel conflict back to its grassroots, we find that the undisputed leader of that part of the Arab world welcomed the Jews home in 1919, desired immediate, large scale Jewish immigration, and expressed the hope that the Arabs might be able to repay some of the Jews' kindnesses. It was a radical, minority Arab element which objected to Jews being on what was considered to be Muslim land, and this element was encouraged to riot and kill by the British themselves. The leader of this radical element and instigator of the riots that took many lives, was appointed by the British even though they were fully aware he was both anti-British and anti-Jew. Had the British firmly honored their pledge and carried out the purpose of the mandate that was given to them; had they exercised their power and authority to crush the radical element, immediately and without partiality, there would not have been wars in **1948, 1956, 1967, 1969, 1973, 1982, 2006, 2008, 2012,** or **2014**. These wars have resulted in the loss of tens of thousands of Jewish and Arab lives. Nor would there have been continuous terrorist strikes against Israeli civilians that have killed, maimed or disfigured a multitude of Israelis, including many women and children. ***The present conflict is, therefore, nothing less than the aftermath of broken promises and British prejudice***.

Forty-five years after pulling out of Palestine, Britain remains impenitent of her actions. She is the fifth largest seller of arms to the Arab states while maintaining an arms boycott against Israel. Even though chemical weapons have been banned from the theatre of war, John Major, the conservative prime minister in 1993, was implicated along with his government in having supplied chemical weapon components worth millions of pounds to Iraq prior to the Gulf War. Britain also strictly adhered to the Arab economic boycott of Israel and refused to introduce a law that would make it illegal. The British industrial-chemical giant ICI made the news in May, 1993, when it issued fresh directives to its department heads not to trade with Israel. An internal memorandum said the firm remains "***committed to recent undertakings to the boycott office not to support the Israeli war effort, and not to import raw materials from Israel***."

An Editorial in the *Jerusalem Post* on December 7, 1992, comments on the Israeli request to Britain for children's gas masks. The request was made in anticipation of an Iraqi missile attack on Israel. Saddam Hussein had pledged to use chemical weapons to "burn up half of Israel" if allied forces led by the United States and Britain attacked Iraq. The appeal for children's gas masks from Britain was "turned down on the grounds ***the equipment could have 'aggressive potential***.'"

A letter to the Editor published in *In Jerusalem* on July 9, 1993, complained that the British Consulate in Jewish West Jerusalem "was closed on Mohammed's birthday as well as the duration of the recent Muslim festival." Obviously, the British government is still wooing their Arab friends at the expense of Israel.

NO ONE HAS TO LOOK FAR to find glaring examples of British hypocrisy. The Queen traveled to Jordan in the 1980's and delivered a speech in which she mentioned "the shame of Israelis occupying Arab land." But what about the British occupations? The carnage of Northern Ireland was a fruit of Irish nationalists fighting for independence from the British, and the 1992 Falkland Islands War was caused by Argentina trying to regain her territory from them also. Many thousands of troops are needed to guard Britain's stake in countries occupied by force. Half of the known world was subjugated by the British through gunpowder and bayonet, and it was the 1939 White Paper against the Jews in Palestine which spelled the beginning of the end of that empire.

Britain absolutely refused to negotiate with the IRA (Irish Republican Army). Indeed, an editorial in London's *Daily Telegraph* published in 1993 was headed, "**Don't talk to terrorists**":

> It is **fundamental to the policy of the government** not to allow terrorists to participate in the political process even by proxy. **Negotiation with murderers and their accomplices is morally repugnant**.

Yet Britain today threatens and pushes Israel to negotiate with the Palestine Liberation Organization (PLO), Hamas ,and Hizb'allah terror organizations, which have killed or maimed tens of thousands of Israeli civilians. Britain never ever had any shame, and it does not now. The only thing that has changed is its name; it is now known as the (dis)United Kingdom.

It's Workers and Student Unions are tripping over themselves to establish boycotts against Israel today, and in October 2015 more than 300 British academics signed a public letter pledging to boycott Israel. Anti-Semitism throughout that nation is soaring, Jews, Jewish buildings, and Jewish cemeteries are being attacked on an almost daily basis and shouts of "**Jews to gas!**" and other foul epithets can be heard at the frequent anti-Israel demonstrations.

The death of a three year old boy by an IRA bomb blast in March 1993 caused an outrage in Britain. But Israel suffers similar tragedies almost daily from the hands of the terrorist groups in Gaza and the "West Bank"— Biblical Judea and Samaria—which are not committed to regaining territory

Britain — Chapter 14

lost in their abortive wars against Israel, but committed to Israel's complete destruction. Britain, however, supports the PLO terrorist organization, holds talks with it, and is pressuring Israel to do the same. It is interesting to note that in the British press, IRA men were and are always terrorists, while Palestinian terrorists are "gunmen," "guerrillas," or "freedom-fighters."

A typical British diplomatic coup took place during the January 1988 visit to Israel of David Mellor, the British Secretary of State for Foreign Affairs. Jim Lederman (an American journalist) records in *Battle Lines: The American Media and the Intifada*:

> With the cameras rolling, the minister suddenly began berating an Israeli colonel for the ill-treatment Israel was meting out to the Palestinians. Mellor had the media stage to himself because **he knew, in advance, that the colonel was forbidden by regulations to reply**, and that, in any case, the officer spoke little English and would have been incapable of responding effectively to the verbal whiplashing. The incident was broadcast around the world.

Mellor, like others before him, had his moment of glory when the eyes of the world were upon him. Mellor is not alone in being an anti-Semite in Britain's parliament; he is accompanied by a host of other anti-Semites, not the least being George Galloway the leader of the far-left **"Respect Party."** Galloway has a history of racism and mouthing-off at Israel and as the candidate for Bradford West he declared his constituency an "Israel-free zone." In an anti-Israel tirade Galloway told a meeting of the **"Respect Party"** that Israelis of any persuasion were "not welcome" in Bradford, where serves as MP. "We have declared Bradford an Israel free zone," he told party activists at the meeting in Leeds:

> *We don't want any Israeli goods. We don't want any Israeli services. We don't want any Israeli academics, coming to the university or the college. We don't even want any Israeli tourists to come to Bradford if any of them had thought of doing so.*
>
> *We reject this illegal, barbarous, savage state that calls itself Israel. And you have to do the same*.

At the time of writing Galloway is campaigning for the 2016 London mayoral elections. Questioned on BBC TV's *Sunday Politics*, he was pressed on the issue whether he intended to try to ban Israelis from London if he wins. Gallaway said that while he was not planning to declare London an "Israeli free zone" it would certainly be his aim **"to encourage the huge swell of pro-Palestinian support in London:"**

I think **Palestine has more supporters in London than anywhere else in the country**. But the mayor is not the pope and the mayor is not the president and is not the prime minister or the foreign secretary.

It was then pointed out that he did not hold any of those posts in Bradford, either, but had called for an Israel-free zone all the same. Galloway conceded he had but admitted that it was impossible to implement:

Of course, it's unimplementable. It's a moral position and my moral position on Palestine is well known.

Galloway's position is well known, as are the positions of several British MPs in prominent positions. The new leader of the Labour Party, Jeremy Corbyn, is a known anti-Israel MP, and is appointing anti-Semites to positions of authority. In November 2015 Britain's Labour Party also voted to cut ties with a well-known security firm which **has business ties with Israel**. The party's national executive committee approved a resolution to boycott G4S, a Crawley-based multinational corporation that employs over 620,000 workers in over 120 countries. G4S has provided security services to Labor events in recent years.

On October 27, 2015, Gerald Kaufman, a self-hating Jewish Labour MP who never misses an opportunity to strike at Israel, gave a speech full of barbs against Israel, even saying that half of the recent wave of Palestinian terrorist murders of Israelis were "fabricated." There is little doubt that the British people as a whole are as anti-Semitic in 2015, possibly even more so, than they were in the 1930s and 1940s. It appears that Labour MPs are trying to outdo former radical Labour anti-Semites like Ernest Bevin.

ISRAEL IS DISMAYED BY THE NUCLEAR agreement struck between Tehran and world powers—Britain was one of the negotiating countries—and considers it to be an existential threat to the Jewish state. Dismissing Israeli objections to the agreement Britain's Foreign Secretary Philip Hammond snidely told Britain's Parliament on July 14, 2015:

The question you have to ask yourself is what kind of a deal would have been welcomed in Tel Aviv. **The answer of course is that Israel doesn't want any deal with Iran—Israel wants a permanent state of standoff**.

In dismissing Israel's objections to the very real possibility of it being annihilated, Hammond walked the all-too-familiar path of British detestation of the Jewish state. And by saying "Tel Aviv" instead of "Jerusalem," Hammond made the point that Jerusalem was not recognized by Britain as being the capital of Israel and its seat of government, which it has been for more than 3,000 years. Britain's time of fear and anguish is drawing nearer by the day:

> *Do not be deceived, God is not mocked; for whatever a man sows, that he will also reap* (Galatians 6:7).

THE SPIRITUAL CLIMATE IN BRITAIN GROWS progressively cooler. Homosexuality, sodomy and witchcraft is rife, and spreading—within and without the Church.

On August 6, 2015, an openly homosexual British ambassador disgracefully presented his credentials to Israel's President Reuven Rivlin in Jerusalem. The sodomite, David Quarrey, introduced his "**spouse**," Aldo Oliver Henriquez, to Rivlin at the President's Residence. Neither they nor the British government have any shame.

Only a tiny percentage (twp percent in 2015) of traditional church members attend services, and as of 2014 more than 1,000 churches have been turned into mosques. Queen Elizabeth II, head of the Church of England, has also officiated at the opening of at least one large mosque, much to the chagrin of God-fearing British Christians.

When Prince Andrew married Sarah Ferguson in August 1986 it was requested that no mention of Israel, Jacob, Jerusalem, or Zion be made during the wedding ceremony in Westminster Abbey. The royal ambassadors of British anti-Semitism rejected over three thousand verses of Scripture in an obvious effort to discomfit Israel and win further Arab approval. The rejection of Scripture for political purposes is more than a rejection of God's Word, it is blasphemy against the LORD. However, it was merely a reflection of the inherent Jew-hatred that permeates British society.

IN LATE **1992,** TWO YOUNG BOYS aged eight and ten, enticed a two-year-old toddler away from his mother in a British shopping mall and brutally killed him outside of the mall. After dragging the body to a railway line it was left to be run over by a train. But these young children only imitated what they observed in the violent, real-life world around them.

While it is not endemic solely to Britain, an established pattern has arisen where murder, gang rape, and other equally heinous crimes are being committed by the very young. The morality of the parents is being handed down to the children.

The disregard for human life shows up clearly in the rising tide of British abortion. The most obvious parallel between the ancient rite of child sacrifice and the practice of abortion is the sober fact that the parents actually kill their own offspring. Clifford Hill reports in *Prophecy Today*, Vol 4, No 4, that:

In the years since abortion was legalized in Britain, vast numbers of babies have been used for various forms of research and for commercial purposes. There have been numerous reports of the use of collagen derived from human fetuses in the manufacture of cosmetics, particularly face creams that claim rejuvenating properties.

Reports from the abortion scene indicate that huge amounts of money are made from the bodies of aborted babies. It is also apparent that less care is given to the mother than to that of a marketable baby. In a letter to a prospective client, As far back as 1993 a British distributor of "products for rejuvenation of skin cells" wrote (the same products price in 2014 is shown bracketed):

> It is therefore **with pleasure I submit the prices for your kind consideration**, as follows: Thymus £40.10/kg. [£101.50 in 2014], Pituitary £102.45/kg. [£259.30 in 2014], Liver £30.92/kg. [£78.27 in 2014], Spleen £79.43/kg. [£201.10 in 2014].
>
> A discount of 15 percent was offered for orders of 100 kg. or more of each "material." Carriage is charged on orders with a goods value of less than £350.00 [£900.00 in 2014]. VAT is extra.

The *Lydia Information Bureau* in Walden, Essex also reports that:

> Investigations in Europe uncovered **the world's largest fetal bank in London** and the fact that abortion **clinics from around the world air-express their aborted fetuses to this bank**. We are told that when possible the babies are taken late term and by "C-section." **They are immediately decapitated, a cell preserving solution is poured into their open throat**, they are then quick frozen and air-expressed to this fetal bank. Here **they are processed into collagen and sold to cosmetic companies around the world**.

First Britain sold out Czechoslovakia, then it sold out the Jewish people. Today, among its multitude of odious sins, it buys the world's unwanted babies and processes them into cosmetics. Britons need to understand that the storms and floods which have been hitting the nation—floods so great they could be seen from 400 miles up in space—are but a taste of troubles to come. Seventy percent of London's inhabitants are Muslim today and Britain now has 85 Sharia courts dealing out Islamic law. Britain is a nation that has gorged itself upon other nations. For this Britain must pay. Britain's sins are many—we have touched only upon a few:

Britain — Chapter 14

a) Murder, perverse and immoral behavior
b) Breaking of political agreements
c) Pride in National Security
d) Using power and wealth to make lesser nations subservient
e) Waging war against Israel
f) Allies of those waging war against Israel
g) Fraudulent, deceitful, and crafty business transactions
h) Rejoicing at another nation's misfortunes (especially Israel's)
i) Extreme cruelty in times of war
j) Homosexuality
k) Sodomy (sexual perversion, including acts with animals)
l) Anti-Semitism—political, racial and religious
m) Rejection of God
n) Rejection of God's Salvation
o) Refusal to hear and live by God's Word
p) Practicing witchcraft, horoscopes and the occult
q) Blasphemy

The judgments are, therefore: **Physical catastrophes and widespread death**; **Destruction of nation** (seven times); **Near annihilation** (five times); **Nation conquered and devastated**; **Annihilation** (two times); and **Judicial cursing or complete destruction of nation**.

THE UNPRECEDENTED WAVE OF MUSLIM REFUGEES and migrants into Britain taking place in 2015 – 2016 will bring its own manifestation of God's judgment. Hundreds of British Islamic jihadists have traveled to Syria and Iraq to join the barbarous ISIL; they learn how to kill, to decapitate, and to rape innocent girls. They will return to their homeland and put into practice what they have learned. In May 2013, two Muslim converts hacked a British soldier to death with meat cleavers on a London street in broad daylight in an attack that shocked Britain. There will be many more such attacks.

BRITAIN IS A NATION THAT URGENTLY, desperately needs to produce another Wesley, the great eighteenth century evangelist. Britain is a nation that wallows in a sea of hypocrisy and shame, doomed to be broken up by the storm of God's wrath—*for* ***the LORD has a controversy with Britain.***

15

China

China is the third largest nation in the world in terms of land (next to Russia and Canada); in terms of population, it is the largest, with 1.5 billion people.

China's ruling government is hard-line communist, which like other communist regimes, imprisons, tortures and executes at will many of its citizens who choose a path other than that of communism. The Chinese Church has felt the sting of communist oppression and aggression; many Christians have suffered terribly at the hands of the Chinese Communist party.

Strict control and censorship of the news media is applied to all events in China. Only that which the leaders allow to be known, is known. Western tourists and journalists are usually the means of getting the truth back to the West, as was the case of the Tiananmen Square massacre in June 1989. Videos were shown in the West of troops firing automatic weapons into crowds of unarmed people. Tanks were shown driving over students trying to block their path. The pro-democracy movement was crushed in Tiananmen Square, as were the bodies of many students, their blood spurted onto the walls. From eyewitness accounts, 2,000– 3,000 people died in that massacre. But the official June 30, 1989, Chinese propaganda "**Report on Putting Down Anti-Government Riot**," with the name of Chen Xitong, mayor of Beijing, attached, says:

> During the whole operation no one, including the students who refused but were forced to leave, died. Tales of "rivers of blood" in Tiananmen Square and the rumor-mongers themselves "escaping from underneath piles of corpses" are sheer nonsense .
>
> ... During the quelling of the counter-revolutionary rebellion, the PLA [Peoples Liberation Army], the armed police, and the public security police fought valiantly and performed immortal feats.

The Western nations were told "not to interfere in China's internal policies." I was in China within three months of the Tiananmen Square tragedy and suffered the same treatment as many other foreigners before me—that of having a full roll of film torn from my camera because I had photographed a scene that was not for Western eyes.

At that time when I was in China the Chinese people avoided Westerners like the plague, they were afraid to be seen in close proximity to a Westerner. There was a noticeable and widespread fear of getting arrested for being a counter-revolutionary. At other times they were always curious to see Westerners up close, we seemed strange to them because we had round eyes and hair grew on our skin.

THE MAINLAND CHINESE PEOPLE HAVE MANY natural talents. They are famous for producing exquisitely fine handcrafts, and they are equally famous for their ability to deceive. The Chinese government says categorically that it is not selling missiles to Iran, while American satellite pictures show missiles with Chinese markings being unloaded from Chinese ships. Prior to the 1991 Gulf War, Chinese envoys were seen entering and leaving Iraq, and much was made in the Western media concerning Chinese (and Russian) peace efforts. But on November 9, 1990, the U.K. based *Intelligence Digest* stated:

> According to reports reaching *Intelligence Digest* from India, both the Soviet Union and China are supplying arms, chemical weapons, food and other essential supplies to Iraq by way of Afghanistan and Iran. Both Moscow and Beijing have assured Saddam Hussein of uninterrupted supply.
>
> The new route via Afghanistan and Iran has been cleared by the strategists in order to bypass the surveillance of U.S. satellites.

How perceptive was Richard Wurmbrand when, years ago, he wrote:

> The communists are wrongly called "Reds." Actually, like chameleons, they assume any color and are masters of deceit and dissimulation.

China, like other large nations already mentioned, relies on arms sales to lower her budget deficit. The *Cedar Rapids Gazette*, on May 6, 1991, ran an article naming China as the fourth largest arms supplier to the Middle East between 1976 and 1990. During those years China sold a large part of the $850 billion in arms calculated to have gone to Iran and the Arab states. But when France sold fifteen *Mirage* fighters to Taiwan in December, 1992, China considered this "unacceptable," and closed the French Consulate in Guangzhou (Canton).

China has an effective arms boycott against Israel and has been somewhat of an implacable enemy for many years. It has consistently denounced Israel for occupying lands won in wars waged against her by the Arab states. Israel, apparently, committed an international sin in Chinese eyes by not only surviving Arab aggression, but defeating the aggressors as well. China, on the other hand, invaded Tibet in 1950 and forced her to sign a treaty making the country a part of China. Anti-Chinese demonstrations erupted in Tibet in 1959, but were violently crushed by Chinese soldiers, forcing the Dalai Lama and many of his followers to flee to India. The Tibetans still demonstrate against the Chinese takeover of their country, and China is still merciless in its quashing of them. These examples of unprovoked Chinese aggression are, according to Beijing, simply a matter of "internal politics."

IN A BID TO HALT CHINA'S natural population growth the Communist regime introduced laws restricting the amount of children any couple may have. Couples living in urban areas are limited to one child only—those in rural areas may have two. Compulsory sterilization of all mothers took place within a few weeks of reaching the allowable limit. As a result of these laws, appalling numbers of female babies were being murdered in their first few days of life to allow the mother another opportunity to produce a son. Many thousands—probably millions—of couples want sons, not daughters. They need sons to work their fields and to provide for them in latter years when they can no longer work themselves—consequently the life of innumerable healthy daughters was unceremoniously snuffed out.

A Chinese woman, pregnant with her second child, fled to the U.S. with her husband and son in order to save the baby. She testified at a hearing of the Congressional Executive Commission on China in December 2015 that:

> The Chinese government data report that **13 million abortions** are performed each year, for an average rate of **35,000 abortions per day**. I personally believe the number is much higher because these statistics only include hospitals that report their figures and most abortions occur in unauthorized 'black' clinics or at home."

She said she believed the number of abortions annually in China is **closer to 20 million a year**.

CHINA IS ONLY NOW BEGINNING TO develop her full potential as a world superpower and is currently wooing the industrial nations. After being an irreconcilable enemy of Israel for many years, China established diplomatic relations in 1992 because it "needs Israeli technology."

Earlier is was said that the Chinese "are famous for producing exquisitely fine handcrafts, and they are equally famous for their ability to deceive." It is a fact that anything of value that is manufactured by the West or developing nations is soon copied—mostly illegally—by Chinese businessmen. Most of these "stolen" goods are sold to the West at prices below what it was possible to manufacture them for in the West. The great majority of manufactured products on the shelves in Western stores are now made in China. Nevertheless, China in 2016 is undergoing an economic earthquake that has impoverished millions of its more affluent citizens by some $3 trillion through an enormous stock crash in June 2015, which was replicated again in January 2016. The ripples going out from these stockmarket crashes are showing up in China's trade figures—foreign investors and buyers of Chinese goods are wary of a possible deepening of the crisis and China's exports have taken a hit.

China is also at the forefront of cyber theft. Chinese hackers break into corporate Western business computers and steal the secrets which have taken businesses years to perfect. The Chinese government, too, has an official cyber department which hacks into Western military computers and steals everything from weapons designs to personal data on military personnel. Virtually the entire Chinese military is equipped with weapons and fighter-jets which have been manufactured according to the plans and specifications hacked from Western military computers.

THE CHINESE COMMUNIST GOVERNMENT IS GREATLY concerned by the growth of Christianity in the country. And the more it persecutes the Church the faster it grows. The Communists have destroyed countless numbers of beautiful church buildings on the pretext that its "paperwork was not in order." Some regions in China have gone on an anti-cross spree and bring cranes to remove crosses from church facades and rooftops. No matter how hard pressed the Chinese Christians have become, Christianity continues to spread like a ferocious wildfire.

A possibility that Christians need to be aware of, is that of China fulfilling apocalyptic Scripture:

> *The number of the army of the horsemen was two hundred million ... I saw the horses in the vision: those who sat on them had* **breastplates of fiery red, hyacinth blue, and sulfur yellow; and the heads of the horses were like the heads of lions; and out of their mouths came fire, smoke, and brimstone** *(Revelation 9:16,17).*

Reports place China's standing army at 2.3 million. On November 26, 2015, *Bloomberg News* reported President Xi Jinping announcing a major overhaul of China's military "to make the world's largest army more combat ready and better equipped to project force beyond the country's borders." Xi Jinping says

China — Chapter 15

China's "defense and military development stands at a new and historic starting line." The favored colors of the Chinese are *"fiery red, hyacinth blue, and sulfur yellow,"* and they have **a history of displaying fiery dragons and lions**.

THERE IS A DEAL OF ANGST in both the West and also in the East over China's building of artificial islands among the Spratly Islands, a group of islands and associated maritime features such as reefs and banks located in the South China Sea. Ownership of the islands is claimed by Brunei, China, Malaysia, the Philippines, Taiwan, and Vietnam, but China is slowly taking possession of most of the South China Sea.

China is extending its military reach hundreds of miles out from its mainland by creating artificial islands through sucking the ocean's bottom up and pumping it onto reefs and shallow banks until it fills whole areas above water level the size of several football fields—large enough to accommodate aircraft carriers at docks, and with sufficient length for runways that can handle large aircraft. China then claims a 12-mile territorial limit surrounding these artificial islands.

China lays claim to almost all of the South China Sea and its fighter-planes are buzzing U.S. and other nation's survey planes, which fly over the international waters of the South China Sea in a game of intimidation and brinkmanship. In October 2015 the U.S. sent a warship very close to one of China's artificial islands in challenge to Beijing's territorial claims in the contested waters. Chinese ships and aircraft warned and tracked the U.S. warship as it came close to reefs claimed by China. Someone will likely soon make a wrong move in the militarizing of these contested waters—with earth-shattering consequences and great loss of life.

The sins concerning China in this chapter are:

a) Murder, perverse and immoral behavior
b) Rejection of God
c) Rejection of God's Salvation
d) Refusal to hear and live by God's Word
e) Suppressing or Hindering the preaching of the Gospel
f) Slavery and Oppression
g) Breaking of political agreements
h) Unprovoked military aggression
i) Extreme cruelty in times of war
j) Allies of those waging war against Israel
k) Anti-Semitism-political, racial and religious
l) Fraudulent, Deceitful, and crafty business transactions

The judgments are, therefore: **Physical catastrophes and widespread death** (two times); **Near annihilation** (four times); **Destruction of nation** (two times); **Defeat with high loss of life**; **Nation conquered and devastated**; and **Judicial cursing or complete destruction of nation**.

CHINA HAS A HISTORY THAT SPANS approximately 5,000 years. In the misty morning of the twenty-first century she is rapidly moving into a more powerful—and deceitful—world influence. But for all her millennia of existence, her iniquity might be like that of the Amorites of old in Genesis 15:16—not yet complete. Unlike the Amorites, however, China will, perhaps, reach the stage of judgment well before another four hundred years, possibly in a matter of just a few decades. But then again, it could be one year, or perhaps five.

On August 3, 2014, an earthquake struck the Yunnan province with a moment magnitude of 6.1. The earthquake killed at least 719 people, injuring more than 2400 others—over 12,000 houses collapsed and 30,000 were damaged. Perhaps that was a forewarning of what is to come.

The dramatic spread of Christianity in China today could possibly hold off judgment until the full number of believers come in. *How long O LORD, how long?—for the LORD has a controversy with China.*

16

The Church

The reader might well ask, "What is a chapter about the Church doing in the section dealing with judgment of nations?" Of course, we all know that the Church is not a nation, but we are told that judgment must begin **first** with the Church:

*For the **time has come for judgment to begin at the house of God**; and if it begins with us first, what will be the end of those who do not obey the gospel of God?* (1 Peter 4:17).

In the book of Revelation we read

I saw another angel ascending from the east, having the seal of the living God. And he cried with a loud voice to the four angels to whom it was granted to harm the earth and the sea, saying, "Do not harm the earth, the sea, or the trees till we have sealed the servants of our God on their foreheads (Revelation 7:2–3).

The marking with ink and the sealing with God's seal is one and the same thing, which is also depicted as being "washed" in the blood of the Lamb:

To Him who loved us and washed us from our sins in His own blood (Revelation 1:5).

This is the New Testament parallel of what the man with the inkhorn did when the of the Lord said to him:

*Go through the midst of the city, through the midst of Jerusalem, and put a mark on the foreheads of the men **who sigh and cry over all the abominations** that are done within it* (Ezekiel 9:4).

*To the others He said in my hearing, "Go after him through the city and kill; do not let your eye spare, nor have any pity. Utterly slay old and young men, maidens and little children and women; but do not come near anyone on whom is the mark; and **begin at My sanctuary**." So they began with the elders who were before the temple* (Ezekiel 9:5–6).

And we have previously discussed that those receiving greater light, receive a stricter judgment (see page 80). The Church has a long and dreadful history of persecution and mistreatment of Jews (see chapter 23 titled *The Great Hatred* in my book *When Day and Night Cease*, or Michael L. Brown's book, *Our Hands Are Stained With Blood*), and the greater portion of the Church today still opposes Israel. Derek Prince, one of the finest Bible teachers ever to have lived, writes in his book, *The Destiny of Israel and the Church*:

> If God permitted the Holocaust to bring the Jews of Europe into line with His purpose, **what will He permit to come on the Church if she, on her side, persists in refusing to fulfill God's revealed purpose for her**?

The object of this chapter, however, is not to sit in judgment upon the Church, but to simply furnish a few observations that might help a Christian respond more positively in adverse conditions. There is a high probability that most Christians born after the start of World War II will find themselves caught up in some calamitous situation, either because of judgment on their personal sin, judgment upon the Church in general, or because they live in a land that is subject to God's judgment.

THAT GOD JUDGES HIS CHILDREN IS a fact of life. Most Christians, if not all, have experienced His chastisement during the process of their individual spiritual development. Usually we are merely spanked by a loving Father who cares for us with an intense love—and for this we should be grateful. But many Christians have gotten sick (this does not imply that all sickness is a consequence of sin), some have suffered public humiliation for their sins, and a number have also had their ministries destroyed. A few languish in prison—sentenced by a court of law, and others are no longer in the land of the living. We need to pay earnest heed to the way we act and live as professing Christians:

> *That is why* ***many of you are weak and ill, and some have died***
> (1Corinthians 11:30 RSV).

I HAVE BEEN PERSONALLY INVOLVED WITH two Christians who died very suddenly. One person managed a Christian bookstore in the downtown section of a leading New Zealand city. From this store I purchased a Bible with a written, lifetime replacement guarantee. Disappointingly, the binding of my new Bible broke after only two weeks of normal use. I returned to the store with the Bible, where the genial staff told me, with some embarrassment, that it was not the manager's policy to make exchanges or give refunds. The manager was out of his office at that time, so I left the defective Bible with the staff and said that I would return in the afternoon.

The Church — Chapter 16

When I came back later, the staff told me that the manager had looked at the Bible but would not replace it, and that they were ashamed to have to tell me this. I took the Bible into the manager's office, laid it on his desk and demanded either another Bible or a refund of the purchase price—he flatly refused and suggested I return it to the publisher. I said to him, "As a manager of a Christian store, you should be ashamed of your business ethics—they are unbefitting to the kingdom of God; you are morally and legally bound to satisfy the terms of the guarantee under which your store sold the Bible." I also added, "**By defrauding God's children you are robbing God Himself**." At my insistence, but showing no signs of repentance, he grudgingly exchanged the faulty Bible for a new one—I thanked him and left the shop.

A few days later, during business hours, I passed by the same store, but it was closed. A notice on the door attracted my attention: "Owing to the sudden death of the manager this shop will be closed for three days ...." I later learned from the staff that within 72 hours of my speaking with the manager, he had suffered a massive heart attack and had literally dropped dead in his office.

The other person who died was a single "professing Christian" woman whom I knew quite well, since she had received treatment at a Christian drug and mental-health rehabilitation ministry of which I had been a staff member. She was extremely rebellious and would not submit to pastoral authority, neither would she receive any correction—often using the most dreadful gutter language when unable to get her own way. Not only could we not help her because of her refusal to obey our authority, but she had a detrimental effect upon the entire program because of her bad influence.

Reluctantly, we put her out of the program and requested that she stay away from the property. Several months later she was discovered sleeping in a staff member's bed, having climbed up a fire escape and entered the building via an open window. We had her take a hot shower, gave her a complete change of clothing, and prepared her a meal. After she had eaten we asked her to leave the property, but she refused and struck one of our female staff. I had the very unpleasant duty of taking her by the arm and escorting her from the premises while she called me every foul and disgusting name imaginable.

The New Zealand Police arrested her a few hours later for some minor misdemeanor, and she died that same evening—alone in a prison cell. An autopsy was held but the cause of death was never determined. According to the coroner's report, she was a "strong, healthy 28-year-old woman."

We should not be surprised at such things—God has not changed since He wrote the book of Acts. Our God is *"a consuming fire"* (Hebrews 12:29)—and we can be sure that the fire has not been extinguished. I cannot help wondering how many other Christians have been struck dead like Ananias and Sapphira (Acts 5:1–10) were, and which have been portrayed as mere happenstance?

I was personally shocked when a good friend, a pastor of a congregation in Arizona, told me that he was weighed down under more than $50,000 of credit card debt. However, he was not alone in being a Christian and purchasing "things" on credit when he could not afford them. Ordering items on credit when a person does not have the wherewithal to pay for them is nothing short of lust and covetousness. The Bible speaks about *"covetousness"* and says it is *"idolatry"* (Colossians 3:5). Credit card debt is therefore ranked by the LORD as covetousness. Coveting things we cannot afford is lust, and lust is linked with witchcraft. The LORD admonishes us:

> *Let your conduct be without covetousness; be content with such things as you have* (Hebrews 13:5).

That says everything needing to be known about Christians getting into debt. Debt is nothing but a briar patch for modern-day Christians. We are warned about the thorns among which the *Sower's* seed—*"the Word of God"*—fell, and which chokes the life of the Son of God out of Christianity.

> *And as for what fell among the thorns, they are those who hear, but as they go on their way they are choked by the cares and riches and pleasures of life, and bring no fruit to maturity* (Luke 8:14).

Unfortunately, it seems the average Christian is only content to be a Christian provided it does not interfere too much with his life-style. His behavioral pattern does not differ greatly from the unchurched. A number of Christian youth organizations have sponsored research into youth behavior, and the results reveal that the only major difference between Christian and non-Christian youth is a verbal one:

> The Christians answer "no" when asked if they would lie, cheat, steal or go to bed with someone, while the non-Christian youth say, "Of course, if it's to my advantage."

Available data from a Barna Group survey in 2014 reveals that viewing pornography on a regular basis is widespread in the U.S. It also found that the number of men identifying themselves as Christians and viewing pornography virtually mirrors the national average. The percentage of

The Church — Chapter 16

Christians that watched pornography on **a daily basis** was **higher** than that of non-Christians. The survey showed that women watch pornography far less than men; however, the ratio of Christian women watching pornography is **higher** than non-Christian women.

IT IS MY FIRM CONVICTION THAT no judgment will come upon any Christian from the hand of the LORD without Him first having given that person clear warnings. The warnings—those checks which we receive in our spirit—are from the Holy Spirit. He is saying, "Son, change your ways." God does not promise to protect Christians from trouble or heartache. Without challenge there is no growth. And *"man is born to trouble as surely as sparks fly upward"* (Job 5:7 NIV).

The LORD does, however, promise to give us the grace and the power to remain victorious in the midst of trouble. When a nation is at war, many Christians also suffer the destruction of their homes, the loss of their employment, and the death of loved ones. This is fact; it is not a failing on God's part. He never promised us anything to the contrary. Faith does not look upon God as a blessing machine. Faith says, in the midst of adversity:

> *The LORD gave, and the LORD has taken away; blessed be the name of the LORD* (Job 1:21).

Christians also need to give thought to judgment for their sins of omission besides their sins of commission. James, the brother of our Lord says:

> *Therefore,* **to him who knows to do good and does not do it, to him it is sin** (James 4:17).

There are things which we know we should do, but for one reason or another we simply do not do them. This could cost many Christians dearly:

> *Then He will also say to those on the left hand, "Depart from Me, you cursed, into the everlasting fire prepared for the devil and his angels: for* **I was hungry and you gave Me no food; I was thirsty and you gave Me no drink; I was a stranger and you did not take Me in, naked and you did not clothe Me, sick and in prison and you did not visit Me.***"*
>
> *Then they also will answer Him, saying, "Lord, when did we see You hungry or thirsty or a stranger or naked or sick or in prison, and did not minister to You?" Then He will answer them, saying, "Assuredly, I say to you,* **inasmuch as you did not do it to one of the least of these, you did not do it to Me***." And these will go away into everlasting punishment, but the righteous into eternal life* (Matthew 25:41–46).

And what about our persecuted Christian brethren? Do we care about those in prison for the sake of Jesus; those being executed; or our sisters being raped? Neither Christians nor churches are showing empathy for them, but we are one body, what affects the hand affects the eye:

> *so we, being many, are* **one body in Christ**, *and individually members of one another* (Romans 12:5).

There is, without question, fierce storms brewing in both our Christian and secular worlds. We dare not allow our faith to be shipwrecked on the rocks of apathy or adversity. If we hold to the belief that God will shelter us in a time of war, from the effects of war, many will — as many have done in the past — renounce faith in God with the first calamity that comes their way. Everything we have belongs to God — all our possessions and all our loved ones — only our sin belongs to us. However, there are promises that every God-fearing Christian can stand upon in times of war and catastrophe:

> *"I will surely deliver you and you shall not fall by the sword; but* **your life shall be as a prize to you**, *because you put your trust in Me," says the* LORD (Jeremiah 39: 18).

> *"I will bring adversity on all flesh," says the* LORD. *"But* **I will give your life to you as a prize** *in all places, wherever you go"* (Jeremiah 45:5).

These promises are personal promises — they are not made to family units (young children are protected by a godly parent) — each individual must have his own faith and his own righteousness:

> *Son of man,* **when a land sins against Me by persistent unfaithfulness, I will stretch out My hand against it**; *I will cut off its supply of bread, send famine on it, and cut off man and beast from it.* **Though these three men, Noah, Daniel, and Job, were in it, they would deliver only themselves by their righteousness**, *says the* LORD GOD.
>
> *If I cause wild beasts to pass through the land, and they empty it, and make it so desolate that no man may pass through because of the beasts,* **even though these three men were in it**, *as I live, says the* LORD GOD, **they would deliver neither sons nor daughters; only they would be delivered**, *and the land would be desolate.*
>
> *Or if I bring a sword on that land, and say, "Sword, go through the land," and I cut off man and beast from it,* **even though these three men were in it**, *as I live, says the* LORD GOD, **they would deliver neither sons nor daughters, but only they themselves would be delivered.**

The Church — Chapter 16

> *Or if I send a pestilence into that land and pour out My fury on it in blood, and cut off from it man and beast,* **even though Noah, Daniel, and Job were in it**, *as I live, says the* LORD GOD, **they would deliver neither son nor daughter; they would deliver only themselves by their righteousness** (Ezekiel 14:13–20).

The promise of receiving life as a prize is strictly an individual matter before God, and is dependent upon our level of faith and righteousness—of which He is the Judge. In order to weather the approaching storm of God's wrath, we need more than a good attendance record at church and we will not make it through by hanging onto another person's coattails. We need more than godly parents or grandparents, godly brothers or sisters. And having an intimate relationship with a godly spouse will not benefit us on that Day:

> *two people will be in one bed; one will be taken and the other left*
> (Luke 17:34 NIV).

We must have an essential, personal, vital, intimate relationship with the risen Son of the Living God. No creed, doctrine, or denomination is going to take us through the coming storm—only He who walks on the waves can deliver us. Peter, the fisherman, was afraid of the wind and waves during a particular storm and cried out:

> *Lord, save me! And immediately Jesus stretched out His hand and caught him* (Matthew 14:30,31).

Jesus stretches out His hands to those in distress every moment of every day. Perhaps He is reaching out to you right now. Cry out to Him, **"Lord, save me!"** Take His hand—He will bring you safely to the other shore. Nevertheless, *the* LORD *has a controversy with the Church.*

17

France

In the last week of November, 1992, President Mitterrand of France made his second visit to Israel—both since the 1991 Gulf War. In interviews with the Israeli news media during the two day visit, he repeatedly declared both himself and France to be "friends of Israel." With more friends like Mitterrand and the French Republic, Israel would need fewer enemies—the facts speak for themselves.

AT THE TIME OF MITTERRAND'S VISIT, *Israel Radio* reported that of the 20 billion dollars France had invested abroad during the previous ten years, only one million had been invested in Israel. Obviously, the French hold to the maxim of not mixing business with friendship.

The purpose of Mitterrand's visits was an attempt to regain French prestige that had eroded over the years—especially since the Gulf War. France was a dominant power in and around the Middle East for over half a century, and this is evidenced by the widespread use of the French language in the Arab world. France was the biggest supplier of arms to Israel until just before the 1967 Six-Day War, when, in a bid to offset growing Soviet influence in the Middle East, it stopped supplying Israel and began instead to sell massive amounts of weapons to the Arabs. The U.S. entered the arena and commenced to supply Israel with arms to counteract the Soviets' strong sphere of influence. America's power grew in the Middle East as it also paid court to the Arabs by selling them more arms than what it sold to Israel. The prominent role of the U.S. in the Gulf War, saw it emerge as the undisputed driving power in the region.

By involving itself in the Middle East "peace process," France hopes to gain some international recognition as a world power—especially among the Arab states. While he was in Israel, Mitterrand was quoted in the *Jerusalem Post* as saying: "A Palestinian state should have come into being in 1948. After all, a nation should have a homeland." Mitterrand knows full well that Jordan was originally created for the Arabs living in Palestine—Britain cut off 77 percent of the land earmarked for the Jewish National Home and gave it for the Arab state of Trans-Jordan. Britain also cut off the Golan Heights from Palestine and gave that to France, which had the mandate for Syria. And when the United Nations, on 29 November 1947, partitioned the remaining 23 percent of Palestine between Jews and Arabs so that each could have a state of their own, the Arabs refused it and chose war instead. But Mitterrands remarks were constructed to earn diplomatic points with the Arabs, not laurels from the Israeli public.

LIKE THE OTHER GREAT NATIONS, THE French Republic's lust for Arab petro-dollars knows few limits. In late January, 1992, the French government opened its doors to George Habash, a villainous Arab terrorist and one of the world's most wanted men at that time. Israel wanted to extradite Habash to Jerusalem to stand trial for his worldwide acts of terror against Jews, but France arranged to have him flown to Tunis where he met with another terrorist boss, Yasser Arafat. The *Middle East Intelligence Digest*, Vol 2, No 10, said of the French actions:

> Their decision to permit into their country one of the world's most notorious terrorists at the risk of being caught in the act clearly indicates at least two things:
>
> 1) That the French Government supports the Palestinian Arab "cause" to such an extent that it considers acts of terror against Israelis excusable, if not justifiable, and
>
> 2) That President François Mitterrand today leads arguably the most anti-Semitic government in Western Europe.

France's record vis-a-vis Israel has deteriorated steadily since 1967, when Charles de Gaulle reopened the floodgates of anti-Semitism in his eagerness to support and be supported by the Arab nations. The nation which was Israel's chief arms supplier before the Six-Day War has since led the crusade against Israel's admission to the European Community, while supplying arms and nuclear reactors to the enemies of the Jewish State.

DURING WORLD WAR II, THE FRENCH government collaborated with the Nazis. It betrayed the Jews and sent many of them to the death camps. In recent years French anti-Semitism has once again taken an upsurge and has now overtaken Britain and Sweden as the most anti-Semitic countries in Europe. Jewish cemeteries have been destroyed or desecrated and, in the city of Carpentras, in May 1990, a Jewish corpse was dug up and defiled. Synagogues have been broken into and set alight—Torah scrolls and prayer-books have been destroyed. An article in *The Jerusalem Post,* July 18, 1993, named France as the second major center in the world for Holocaust revisionism with overt dissemination of materials denying the

Holocaust ever happened. The article stated that revisionist material is spreading "from France to the rest of the European continent, to the Third World, India and Japan."

It was posited above that François Mitterrand led what was perhaps the most anti-Semitic government in Western Europe in 1992; little has changed in 23 years. Current president François Hollande continues to keep Israel at arm's length, continues France's weapons boycott against Israel, and promised to introduce a resolution to the U.N. Security Council in 2015 that would stipulate worldwide recognition of Palestine within 1967 borders and East Jerusalem as its capital.

An immoral liberal, François Hollande campaigned on a pledge to bring in homosexual marriage and adoption for homosexual couples, and as president, in keeping with his election pledge, signed a law in May 2013 stipulating that:

> marriage is a contract between two persons who are either of the same sex or of a different sex.

About 7,000 homosexual couples were married under the new law in France in 2014. In May 2015, two years after homosexual marriages were legalized in France, United Protestant Church of France, the fourth-largest religious group in the country, voted for its pastors to give their blessing to homosexual couples.

Hollande is no newcomer to immorality. He cohabitated for over 30 years with Socialist politician Ségolène Royal, with whom Hollande has four children. Hollande split from Royal and after only a matter of weeks was in another relationship with French journalist Valérie Trierweiler. Trierweiler moved into the Élysée Palace with Hollande and became his mistress and France's First Lady when he became president for a second term.

The French government of today, as in Mitterrand's day, purports to be "Israel's friend," but in reality it is equally as anti-Semitic and as immoral as at any time in the past. And with so many recent attacks being made against Jews and Jewish institutions that French Jews are fleeing to Israel in droves for safety.

In March of 2012, Mohammed Merah, a Muslim jihadist of Algerian descent, shot dead a teacher and three children at a Jewish school in the city of Toulouse. In January 2015, another jihadist, Amedy Coulibaly, the son of immigrants from Mali, burst into a kosher supermarket in Porte de Vincennes and killed four Jewish customers—two days after brothers Said and Cherif Kouachi, with whom Coulibaly liaised, killed 12 people at the offices of satirical magazine *Charlie Hedbdo*, which was known for its satirizing of religion, including Muhammad, the founder of Islam. Couple these latest massacres of Jews with a myriad of violent or verbal attacks against other members of the Jewish community and we see a returning of the Nazi era in Europe.

In 2014 – 2015 more French Jews immigrated to Israel than at anytime since the founding of the Jewish state. France is the most anti-Semitic country in all of Europe at this time in history.

F‍RANCE'S INVOLVEMENT WITH MIDDLE EAST POLITICS has a long history. A secret treaty—the Sykes-Picot Treaty—was made between Britain and France in 1916. Under its terms, France received Syria, Lebanon, and all Palestine north of a line drawn from Acre to the Sea of Galilee. The French were rebuffed in their bid for all of Palestine, but they did succeed in dividing off a sizable portion, until Israel captured it in the 1948 War of Independence.

Since Algeria gained independence from France in 1962, France has pursued a consistent pro-Arab policy. France is the third largest supplier of arms to the Middle East, after Russia and the United States. Like Russia, China and Britain, France maintains an arms embargo against Israel, while selling billions of dollars in arms to the Arabs. France constructed the Osiraq nuclear reactor on the outskirts of Baghdad that Iraq was using to produce a nuclear bomb. On June 7, 1981, Israeli fighter-planes made the hazardous journey across enemy air space—refueling during flight—and reduced the reactor, the laboratories, and the major outbuildings to rubble. This operational feat set Iraq's nuclear program back for years—for which the world should be eternally grateful. Needless to say, France condemned Israel's actions and rebuilt the reactor.

Israel, currently rated the fourth most powerful fighting force in the world (see page 61), is placed ahead of France. And rated as the fifth world nuclear power, sharing equal place with Britain, Israel only lags slightly behind France in terms of **known** nuclear capabilities.

F‍RANCE IS REGARDED AS A CATHOLIC country, but the rapidly weakening influence of the Roman Church is evidenced by the equally rapid rise in French divorces. The Protestant Church long ago relinquished her second largest French religion status to the Muslims. In place of Christianity, Islam, immorality and AIDS are spreading like wildfires. As seen above, homegrown Islamic jihadists who identify with ISIL are becoming active within France. Many French jihadists will return from the fighting in Iraq and Syria and bring with them experience in mayhem and murder, as they did on November 13,

France — Chapter 17

2015. Three groups of Muslim jihadists attacked in six places in the heart of Paris, killing 129 and injuring 352, some (99) critically. France has begun to reap the fruits of its pro-Arab, anti-Israel policies and has gotten a small taste of what Israel has been experiencing for 67 years. For France, there is much more to come.

The period of prosperity France enjoyed in the 1980s and 1990s has drawn to a close. Many French businesses are now struggling to survive, and unemployment is heading toward a record high. The unemployment rate in France hovered at around 10.6 percent in March of 2015, and a further 26,000 joined the ranks of the unemployed the following month. All the Jews fleeing to Israel helps to make unemployment figures look rosier than they actually are.

French power has been declining for 40 years. The coming economic and physical cataclysms are a consequence of past and current political, national, and religious sins:

a) Breaking of political agreements
b) Discriminating against strangers (includes racial discrimination)
c) Using power and wealth to make lesser nations subservient
d) Appropriating Israel's land
e) Murder, perverse and immoral behavior
f) Allies of those waging war against Israel
g) Anti-Semitism-political, racial and religious
h) Rejection of God
i) Rejection of God's Salvation
j) Refusal to hear and live by God's Word
k) Adultery, Divorce and Sexual Lusts
l) Homosexuality
m) **Sodomy** (sexual perversion, including acts with animals)

The judgments are, therefore: **Destruction of nation** (four times); **Physical catastrophes and widespread death** (two times); **Judicial cursing or complete destruction of nation**; **Near annihilation** (three times); **Annihilation** (two times); and **Collapse of nation**.

France, the nation that lost its honor during World War II, and its empire in the 1960's, is continuing her downward plunge toward full judgment. May her few remaining Christians rise up with a battle cry on their lips—*Repent! For the* Lord *has a controversy with the French Republic.*

18

Germany

Endowed with brilliant minds, Germans manufacture precision-made goods—exporting automobiles and appliances that are unmatched by any country in the world. But unfortunately, the German ability to produce murder apparatus—exporting death and suffering to the four quarters of the earth—is also unmatched by any other country in the world.

The belief in Aryan superiority has cost the lives of many, many millions of people. Just one man, Adolf Hitler (whose radically anti-Semitic book *Mein Kampf* was republished in Germany in January 2016), brought more misery, pain, and death in six years than did hundreds of world leaders throughout several centuries. Hitler's insane desire to create a "greater Germany" by subjugating surrounding countries, led to the blitzkrieg—an avalanche of German troops and armor that crushed their neighbors' opposition. Much of Europe's earth is stained red to a great depth with the blood of the masses shed by Germans. The mountains, hills, lakes, rivers, rocks and trees have no capacity to retain memories of atrocities committed before their eyes, but man and history do not forget. Seventy years after the end of the second World War, multitudes of men and women—scattered like straw around the world—nightly relive in their dreams the horrors of German savagery.

Politicians, especially German politicians, would have us believe that they have changed, but:

Can the Ethiopian change his skin or the leopard its spots? Then may you also do good who are accustomed to do evil (Jeremiah 13:23).

Cornelius Tacitus, one of the greatest Roman historians, provides important knowledge about ancient Germany. He wrote in 98 AD:

Many noble youths, if their native land is stagnating in a long period of peace and inactivity, deliberately seek out other tribes which have some war in hand. For the Germans have no taste for peace.

Another historian, Edward Gibbon, who lived in the eighteenth century wrote, in *The History of the Rise and Fall of the Roman Empire*:

To solicit by labor what might be ravished by arms was esteemed unworthy of the German Spirit.

Apparently, the two World Wars in the twentieth century that took some 60 million lives, and for which Germany was directly responsible, were not departures from the established German norm, but indicative of it.

It is also apparent that in postwar Germany there are relatively few new Germans. The pride, the arrogance, the disdain for anything and anyone non-German led to the riots in Rostock and other cities. The deaths of foreigners, and the destruction of their homes by Neo-Nazis show that many German hearts remain unchanged. *Newsweek*, September 7, 1992, quoted a middle-aged German man outside a shelter housing Romanian refugees in Rostock, after it was fire-bombed: "We all want the same thing—to get rid of them."

An article on the riots in the same magazine quoted a woman who "applauded" a "swarm of teenagers" that attacked and set on fire a building housing foreigners, "I cheered and cheered," she said with a smile, "Someone should have given those boys a bouquet." And the approving crowd chanted, "Hang them all!" and "Germany for the Germans!" A *Reuter's* report from Bonn, November 13, 1992, said that 24 soldiers

> were caught attacking immigrants while off duty or spreading Nazi propaganda.

According to *Dispatch From Jerusalem*, 4th Quarter, 1992, there were 1,900 reported German attacks against foreigners and Jewish memorials in 1992. Moshe Kohn, writing in "View from Nov," the *Jerusalem Post*, November 13, 1992, says:

> I understand the latter-day Nazis: they are Nazis (not "Neo Nazis," but Nazis), dedicated to hatred of and violence against the different.

An Israeli journalist, Yaron Svoray, worked under cover for five months among Germany's Neo-Nazi organizations. He said that neo-Nazi numbers are substantially higher than "official" government figures, and that some of the groups boast of police "help." When arrested at a demonstration, he and some Neo Nazis, "were quietly released 'with a wink.'"

POSTWAR GERMANY IS SAID TO BE "a different Germany," but a Germany in which people are being burned because they are not Germans is not "a different Germany." Wartime Germany burnt millions of Jews in specially built crematoriums after first gassing them in sealed chambers. Historian Martin Gilbert in *The Holocaust: The Jewish Tragedy,* quotes from an address by Heinrich Himmler to his senior SS officers on October 4, 1943:

Germany — Chapter 18

The extermination of the Jewish race ... it's our program—elimination of the Jews and we're doing it, exterminating them ... We had the moral right, we had the duty to our people, to destroy this people ... we have exterminated a germ.

Six million European Jews—the old, the young, babes at the breast, male and female alike—were systematically butchered and buried, or gassed and burned.

William L. Hull, in *The Fall and Rise of Israel*, says:

> Hitler's *Judenrein* after his rise to power was not Germany's introduction to hatred of the Jews; he merely intensified and increased anti-Semitism in both Germany and Austria. One has but to recollect the persecution of Jews in Germany during the Middle Ages; the ghettos; the slaughter of Jews in Germany by the Crusaders; and later the renewal of this mass hatred in the days of Bismark, to realize, as Jabotinsky maintains, that anti-Semitism is endemic in Germany.

IN APRIL, 1943, 1,200 POLISH JEWS of the Warsaw Ghetto—the last vestiges of the Polish capital's once great Jewish community—fought, against hopeless odds, the German murderers of their people. They did not expect to survive German counter attacks and very few did, but the uprising became a symbol of Jewish determination. On the fiftieth anniversary of the Warsaw Ghetto Uprising, Israel's Prime Minister, Yitzhak Rabin visited the site in commemoration of the ghetto fighters, and said:

> Here, on this square kilometer, stood the Warsaw Ghetto, a remnant of the 400,000 Jews who lived in this city, and the city is empty. Where are the writers? Where are the rabbis? The doctors? The musicians? Where are the simple folk? And where are the children? Scorched earth and a scorched people. My people are no more.

MARTIN GILBERT'S BOOK, *THE HOLOCAUST*, contains nearly 1,000 pages of eyewitness accounts of the most gruesome suffering ever endured by any race of man. Kurt Gerstein, chief of the Waffen SS Technical Disinfection Services, gave testimony before the Nuremberg War Crimes Tribunal of how, with stopwatch in hand, he monitored the opening, clearing, and preparation of a gas chamber at the Belzec death camp for the next batch of victims. He recalled that after the doors were opened:

> The people were standing like columns of stone, with no room to fall or lean. Even in death you could tell the families, all holding hands. It was difficult to separate them while emptying the room for the next

batch. The bodies were tossed out, blue, wet with sweat and urine, the legs smeared with excrement and menstrual blood. Two dozen workers were busy checking mouths which they opened with iron hooks ... Dentists knocked out gold teeth, bridges and crowns with hammers.

Christian Wirth [the camp commandant] stood in the middle of them. He was in his element and, showing me a big jam box filled with teeth, said, "See the weight of the gold! Just from yesterday and the day before! You can't imagine what we find every day, dollars, diamonds, gold!"

Perhaps Gilbert's book should be compulsory reading for every German for ten consecutive decades. It could take that long to instill some sense of guilt for their past actions. After the carnage inflicted upon the world by the German forces in World War II, German politicians and policy makers now treat the allied counter-attack as the moral equivalent of Germany's aggression. They officially protested at homage paid by the British to the soldiers who took part in that attack. Germany bombed London for 57 consecutive nights, and Britain retaliated by bombing German cities in return. When the Queen of England visited Dresden in 1992, the Germans threw eggs, tomatoes and apples at her because of the damage done to their city.

MARTIN LUTHER, THE SIXTEENTH CENTURY GERMAN who lead the Protestant Reformation, called for the burning of Jewish synagogues, destruction of their homes, and urged that all Jews be put "under one roof, or in a stable, like Gypsies." He called the Jews "poisonous bitter worms," and advocated they be stripped of their possessions and driven out of the country for all time. And more than one history book records that the mass-murder taking place in World War II extermination camps ceased on Sundays. This was to allow the thousands of German "employees" to attend church—often with their families. The German Church is said to have undergone real repentance, but this can only be true in part, because when a friend of mine recently visited the country and stayed in the home of a prominent German Christian family, he was cautioned by the head of the house: "You can talk about Israel, but don't mention Jews to my father." Can a man love *"the King of the Jews"* while hating His family according to the flesh? The Bible says he cannot.

GERMAN CHEMISTS PRODUCED VAST QUANTITIES OF lethal, inexpensive poison gas—"Zyklon-B"—for the extermination of millions during World War II. German engineers then built the death machine that most effectively

Germany — Chapter 18

utilized the gas. This same expertise is being exported to sworn enemies of Israel. In June 1993 Arie Stav, of Tel Aviv's *Nativ Center for Policy Research*, wrote an article entitled "On the threshold of Critical Mass. Part II":

> In the matter of weapons of mass destruction, and especially chemical weapons, Germany—with its highly developed chemical industry, led by J.G. Farben, and with its years of practical experience in Auschwitz and Treblinka—is the uncontested champion. Not only are 100 of the 300 firms supplying weapons of mass destruction German; but their share of the profits is around 70 percent. Heading the list, are of course, the three chemical giants Hoechst, Bayer and BASF. True to the traditions of the mother firm, J.G. Farben, the properly licensed Germans are constructing "pesticide" plants in Iran. **[German dictionaries and encyclopedia define "Zyklon-B" as "a pesticide for control of plant lice".]**
>
> Mercedes Benz supplies missile engines, while Rheinmetall, Mannesmann and Siemens construct munitions factories and supply the infrastructure and equipment for nuclear reactors. Bosch, AEG and Braun are subcontractors for the specially created firm OTRAG—responsible for the construction of the chemical weapons center at Rabta. Frankfurt-based Deuteronomysche Bank finances the deals with the Libyans. Thyssen and Siemens are involved in the new plant being constructed at Sabha. Audi is negotiating for the construction of a "pharmaceutical" plant near Damascus. ...
>
> Outstanding amongst those nations for which greed is a primary driving force, is the special case of Germany—first among purveyors of death by chemical, biological, and nuclear means. By virtue of its surrender terms of 1945, Germany is forbidden to develop and manufacture within its borders a long list of weapons, from missiles to nuclear systems. **Germany evades this ban by producing such items in Arab countries**, thus retaining its primacy as a weapons manufacturer, without breaking any laws. It is worth mentioning that this is exactly what the Germans did after signing the Versailles Treaty, which also forbade them to produce advanced weapons. At that time they made them in Soviet Russia. [The Versailles Treaty formerly ended World War I on June 28, 1919. It laid the blame on Germany for starting the war and held it responsible for the resulting damage. Reparations to be paid by Germany was set at 132 billion gold marks.]

THE REUNIFICATION OF GERMANY IN OCTOBER 1990 created apprehension in the hearts of many nations—especially Israel. With the new UN Conventional Arms Register listing Germany as the sixth largest supplier of arms in the world, and considering German history, a united, mentally aggressive, economically strong Germany is cause for alarm.

In 2005 the International Atomic Energy Association (IAEA), the UN's nuclear watchdog, found that Iran was not complying with its international obligations. International economic and trade sanctions were applied because of Iran's pursuit of nuclear weapons. A number of countries found ways to circumvent the sanctions and a few German business giants like Siemens openly flouted the sanctions and continued with a "business as normal" approach, thus they helped Iran become a nuclear threshold state.

THE GERMAN ECONOMY, HOWEVER, BEGAN A nose-dive from the moment of unification. According to an article in the *Jerusalem Post, International Edition,* December 19, 1992:

> Realistic estimates are that one out of three, or even one of two east Germans are unemployed.

Another article, from the financial pages of the *Jerusalem Post*, June 4, 1993, reports that the West German economy had suffered a sharp decline—"the worst slump in thirty years."

The 2007 – 2008 Global Financial Crisis ate out the reserves of many nations, causing some to go belly-up and others to teeter upon bankruptcy. Under Chancellor Angela Merkel's leadership Germany weathered the storm by introducing severe austerity measures, which was good fiscal responsibility.

HITLER SOUGHT TO CREATE "A PURE Aryan race" by exterminating all Europeans whose ancestry was not Aryan. Today, Germany is going in the opposite direction. For a "German" Germany to survive, its birthrate must rise from the current 1.3 babies per woman to a 2.2 replacement rate to even remain static. It would appear that Germans actually prefer dogs to children. Germany's population is forecast to decline by 23.4 million by 2050; only by absorbing 450,000 new immigrants **per year** can it maintain its current population unless a cultural revolution takes place among German women. *De facto*, Germany has already become a society of immigrants; the 2015 migrant influx will only exacerbate that. Hitler must be turning in his grave.

CHANCELLOR ANGELA MERKEL, HOLDING A DOCTORATE in Physical Chemistry, entered politics in the aftermath of the 1989 revolutions against Communist one-party rule. Working her way upwards through the rank and file of German politicians she became the first female Chancellor of Germany in 2005, and 10 years later continues with her long reign as the most powerful woman in the world. Leading Europe's most vibrant economy, Merkel is the longest-serving elected EU head of state. Merkel's fiscal acumen fought off a national recession during the global economic crisis and she has consolidated Germany's economic clout. Merkel has used her political power against ISIL (a.k.a. Islamic State), by breaking the post-Nazi-era taboo of direct involvement in military actions and is sending arms to the Kurds fighting the brutality of ISIL.

Homosexuality is endemic in Germany, and while Germany has had civil partnerships for same-sex couples since 2001, Chancellor Merkel has no plans to push for the legalization of same-sex marriage, despite the overwhelming support for homosexual marriage in Europe, Scandinavia, and Nordic countries. Germany remains one of the only countries in Western Europe where homosexuals cannot legally wed.

Chancellor Merkel has favored Israel with state-of-the-art German defensive weaponry, and her government has heavily subsidized the cost of Israel's six Dolphin-Class submarines. Germany continues to pay reparations to Jews and to Israel for the terrible sufferings and trauma the Jews were subjected to under the Nazis. Since 1952 until November 2012 Germany had paid out $89 billion in reparations to Jews. Merkel has addressed Israel's Knesset (Parliament) and often defends Israel against diatribes from leaders of countries opposed to Israel's existence.

Chancellor Merkel has shown true personal repentance for the repungant, bestial deeds of the Nazis and Israel considers her to be a true friend. Many German Christians also have a true love for Israel and are generous in their support for the Jewish state, but will the repentance of the minority be sufficient to prevent the destruction of the majority? Anti-Semitism and Jew hatred in Germany still raise their heads from time to time.

GERMANY REPEALED HER REFUGEE LAWS SINCE the neo-Nazi riots began against foreigners in 1992. This had effectively sealed its borders against foreigners, and was a victory for the Nazis. However, with Merkel at the helm, Germany has shown willingness to accept large numbers of refugees, albeit amid some violent protests.

Due to Merkel's rethinking on asylum for refugees, Germany has become the main destination for migrants arriving on the EU's eastern borders. Germany admitted 1.1 million asylum seekers in 2015 and in early 2016 there had been no staunching of the human flow into the country. At the time of writing some 516 criminal complaints of theft, rape, and fondling of young German women on New Year's eve in Cologne have been filed against predominantly North African male refugees and migrants. Police in Hamburg and other cities are also dealing with similar complaints against "foreigners." A criminal and terrorist element was not unexpected with such a tidal wave of refugees. Chancellor Merkel optimistically said:

> Germany is a strong country—we will manage.

Following a spate of arson attacks on refugee shelters and anti-migrant demonstrations Merkel also said there would be "no tolerance for those who question the dignity of other people."

Merkel's response has been a far cry from the Germany of 70 years ago. With continued leadership like hers, together with an increase in national repentance, Germany could forestall judgment for decades to come. On the other hand, the tsunami of Muslim refugees that began in 2015, may be in itself be part of the bitter pill of judgment for Germany, a nation with a long history of racism. With so many hundreds of thousands of Muslims being given sanctuary in Germany, it will not be long before terror attacks like those carried out in Paris happen. Muslims do not assimilate into the cultures they are received into, they form Muslim ghettos into which non-Muslims are not welcome. There seems to be little doubt that the Islam which the refugees are bringing in, coupled with that already in Germany, will, in time, greatly overwhelm Germany's predominantly Catholic population.

The "refugees" are being enjoined by top Al-Aqsa Iman Sheikh Muhammad Ayed to **breed with European citizens in order to capture their countries**. The Qur'an definitively states that "whoever emigrates for the cause of Islam will find abundance." Moving to a different land in order to spread Islam is considered "meritorious." *The Independent* reported on September 11, 2015, that Saudi Arabia, which cultivates the strictest Wahabbi sect of Islam, has responded to the growing number of Muslims fleeing the Middle East for western Europe—by offering to build 200 mosques in Germany, or one mosque for each 100 Muslim refugees that entered Germany over the weekend.

The sins of Germany touched upon in this chapter are:
a) Murder, perverse and immoral behavior
b) Breaking of political agreements
c) Unprovoked military aggression

Germany — Chapter 18

d) Military aggression to enlarge territory
e) Discriminating against strangers (includes racial discrimination)
f) Pride in national security
g) Fraudulent, deceitful and crafty business transactions
h) Allies of those waging war against Israel
i) Extreme cruelty in times of war
j) Anti-Semitism-political, racial and religious
k) Homosexuality
l) **Sodomy** (sexual perversion, including acts with animals)

The judgments are, therefore: **Physical catastrophes and widespread death** (two times); **Destruction of nation** (four times); **Defeat with high loss of life**; **Acceleration of nation's destruction**; Nation conquered and devastated; and **Judicial cursing or complete destruction of nation**.

Germany's history of instigating bloodshed is simply appalling. Her preoccupation with an assumed superiority has caused the greatest losses of life in world history. The systematic murder of millions of God's chosen people in the most bestial fashion—the avowed determination to exterminate every last Jew in Europe—has no counterpart in the world's book of horror stories. Martin Gilbert, in *The Holocaust*, quotes a high ranking SS officer:

> *There are only two superior peoples—the Jews and Germans. The question is, which one will dominate?*

No nation or empire has survived to tell of its conquest of the Jews—and *the LORD has a controversy with Germany.*

19

Iran

In 1947, Iran (ancient Persia) was among 13 countries that voted against the United Nation's Partition Plan for Palestine. In 1949, twelve months after Israel became a state, Iran voted against Israel's admission to the United Nations. Nevertheless, following Turkey, Iran became the second Muslim-majority country to recognize Israel as a sovereign state. In 1953, a joint CIA-British *coup d'état* overthrew the democratically elected prime minister of Iran, Mohammad Mosaddegh, essentially giving the U.S. and Britain control of the Iranian oil business. While the *coup* empowered pro-Western Mohammad Reza Shah Pahlavi, it set the stage for the Islamic revolution in 1979 and generations of anti-American hatred in Iran.

After the overthrow of Mosaddegh relations between Israel and Iran significantly improved. The Shah saw himself first and foremost as a Persian king, and in 1971 held an extravagant celebration of the 2,500th anniversary of the pre-Islamic Persian monarchy. In 1976, he formally replaced the Islamic calendar with a Persian calendar.

Israel steadily built good diplomatic and commercial relations with the Shah, or King, of Iran, who ascended the throne in 1941, and sold Iran all manner of goods, including Israeli-made weapons.

Following protracted protests against his rule by Iranian Islamists, the Shah, the last of the Persian monarchs, was forced to flee the country on January 6, 1979 and 14 days later, Ayatollah Ruhollah Khomeini, the spiritual leader of the Islamic revolution, returned after 15 years of exile and took control of Iran. On February 11, 1979, Iran's Pahlavi dynasty was completely overthrown. After the revolution, Khomeini's fanatical interpretation of Islam took firm hold and Iran severed all diplomatic and commercial ties with Israel; Iran's Islamic government categorically refuses to recognize the legitimacy of Israel as a state; it has repeatedly threatened to annihilate it.

THE IRAN–CONTRA SCANDAL OCCURRED DURING the second term of U.S. President Ronald Reagan's administration and dragged Israel into a U.S. machination. Unbeknown to President Reagan, administration officials secretly facilitated the sale of arms to Iran—which was the subject of an arms embargo at the time—having been designated a State Sponsor of Terrorism in January 1984, and thereby prohibited from purchasing arms. U.S. assistance from Israel was necessary to effect weapons sales to Iran through an intermediary to the Islamic republic, by which the U.S. hoped to secure the release of seven U.S. hostages held in Lebanon by Hizb'allah, a terror group with Iranian ties to the Army of the Guardians of the Islamic Revolution. The plan was for Israel to ship the weapons to Iran, and then the U.S. would resupply Israel and receive the Israeli payment. Iran at the time was in the midst of the Iran–Iraq War—a war in which both sides used tons of poison gas against each other—and Iran could not find Western nations willing to supply it with weapons.

The concept of the plan was for Israel to ship weapons to a supposedly moderate, politically influential group within Khomeini's regime. The recipients were to do all in their power to secure the release of the U.S. hostages. Israel demanded the sale of arms to Iran meet high level government approval in the U.S., and when Israel was assured the U.S. government approved the sale, it agreed to sell the weapons. However, the plan was modified in the U.S. and went horribly wrong: America was caught swapping weapons for hostages, which was against U.S. policy; U.S. officials padded the price of the weapons as did the greedy arms dealer—the price of the weapons deal was padded by over 60 percent, which incurred the wrath of the Iranians and Israel became the scapegoat. Part of the payment went to fund Contra rebels in Nicaragua trying to topple the Sandinista government in yet another U.S. machination. None of the hostages in Lebanon were released.

MUHAMMAD WAS RESPONSIBLE FOR THE INTRODUCTION of Islam into the world, and Islam is responsible for keeping the Muslim world locked into the dark ages. Mohammad preached:

A day and night of fighting on the frontier is better than a month of fasting and prayer.

Islam is a cruel religion—the continual media reports, along with videos uploaded to YouTube, of beheadings by knife, machete or exploding necklaces; the burning of captives alive; the drowning of captives; the forcing of captives to kneel on top of explosives buried in the ground before detonating, prove the lie that Islam is a religion of peace. Islamists who act true to the Qur'an (Koran) are cruel, indeed, they are savage.

The adherents of Islam are repeatedly exhorted in the Qur'an to kill for the sake of Allah, and where the Sharia law is in effect, there can be no resisting Islam or turning to another religion or faith. To do so invites death—by sword, hanging, stoning or crucifixion.

Christianity is barely tolerated by the leaders of Iran's extreme brand of Shia Islam. Numbers of Christians, predominantly pastors, get arrested on false charges and are thrown into rat-infested jails, tortured, and often hanged for crimes against the state, even in the face of international outrage.

Public executions are common, usually by hanging, but sometimes by stoning, and often there are hangings of six or ten people at a time. Amnesty International say executions in Iran surpassed 1,000 in 2015. According to the United Nations, Iran's government executed at least 82 people shortly following Hassan Rouhani election as president in June 2013. Not voting according to the Supreme Leader's choice cost these people their lives.

AYATOLLAH KHOMEINI WAS A FANATICAL ISLAMIST who perceived his destiny to be the restorer of the ancient Persian Empire which ran from Macedonia in Greece right through to India, and encompassed Armenia, Afghanistan, Pakistan, Syria, Libya, Lebanon, Israel, the Palestinian Territories, most of modern Egypt, and the islands of Crete and Cyprus. This restored Persian Empire would be administered according to Khomeini's interpretation of Islam and strict Sharia law. For Khomeini it was a given that the Empire would need to be taken back by use of the Islamic sword.

Iran foments wars using Islamic brutality throughout the Middle East for the purposes of resurrecting the ancient Empire, this time under intolerant Islamic rule. It is also working for the eradication of Israel, which is most essential if Iran is to take possession of Israel's territory. Iran has a firm foothold in Lebanon with its Hizb'allah proxy, and it has Hamas and Islamic Jihad as proxies in Gaza. Hizb'allah and Islamic Jihad have both spread their tentacles into Syria where Iran has around 1,000 of its own troops fighting to keep Bashar al-Assad in power. They are establishing bridgeheads on the Golan Heights with the view to attacking Israel at an opportune time.

Those fighting against Iran and its proxies are severely hampered due to Iran's financial power and its weapons supply. Israel will not be a pushover, it has a strong military and powerful defensive and offensive weapons. Iran is content not to push Israel too far at this time; Iran must first consolidate its hold on Iraq, Yemen, Lebanon, and Syria.

Iraq is in a turmoil, and if it was not for the Kurdish fighters it would have succumbed completely to either ISIL or Iran, each of which hold large areas of blood-soaked Iraqi territory.

If al-Assad of Syria manages to survive he will be under Iran's thumb. Syria is central to Iranian strategic thinking. Mehdi Taaib, who heads Ayatollah Ali Khamenei's think tank, said:

Syria is the 35th district of Iran and it has greater strategic importance for Iran than Khuzestan [an Arab-populated district inside Iran]. By preserving Syria we will be able to get back Khuzestan, but *if we lose Syria we will not even be able to keep Tehran*.

The Commander of the Quds Force of the Revolutionary Guard Corps is Qasem Suleimani. Suleimani has prepared an operational plan named after him, which is based upon the establishment of a 150,000-man force for Syria, the majority of whom will come from Iran, Iraq, and a smaller number from Hizb'allah and the Gulf states.

Interviews with Afghan fighters and relatives of those killed in Syria point to a strong recruitment drive among the waves of Shiite Hazara refugees by Iran's Revolutionary Guards Corps. The young Afghan refugees seek shelter in neighboring Iran from decades of war that has torn their country apart, but they have gotten ensnared in another war and are used as "cannon fodder" by Iran.

Yemen is being torn apart by the Shia Houthis. Ansar Allah, the Houthi's military wing, is another of Iran's proxy militias. Iran sees Yemen, particularly the northern Shia sector, as a suitable staging ground for troublemaking activity against Saudi Arabia, its main Sunni Islam religious-political rival in the Middle East. (The real war in the Middle East is the war within Islam itself—Shia Islam versus Sunni Islam. Iran heads the minority Shia branch of Islam, Saudi Arabia heads the much larger majority Sunni branch.) According to media reports in November 2014, there are hundreds of thousands armed and organized Shia and Sunni Muslim men fighting each other in Yemen. Sana'a, Yemen's capital, fell to Iran in September 2014.

SAUDI ARABIA BEGAN AIRSTRIKES AGAINST HOUTHI strongholds in Yemen and the Houthis have launched Iranian SCUD missiles into Saudi Arabia. Ali Akbar Velayati, former Iranian foreign Minister, and current adviser to Iranian Supreme Leader Ali Khamenei, was asked about the effects of the revolution in Yemen and he responded with:

> The important issue is that *the road to freeing Palestine passes through Yemen* since Yemen has a strategic location and is near the Indian Ocean, Gulf of Oman, and Bab al-Mandeb.

Ali Riza Zakani, a member of the Iranian parliament and who is close to Khamenei, said, with the hallmark defiance that portrays Iran's foreign policy:

> Four Arab capitals, **Beirut**, **Damascus**, **Baghdad**, and **Sana'a** have already *fallen into Iran's hands and belong to the Iranian Islamic Revolution*.

Iran — Chapter 19

Anis A. Shorrosh, in his book *Islam Revealed: A Christian Arab's view of Islam*, points out that Ayatollah Khomeini, the former fanatical leader of Iran who ousted the Shah and brought a resurgence of fundamental Islam to the Middle East, even preached that:

> *the purest joy in Islam is to kill and be killed for Allah.*

Let us be clear on one point: Allah, the god of Islam, is not the God of creation and the Bible, nor is he the God whom Christians worship. **Allah is a demonic spirit which inspires its followers to commit demonic acts in its name**. In *Sura* 12:39 the Qur'an confirms that Allah is an idol when it says:

> *We will serve no idols besides Allah.*

Until the mid-1990s it was unheard of for the media to portray Allah as God, but the leftist media and its overtly liberal journalists quickly adapted to political correctness and now do so incessantly.

A PAPERBACK COPY OF THE NEW Testament is approximately the same size at the Muslim Qur'an. In the New Testament there are 57 **direct** commands to "love." Christians are commanded to *love* God; *love* their enemies; *love* their neighbors; *love* their wives; *love* one another, etc. In addition to the **direct** commands there are 191 other instructions about "*love*" (not including usage like *"they love the best seats"*). Conversely, in the Qur'an, the word "love" does not appear even one time. It does, however, contain 143 verses which instruct Muslims to kill and fight for Allah. It also instructs Muslims to beat their wives in order to keep them in line.

In the Qur'an Israel, both as a nation and a people, is destroyed; the Jews are cursed by Allah and have been turned into pigs and monkeys—Muslims are to fight and kill them wherever they find them. Thus we have most of the billion-plus Muslims railing at Israel and attacking Jews virtually wherever they are found. For an Islamist there is no possible way to reconcile Islam and the existence of Israel—that would mean the Bible is true and the Qur'an a lie.

There are many Iranian Jews living in Israel, but 99.9 percent of them came before the 1979 Islamic Revolution headed by Ayatollah Khomeini. Those that remained are virtual prisoners, unable to leave Iran and must kowtow to the Islamic leaders, saying only what they are told to say. Numbers of Iranian Jews attempting to reach Israel simply disappeared. On July 27, 2015, Israel's *Mossad* intelligence service ended two decades of speculation over the fate of three Iranian Jews who vanished in 1997 while attempting to emigrate to Israel. The *Mossad* confirmed that the three men were killed by Iranian authorities when the escape plan went wrong.

Iran's hatred of Jews knows no bounds. In 1994, in an interview with the BBC, the leader of the Iranian funded Hamas Islamic terror group said:

> *You don't understand ... Islam can never negotiate or recognize Israel.*

Iran goes further than most Islamist countries, it trains and equips fighters to terrorize Israelis and sends arms and explosives to President Bashar al-Assad of Syria, and terror groups like Hamas, Islamic Jihad, Hizb'allah *et al*.

An article in the *Jerusalem Post*, taken from a report published in the *Telegraph* on May 3, 2015, showed that Iran had stepped up its efforts to support Hamas in Gaza, transferring tens of millions of dollars to Hamas's military wing to help with the rebuilding of tunnels and the restocking of missile arsenals destroyed by Israel during 2014's Operation Protective Edge.

A former adviser to Iran's defense ministry says Tehran will seek to arm Palestinians in the West Bank with "strategic weapons" including missiles to target Tel Aviv and Haifa. He says:

> *A new front must be opened from the West Bank, after it has been armed, especially with missiles*, because we know very well that the distance between the West Bank and Tel Aviv, Haifa, and other areas is much shorter than the distance from Gaza.

Iranian Deputy Foreign Minister Morteza Sarmadi said on July 16, 2015, that Israel plots discord among Muslims and is the root cause of extremism in the Islamic world. This is merely an echo of what Saddam Hussein said in December 1990:

> *We consider that the responsibility for the problems, for the Arab conflicts, fall on Israel.*

Nothing changes in Islam—Israel will forever be its scapegoat.

On August 12, 2015, Iranian Foreign Minister Mohammad Javad Zarif said that Iran's main challenge was "confronting the extremist Zionist regime." Iran's strategy is to totally surround Israel with armies and militia groups who can attack and destroy Israel. Iran's leaders have for years spewed forth hatred of Israel on an almost daily basis:

> *The Zionist regime is a wound that has sat on the body of the Muslim world for years and needs to be removed.*

Iran — Chapter 19

The very existence of the Zionist regime is an insult to humanity.

The Zionist regime and the Zionists are a cancerous tumor.

Israel must be wiped from the map.

Israel is a stinking corpse that is destined to disappear.

Israel will be destroyed.

Israel is a virus that must be eradicated.

the ultimate goal of world forces must be the annihilation of Israel.

The West has abandoned Israel, which paves the way for the Islamic regime to annihilate the Jewish state.

Israel should be annihilated and this is our ultimate slogan.

If one day, the Islamic World is also equipped with weapons like those that Israel possesses now, then the imperialists' strategy will reach a standstill because the use of even one nuclear bomb inside Israel will destroy everything. . .

One Iranian gun-type uranium nuclear bomb, crudely built along the line of Little Boy dropped on Hiroshima, would have an instant kill radius of about 3 miles. If the Iranians delivered the weapon via a Hamas controlled "West Bank" or an Iranian mini-sub off Tel Aviv's coast, they could eradicate the Jewish state in an instant. There could be 2,000,000 killed and an additional 2,000,000 Jews in the coastal plain itself irradiated or wounded. The instant murder of 2,000,000 Jews and additional wounding of another 2,000,000 Jews out of a population of 6,000,000 would make for a rapid demise of the State of Israel.

Again on July 7, 2015, former Iranian president Akbar Hashemi Rafsanjani said that he was confident that the

forged and temporary Israeli entity would be wiped from the map.

Also on the same day Iranian Defense Minister Brigadier General Hossein Dehghan said the Jewish state was:

responsible for the disunity among Muslim countries and stood as a symbol of terrorism, infanticide, occupation, aggression and genocide.

On September 24, 2015, Major General Ataollah Salehi, Iran's Army commander, said:

Iran is eager to face down Israel militarily and destroy it. Iran will "annihilate Israel for sure."

And Iran is the country with which the six world powers just signed a nuclear agreement? Iran habitually makes the above type of malignant comments concerning Israel. It is past time that leaders of world powers take this seriously rather than forging agreements giving Iran a green light to produce nuclear weapons. If history has taught us anything, it has taught us that those with unlimited power create unlimited rivers of blood and misery.

For years Iran has attempted to hide its nuclear weapons program; it has denied at least a thousand times that it is attempting to create an atomic bomb. Israel, however, knows what is in store for it if Iran obtains a nuclear bomb. Israel has worked tirelessly to disrupt progress by assassinating a number of Iran's nuclear scientists, introducing several types of malware into Iran's nuclear computer systems, etc. Slowly, the West began to wake up to the reality that Iran was indeed working at top speed on its production of nuclear weapons and applied sanctions to bring Iran into line.

The International Atomic Energy Agency (IAEA) has been hindered in its efforts to monitor Iran's nuclear program, which Iran claims to be solely for domestic purposes. The IAEA knows that Iran has experimented with refined uranium and tested nuclear triggers, but cannot prove it because Iran is more cunning than a fox and cleans up its sites with bulldozers, or pours concrete over entire areas to conceal traces of radiation prior to an inspection.

For 20 months the six world powers—United States, Russia, China, Britain, France, and Germany—negotiated with Iran to limit its nuclear program in return for the lifting of sanctions. The deadline for reaching a deal was November 24, 2014, but by persistent subterfuge Iran managed to extend the deadline time and time again. As each deadline approached there were further concessions made by the world powers, and more gains made by Iran. Finally, on July 14, 2015, it was announced that a deal—the Joint Comprehensive Plan of Action (JCPA)—had been reached and that Iran had been prevented from making atomic bombs. However, the deal is sham, a complete farce, the agreement contains more holes than a colander and is unacceptable to many nations, especially to Israel. It will in no way prevent Iran from producing nuclear weapons. The agreement only delays by years the production of a bomb, which, given Iran's history of deceit, will see it covertly working at full steam to produce it years ahead of time. U.S. President Barack Obama was only interested in the prestige of getting a deal approved for legacy reasons and his friend Alan Dershowitz, a Professor of Law, Emeritus, at Harvard Law School, said:

Iran — Chapter 19

Obama gave Iran a green light to build nuclear weapons.

After the signing of the deal Iranian President Hassan Rouhani said that *Iran's ability to negotiate without giving up its nuclear program* had "charmed the world."

On November 20, 2014, *Fox News.com*'s Adam Kredo, a nuclear expert, published a report from Vienna where the world powers and Iran were negotiating. The report, authored by former European Parliament Vice President Alejo Quadras, and endorsed by former U.S. Ambassador to the U.N. John Bolton, former U.S. Under Secretary of State for Arms Control and International Security Robert Joseph, says that Iran never halted its clandestine nuclear weapons program despite repeated assurances to the contrary. The report showed that Iran continues to hide a great deal of its nuclear work and it shed new light on Iran's current and ongoing research into the creation of a nuclear warhead.

The findings coincided with comments issued two days earlier by the head of the IAEA stating that Iran still refuses to explain its research into an atomic weapon:

> Iran has vigorously pursued its ambitions to obtain nuclear weapons. *There are no serious indications that Tehran has stopped or abandoned this project or intends to do so. On the contrary, all the available information points to the conclusion that it has resorted to further secrecy and concealment to keep its program intact and unhindered*. Further revelations and information all point to the fact that a military program and military related activities are at the heart of the Iranian nuclear program.
>
> Tehran has worked systematically on all the necessary aspects of obtaining nuclear weapons, such as enrichment, weaponization, warhead, and delivery system at some stage. In other words, *Iran has worked on specific programs and projects to master all necessary aspects of obtaining a nuclear weapon*.

Iran is devious and deceitful in all its dealings with the West. The West was duped, first by Obama's lust for the limelight, and then by Iranian subterfuge. This the world powers could not—did not want to see—because the pot of gold dangling at the end of the sanctions rainbow dazzled them. After the deal was signed in July, leaders of France, Britain, and Germany tripped over each other in their frantic rush to initiate trade with Iran. The ending of sanctions will infuse up to $150 billion into Iran's economy; billions will be spent to foment unrest, not just in the Middle East, but all around the world.

ISRAEL HAS A POLICY OF "NUCLEAR AMBIGUITY," neither confirming nor denying that it possesses nuclear weapons. However, whistleblower Mordechai Vanunu, a technician from 1976 – 85 at Israel's nuclear facility at Dimona, revealed evidence of Israel's nuclear program to Britain's *Sunday Times* in 1986, which included dozens of photographs. Nuclear experts concluded that Israel had produced some hundreds of nuclear warheads. Vanunu, who converted to Christianity, said that he had an obligation to reveal to the world the quantities, the numbers, the types of weapons Israel had produced. Vanunu spent 18 years in jail for treason and was released in 2004, but is not allowed to leave the country for security reasons. He is shunned in Israel as a traitor and laments the fact that he has no friends.

In an unusual departure from years of nuclear secrecy, Israel's military censors permitted Vanunu to give an interview to primetime Israeli television on September 4, 2015, a move that took Israel close to acknowledging the existence of its nuclear arsenal. No doubt his interview was a deliberate act on the part of the Israeli government—a warning to Iran. Vanunu told the world *inter alia*:

This Jewish state has 200 atomic hydrogen bombs, atomic weapons, neutron bombs . . .

On pages 61 and 129 – 130 there are excerpts from a secret document that was declassified (much to Israel's chagrin) by the Pentagon that Israel had the codes to produce hydrogen bombs—considered to be 1,000 times more powerful than atomic bombs. In a nuclear exchange with Israel (it has six submarines equipped with nuclear-tipped missiles) Iran is likely to be hoist by its own petard.

Haman, the villain of the Book of Esther, was a Persian who plotted to kill all the Jews throughout the entire Persian Empire, but his plot backfired and he ended up being hung on the 70-foot—21.3 meter—high gallows that he had constructed to hang Mordechai the Jew on. The spirit of Haman was apparently very much alive and active in Khomeini, and has been in all the fanatical Islamist leaders of modern Iran who have followed Khomeini. Haman's end was not a pleasant one and Iran will rue the day that it enters into a full-blown military conflict with Israel.

The sins touched upon in this chapter are:
- a) Murder, perverse and immoral behavior
- b) Suppressing or hindering the preaching of the gospel
- c) Pride in National Security

Iran — Chapter 19

- d) Using power and wealth to make lesser nations subservient
- e) Waging war against Israel
- f) Allies of those waging war against Israel
- g) Rejoicing at another nation's misfortunes (especially Israel's)
- h) Extreme cruelty in times of war
- i) Anti-Semitism—political, racial and religious
- j) Rejection of God
- k) Rejection of God's Salvation
- l) Refusal to hear and live by God's Word
- m) Slavery and Oppression
- n) Unprovoked military aggression
- o) Military Aggression to enlarge territory
- p) Fraudulent, deceitful, and crafty business transactions

Iran's judgments are: **Physical catastrophes and widespread death** (two times); **Destruction of nation** (seven times); **Near annihilation** (five times); **Nation conquered and devastated**; **Defeat with high loss of life**; **Accelerated destruction of the nation**; and **Judicial cursing or complete destruction of nation**.

Iran is a nation drowning the Middle East in blood. It will likely drown in a sea of its own blood—*for the LORD has a controversy with Iran*.

20

Iraq

On September 22, 1980, Iraq attacked neighboring Iran, saying it was after territory that had belonged to Iraq in times past. The war waged on for eight years, and ended without Iraq ever obtaining its objective. Newspapers and magazines reported that Iraq used poison gas on Iranian troops and civilians, and also on its own Kurdish population. Thousands of Iranian corpses were reported to have been piled high—stacked head to toe in Iraq's northern marshes—and used as roads for Iraqi tanks. Over ten million lives were lost in the war.

In a pre-dawn attack on August 2, 1990, the Iraqi war machine rolled across neighboring Kuwait's border. Within a few hours hundreds of Iraqi tanks were in the capital, Kuwait City, and by the close of day, Kuwait had fallen to the Iraqi invaders. Iraq claimed that Kuwait, too, was part of Iraqi territory.

Amidst widespread looting, rape and murder, Iraq consolidated her forces throughout Kuwait, and began to mass troops and armor close to the border of Saudi Arabia. Any invasion of Saudi Arabia constituted a threat to U.S. oil interests, and the U.S. hastily began putting together an alliance of many nations prepared to make a concerted effort to drive Iraq from Kuwait. The Iraqi president, Saddam Hussein, said on December 27, 1990, in an interview with *Tele 5*, a private Spanish television network:

> *We consider that the responsibility for the problems, for the Arab conflicts, fall on Israel ... if we must suffer the first blow, whether at the front or here in Baghdad, and whether or not Israel participates directly in the aggression, they will suffer the second blow in Tel Aviv.*

Saddam Hussein kept his word. When coalition hostilities broke out in January 1991, Iraq launched SCUD missiles against Israeli population centers. The allies quickly drove the Iraqis from Kuwait, but not before Saddam fired 39 missiles at Israel, destroying or damaging several thousand Israeli homes. Millions of Israelis—all wearing gas masks—sat in specially sealed rooms and bomb shelters, which kept fatalities to a minimum—two persons from direct hits, and a few elderly folk from shock related heart attacks.

Allied losses in the Gulf War were less than 200, but Iraqi losses are believed to be around 20,000. The world's news media mentioned Israel's restraint many times, amazed that it just absorbed the Iraqi missiles without retaliating against the aggressor. After the war, on March 8, 1991, the *Hong Kong Standard* published details of Israeli plans to hit back at Iraq:

> *It called for an armed sweep through western Iraq by helicopter gunships and "significant ground forces." These would include commando teams, all protected by Israeli air force planes that would have secured an air "corridor" through Jordan or Saudi Arabia to support the operation.*

But Israel did not activate her plans. The United States denied Israel the satellite information on Iraqi troop and armor movements, and as we have said on page 132, the crucial IFF—the International Friend or Foe identification codes. Without these codes Israeli planes might well have been brought down by the allies. Even more likely—since the IAF is perhaps the most battle hardened air force in the world—a number of allied planes would probably have succumbed to the Israelis (In the first few days of the Lebanon War in June, 1982, the IAF brought down 96 Syrian MiG fighter-planes without a single loss to itself). In effect, the United States humiliated Israel by denying her the right to defend her citizens.

For Israel to sit idle, while being subjected to missiles raining down upon her most densely populated areas, could be construed by Iraq and other Arab states as weakness. A *Jerusalem Post* editorial in February 1991 said:

> This country [Israel] cannot afford to be known as the paper tiger of the Middle East.

And an unnamed military official said:

> We will punish Iraq in our own time and in our own way, but you don't hit a man when he is down.

After the destruction of Iraq's Osiraq nuclear reactor in the suburbs of Baghdad in June 1981, few would doubt Israel's ability to carry out its promise to repay Iraq for the missile attacks.

BEING DRIVEN OUT OF KUWAIT BY the allies will not dampen Iraq's primordial quest for the oil-rich Arab emirate. *TIME International*, October 8, 1990, quotes Saddam Hussein as saying:

> Kuwait belongs to Iraq, and we will never give it up even if we have to fight over it for 1,000 years.

Why did Iraq pursue waging war against neighboring fellow Arab countries? Why did Saddam Hussein have such an obsession to destroy Israel? Because

Iraq — Chapter 20

the Iraqi president firmly believed that he was a neo Nebuchadnezzar—destined to lead Iraq into the greatness that once belonged to ancient Babylon.

Nebuchadnezzar's kingdom extended from the Persian Gulf to the Mediterranean, taking in land currently occupied by Kuwait, Syria, Jordan, Israel, parts of Turkey and Egypt, as well as Iraq.

The reason for the Kuwait attack is obvious when we consider that it was part of the Babylonian Empire. Former King Hussein of Jordan went against world opinion and allied himself with Iraq in the Gulf War because he well understood Iraqi plans. Saudi Arabia was the ancestral home of the Hashemites, whom Britain displaced and located in what is now Jordan or, more correctly, the Hashemite Kingdom of Jordan. Saddam's plan was to conquer Saudi Arabia and give it back to King Hussein of Jordan. King Hussein would then hand Jordan to Saddam for inclusion into "greater Iraq"—the new Babylon. Yasser Arafat, the late PLO terrorist leader embraced Saddam also, because he thought that he would take control of the vacated Jordan. Syria sided with the allies against Iraq because it knew her days were numbered if Saddam won the war. Syria had backed Iran in the eight year Iraq-Iran war for the same reason.

Saddam Hussein's obsession with destroying Israel was because Nebuchadnezzar's greatest claim to fame was his destruction of Israel—hence the reason Israel was to receive the first retaliatory blow in the Gulf War. Saddam believed it was his destiny to destroy Israel, and then his claim to being a neo Nebuchadnezzar would be established for posterity.

BABYLON, KING NEBUCHADNEZZAR'S CAPITAL, WAS BUILT on both banks of the Euphrates River and was connected by a vast bridge. The city was protected by a continuous double wall 81 feet (25 meters) thick and 28 miles (45 kilometers) long. The Hanging Gardens of Babylon were one of the seven wonders of the ancient world. Nebuchadnezzar's palace had 700 rooms. (Turkey's new president, Recep Tayyip Erdoğan, has had a $600 million palace built that contains **1,000** rooms covering a total floor area of 3.1 million square feet (288,000 square meters), the palace is four times the size of Versailles—the Middle East is replete with megalomaniac rulers.)

All that remained of Nebuchadnezzar's Babylon was some ruins 55 miles (88 kilometers) south of Baghdad. In the early 1970's work began on the reconstruction of ancient Babylon. Up until the 1991 Gulf War, thousands of workers were employed on the site in the middle of the Iraqi desert, and completion was expected sometime in 1994. The newly constructed Babylon was to be Saddam's city and home. Antonio Caballero, quoted in

World Press Review, February, 1990, says that "60 million bricks had been laid so far," and that every six and-a-half feet (two meters), on every row, there is a brick with the inscription:

> The Babylon of Nebuchadnezzar was reconstructed in the era of Saddam Hussein.

After the cessation of hostilities between Iraq and neighboring Iran, the Iraqi government began hosting an annual four week "Babylon Festival," showcasing the government's efforts to rebuild the city. The official seal for the festival was a portrait of Hussein beside the ancient Babylonian king. Charles Dyer, a Dallas Theological Seminary professor, said:

> The portraits are drawn so that Nebuchadnezzar bears a striking resemblance to Hussein.

Also, stretched across the gateway to the new Babylon, were two figures reaching out to shake hands: on the right was Saddam Hussein, on the left was Nebuchadnezzar.

The rebuilding of Babylon was important to the Iraqi people because it united them against their two foes—Iran and Israel. It was the ancient Persians (Iranians) who destroyed Nebuchadnezzar's Babylonian empire (another reason for the attack on Iran in 1980), while Israel was once decisively beaten by the forebears of the current Iraqis. The Iraqi people believed in Saddam—they believed he would lead them to greatness, and the city of Babylon was their link to past glory.

ISRAEL UNDERSTANDS THE IRAQI MENTALITY, AND that the destruction of the reconstructed Babylon would have dealt a death blow to Saddam Hussein's aspirations of being a neo Nebuchadnezzar. Israel still has a score to settle with Iraq and has a point to prove. Obviously, with the remnants of Iraqi army, Iranian and Hizb'allah fighters battling ISIL in Iraq, Israel's settling of the score will have to wait.

Iraqi sins mentioned were:

a) Breaking of political agreements
b) Discriminating against strangers (includes racial discrimination)
c) Pride in national security
d) Unprovoked military aggression
e) Waging war against Israel
f) Allies of those waging war against Israel
g) Rejoicing at another nation's misfortunes (especially Israel's)

Iraq — Chapter 20

h) Extreme cruelty in times of war
i) Anti-Semitism-political, racial and religious

The judgments are, therefore: **Destruction of nation** (five times); **Physical catastrophes and widespread death**; **Defeat with high loss of life**; **Near annihilation**; **Nation conquered and devastated**; and **Judicial cursing or complete destruction of nation**.

THE FIRST EDITION OF THIS BOOK WAS PUBLISHED IN SEPTEMBER 1993— exactly 22 years ago to the day at the time of writing. The above lists of sins and judgments are the same as those printed in that first edition. Readers should now compare the list of judgments with what is taking place in Iraq in 2015, and what has taken place historically in Iraq in the years since the book *SAGA* was first published.

Judgment for Iraq obviously began in 1991 with the Gulf War, but after it was defeated it showed no sign of repentance. Rather, Saddam Hussein remained cocky and belligerent, and obstructed the Western powers, which had delivered him such a humiliating defeat. The West was probing Iraq's WMD (Weapons of Mass Destruction) programs and abilities and U.N. inspections during the mid-1990s uncovered a variety of prohibited weapons and technology scattered throughout Iraq. Saddam's continued flouting of the U.N. weapons ban and its repeated interference with the inspections caused the U.S. to bomb several military sites, after which Iraq refused entry to U.N. weapons inspectors entirely.

The cat and mouse game continued until March 2003 when U.S. President George W. Bush declared an end to diplomacy and gave Saddam 48 hours to leave Iraq. As was expected, Saddam refused to leave and the U.S. and allied forces dropped bunker-buster bombs on bunkers where it was thought Saddam may be hiding. Saddam, however, was no fool; he shipped off most of his chemical arsenal to his ally Syria, to Bashar al-Assad who has used some of the weapons against those fighting his regime in Syria's long-running civil war that began in early 2011.

In April 2003, after a punishing air campaign, U.S. and British forces invaded Iraq. Baghdad fell on April 6 and other cities followed. Several hundred U.S. troops were periodically injured when hastily buried chemical-filled artillery shells were disturbed. On May 1 the major fighting was over and forces concentrated on finding the Iraqi leaders who had fled. A disheveled and dirty Saddam Hussein, with long hair and an unruly beard, was discovered hiding in hole on December 13, 2003. He was handed over to Iraqi authorities in June 2004 and was subsequently convicted of crimes against humanity and ignominiously hung on December 30, 2006.

Iraq has been plagued with internal political squabbling which the U.S. could not settle. U.S. troops "trained" Iraqi forces to take over and pulled out in 2011. Opposing local militias fought each other for preeminence and Islamic State (ISIL) stepped into the vacuum. ISIL became the dominant force that today occupies large areas of Iraq and has continued tearing the country apart—a number of ISIL's top commanders are former high-rank officers from Saddam Hussein's élite fighting units. The semi-trained Iraqi forces literally ran away from the battle-hardened ISIL forces, abandoning their American supplied small arms, heavy artillery, trucks, and some 2,500 armored Humvees.

Iraq has been ravaged by war, crushed into rubble and dust, with large areas totally under the control of the barbarous ISIL; the carnage continues—*for the* L*ORD* *has a controversy with Iraq*.

21

Israel

In addition to what has previously been written concerning Israel on pages 13 – 70, we need to consider the judgment that must most certainly fall upon this country due to its ongoing sin and perversity. Apparently, Israel has learnt nothing from its soul-destroying history of destruction and enslavement. Certainly, Israel is back on its ancient land, having enjoyed the constant help of its *Holy One* in its latest establishment. However, from a reading of the punishments that came upon the nation in the past, following repeated warnings, it is patently obvious that its *Holy One* will not turn a blind eye to its present sins just because Israel is His *"chosen people,"* and the one whom He personally calls the *"apple of My eye"* (Zechariah 2:8).

The gratitude which the early *halutzim* (pioneers) expressed to the LORD for their deliverance from the horrors of the Nazi Holocaust and for the privilege of being in their God-given land after almost two millennia, has, for the most part, been lost to the current generation. Today's youth in Israel do not like to get their hands dirty with manual work and a large percentage dodge having to serve in the Israel Defense Forces (IDF), they want to be protected by the army, but do not want to serve in it, especially in the front line fighting units.

The massive Russian *aliyah* (immigration), resulting from the fall of the Union of Soviet Socialist Republic (USSR) in September 1991 (see page 108), brought over a million Russian Jews came to Israel. It also brought overt racism and organized crime (60 percent of the Russian immigrants were subsequently found not to be Jewish—they obtained their papers by bribing officials with either money or sex). Russian-style mafia crime rings required a special force of Israeli police to deal with them. A major *aliyah* of Ethiopian Jews had taken place in May 1991, only weeks before the great wave of Russian Jews. The majority of Russian Jews instantly hated the dark-skinned Ethiopians and knife fights were common between them, even one time in an elevator.

The Israelis were happy to see both the Russian and Ethiopian aliyahs, but the rising crime rates fueled by the Russian immigrants caused many Israelis to dislike the Russians, which continues until today. Given time, the Ethiopians were discriminated against both by the government and the general public and it is ongoing in 2016 although some steps are being implemented by the government to reverse this stain upon Israel. With the constant terror attacks by Palestinians against Israelis over the years there is a wariness among Israelis to employ Arabs, and they are discriminated against by both the government and the public.

The Israeli government is always touting that Arabs receive equality in Israel, but that is far from the truth. Arab neighborhoods receive far less than what Jewish neighborhoods get in the way of finance and services, and this is a constant cause of friction in the country. If the Arabs were truly given equality with Jewish citizens in Israel we would see a huge and immediate drop in Arab violence against Israelis.

Israel boasts of having the most liberal homosexual laws in the Western world, as if that is something for God's people to brag about. Worse still is the fact that Tel Aviv is promoted by Israel's Tourism Ministry as the homosexual capital of the world. And this was borne out by *Mail Online* in a January 24, 2012 article:

> *Tel Aviv has been named the world's number one gay city. The Israeli metropolis beat out competition from New York to top a survey carried out by American Airlines and GayCities.com to find the most popular destination for gay travelers. It landed a staggering 43 per cent of the vote, way ahead of runner-up New York's 14 per cent and third-placed Toronto with 7 per cent.*

The 2015 Homosexual Pride parade in Tel Aviv brought together 180,000 homosexuals from all across the world. Some of the perverts romped naked in Tel Aviv streets. Homosexuals also hold an annual parade in Jerusalem, *"the city of the great King"* (Psalms 482), *"the throne of the LORD"* (Jeremiah 31:17). Some religious Jews have attempted to ban the parade and in 2005 the then ultra-orthodox mayor of Jerusalem, Uri Lupolianski, turned to Israel's High Court to prevent the parade. The Court sided with the homosexuals and ordered Lupolianski to pay the costs of the parade.

That year an ultra-orthodox Jew, Yishai Schlissel, stabbed three participants in the parade and subsequently served a 10-year prison sentence for "attempted murder." Three weeks after his release from prison the 2015 parade was held and Schlissel stabbed six of the participants—a teenage girl died. At the time of writing Yishai Schlissel has not been sentenced, but it is unlikely that he will ever be freed from prison. Thousands turned out for the teenager's funeral and the international community was aghast at the stabbing. It was outraged because it is itself so perverted

Israel — Chapter 21

and immoral that it cannot see the provocation that a homosexual parade of thousands in the holy city causes. The *"great King"* in whose city the perverted parades takes place says that homosexuality is an *"abomination"* (Leviticus 20:13). Just because there are millions of perverted people in this world today does not mean that their behavior is acceptable to God:

> *Do not be deceived. Neither fornicators, nor idolaters, nor adulterers, nor homosexuals, nor sodomites, nor thieves, nor covetous, nor drunkards, nor revilers, nor extortioners will inherit the kingdom of God*
> (1 Corinthians 6:9–10).

THE ABOVE SCRIPTURE TELLS US THAT *"extortioners will not inherit the kingdom of God."* Israel is full of extortioners. Israeli politics is as corrupt as politics can possibly be. Israelis will quickly vote for a corrupt candidate over a clean candidate, they believe that corrupt people get the job done better because they are pushy. Numbers of Israeli politicians are in prison today for any number of offenses. One politician, Arieh Deri, the leader of the Shas ultra-orthodox party, was found guilty of fraud, embezzlement, and taking $155,000 in bribes while serving as Interior Minister. He was given a three-year jail sentence in 2000 of which he only served 22 months. Released from prison Deri was prohibited from entering politics for seven years. Eli Yishai had been leading the Shas party and as soon as Deri was eligible to enter politics he finagled himself back into the driving seat of Shas, was elected to the Knesset (Parliament) in 2015 and has one again become the Interior Minister, the position that he had abused previously. Tens of thousands of Israelis protested Deri's appointment as a minister, but the Attorney General's 23-page ruling was that while Deri's appointment caused legal problems, it was still not against the law. The most damning part of the ruling was: "Deri is not 'someone who has recognized his sins and taken responsibility for his actions.'"

Deri is merely an example. Former Ashkenazi chief rabbi of Israel Yona Metzger was indicted on multiple charges of fraud, theft, conspiracy, breach of trust, money laundering, tax offenses and accepting bribes involving more than $2,600,000 in October 2015. The ultra-orthodox leaders have no shame, they are still *"lovers of money"* (Luke 16:14).

But pilfering from the public till and taking bribes are not the only occupations of the ultra-orthodox religious Jews. On December 15, 2015, the police revealed that the work of an undercover *Haredi* (ultra-orthodox) police agent operating in Jerusalem's insular ultra-Orthodox neighborhood of Mea Shearim and in the *Haredi* neighborhoods of Beit Shemesh had led to the arrests of 45 residents involved in the trafficking of drugs and sale of illegal firearms. The agent succeeded in procuring large quantities of drugs, including "dozens of kilograms" of controlled substances, a stolen car, two Karl Gustav machine guns, an M-16 assault rifle, and ammunition for the firearms.

The agent said that the drug scene in Mea Shearim, which became active late at night, amounted to a parallel society. There was "Mea Shearim of the night," he said, and a very different "Mea Shearim of the daytime."

Former prime minister and mayor of Jerusalem Ehud Olmert is currently appealing an eight-month prison sentence for "graft," which had been tacked onto a longer sentence for taking bribes in what has been described as "the largest corruption case in the country's history." Olmert will also have to pay many thousands of dollars in fines. The Prison Service is reportedly building a VIP Wing to house Olmert and other politicians of note, like former president Moshe Katsav who was handed a seven-year sentence for rape in 2011. Prominent Israelis convicted of serious crimes is almost endless. They seem to run after corruption like deer run after water in the desert.

In October 2015, the Israeli police completed an investigation into corruption in governance and recommended **that 36 public figures, including two former ministers**, both of the predominantly Russian immigrant party *Yisrael Beitenu* (Israel our Home), be put on trial. A total of 480 people were questioned in the investigation and NIS25,000,000 ($6,438,000) was confiscated.

Israeli police both investigate and are the investigated. In January 2015 a high-ranking police official was placed under arrest for sexual misconduct, **making him the fifth senior police official—commanders and deputy commanders—to be accused of sexual misconduct or corruption** since August 2013.

In June 2014 police questioned former IDF chief of staff Gabi Ashkenazi for the third time in less than a week about his part in a corruption scandal involving Israel's political and military leaderships between 2009 and 2011.

At the time of writing the Attorney General Yehuda Weinstein was expected to close the case against Ashkenazi after state prosecutors determined there was not enough evidence to indict him for his alleged involvement in a high-level corruption scandal. Weinstein's decision, which was expected to be officially announced within a few weeks, would come against the recommendation of police, who had determined that there was enough evidence to charge Ashkenazi with breach of trust and delivering classified information to journalists.

Israel — Chapter 21

In November 2015 two senior Foreign Ministry officials were also indicted for bribery and theft. Also in November, former Bat Yam mayor Shlomo Lahiani was to begin his prison sentence for corruption and breach of trust.

In December 2015 the Tel Aviv court rejected former Ramat HaSharon mayor Yitzhak Rochberger's request to shorten the period of moral turpitude connected to his conviction for fraud and breach of trust.

On December 21, 2015, the *Times of Israel* reported that police had arrested a number of high-ranking local officials on allegations of involvement in bribe-taking, tax offenses, fraud and other crimes. A total of 12 suspects were arrested, including several officials from the Mateh Yehuda Regional Council. Two of the suspects, including a senior municipal official, are also suspected of sexual offenses against several women. Police suspect a senior municipal official and several other people ran a corruption racket to hand out political favors in return for bribes, all while falsifying documents, evading taxes and money laundering.

In January 2016 Ashkelon Mayor Itamar Shimoni was arrested on suspicion of rape, corruption and bribery. And so it goes on.

Israel has a special place in the heart of God, but there is no way that He will to close His eyes to Israel's continual sin and religious apostasy. Israeli society, it seems, is corrupt all the way to the core—from the highest level down to the lowest level of governance, as well as every section of the national security.

WITH THE RISE OF ANTI-SEMITISM IN FRANCE and especially in the aftermath of the coordinated terror attacks in Paris on November 13, 2015, French Jews are fleeing to Israel for safety. Rogel Alpher, a columnist for the liberal left-wing newspaper *Ha'aretz*, took it upon himself to tweet advice to them:

> *Jews of France, stay in France. Don't flee Muslim facism [sic] into the arms of Jewish fasicm [sic]. Nothing for you in Israel.*

Alpher was attempting to get some advance publicity for an article that speaks for hundreds of thousands, if not millions, of Israelis. In the opening paragraph of the piece titled "**Jews of France, There Is Nothing for You in Israel**," published on Saturday, November 21, 2015, Alpher wrote:

> There is no God, he did not appoint you as the chosen people and he did not promise you the land of Israel. You have no rights here. Israel has stopped being the Jewish state. It is a binational apartheid state in which Palestinians live under an occupation that denies them their basic human rights. The Zionist enterprise is dead. Committed suicide.

There is a plethora of Israelis who would agree wholeheartedly, either in part or in total of what Alpher wrote. These people have no belief either in God or in their nation. Their day is coming to an end. Israel will get its fill of judgment even before other nations get theirs.

> *Do not be deceived, God is not mocked; for whatever a man sows, this he will also reap. For* **the one who sows to his own flesh will from the flesh reap corruption**, *but the one who sows to the Spirit will from the Spirit reap eternal life* (Galatians 6:7–8).

The Lord *also has a controversy with Israel.*

22

Japan

On December 7, 1941, Japan launched an unprovoked, unannounced attack on the American naval base at Pearl Harbor, in the Hawaiian islands. The attack, which lasted less than two hours, took the lives of more than 2,500 people, wounded some 1,000 others, and damaged or destroyed 18 American ships and nearly 300 airplanes. Almost half of the casualties from the attack occurred on the battleship USS Arizona, which was hit four times by Japanese bombers. The U.S. fleet suffered enormous damage and the U.S. formally declared war upon Japan the following day; four days later Germany and Italy declared war upon the U.S. On August 6, 1945, America dropped an atomic bomb on the Japanese city of Hiroshima, causing around 100,000 fatalities. Three days later another atom bomb was dropped on the city of Nagasaki and at least another 70,000 people died. On August 14, 1945, Japan surrendered and was under allied occupation until 1952.

Since 1952, Japan's economy has expanded at a rapid rate, and today Japan is a member of the Group of Eight (G-8)—the eight wealthiest industrialized nations in the world.

For all practical purposes, Japan has no Jewish community and no history of anti-Semitism. But like some of the other members of the G-8, in order to siphon Arab petro-dollars into her coffers, Japan introduced her own version of anti-Semitism. Not only is the Japanese news media noticeably anti-Israel, but it is careful to censor from the eyes and ears of Japan's masses that which does not enhance her trade with the Arab states. David Bar-Illan, the former Executive Editor of the *Jerusalem Post*, wrote in his "Eye on the Media" column, January 19, 1993, that:

> Only the Arab propaganda version of Palestinian history has been presented, and rebuttals are not permitted.
>
> New York Mayor Ed Koch's attack on the Arab boycott before hundreds of reporters in Tokyo in 1987 was blacked out.

A statement by Japan's financiers, that Jews were responsible for the 1987 stockmarket crash that cost the Japanese 28 percent of their investments, was widely published. At the same time, Bar-Illan says a statement refuting this view was blacked out. Apparently it is acceptable for the Japanese media to publish accusations against Jews, but unacceptable to publish refutations.

Israel Radio, July 29, 1993, reported that a Japanese newspaper had published an advertisement depicting Japan as the last enemy standing in the way of a "Jewish conspiracy to control the world."

The report said American Jewish leaders were "outraged," but that the editor of the newspaper "planned no apology." The Japanese media has a history of publishing deliberately fabricated anti-Israel, anti-Jew material, and allows no rebuttal. Meir Rosenne, a former Israeli ambassador to the U.S. and France, says Japan is:

> the archetype of a country with an anti-Semitic movement but no Jews.

IN JULY 2013 A DUTCH WOMAN came forward to confirm that occupying Japanese forces rounded up and placed Jews in Indonesia into a separate internment camp during World War II, where they were subjected to beatings and near-starvation rations. Anne-Ruth Wertheim, a former senior high school teacher now living in Amsterdam, confirmed the camp's existence — she is a living witness of the camp.

In January 1944 Wertheim was sent to an internment camp for women and children in Jakarta along with her mother, older sister and younger brother. At that time, she was nine years old. In September 1944, a Japanese officer told internees in the camp, "If even one drop of Jewish blood flows in your bodies, tell me."

In the camp, iron bars were fixed on the windows. Boards measuring less than 20 inches (50 centimeters) in width were placed in rows to serve as beds. Two-thirds of the people in the camp were Jewish.

Harsh disciplinary measures were observed in the camp. If internees did not bow sufficiently to Japanese soldiers, they were struck by camp staff and all the prisoners would then be forced to stand in the hot sun for hours to take collective responsibility for the infraction. Meals in the camp consisted of only one scoop of rations per day. With such near-starvation rations, women stopped menstruating and children became stunted.

It is not known why Japan isolated Jews from other civilians, but it is a fact that in those days incidents of persecution against Jews were taking place in Japan. However, discrimination against Jews appeared to be stronger in areas occupied by Japan.

In the Netherlands, diaries of people who were internees in the detention camps in Indonesia have been published since the 1970s — those diaries have attracted little attention however.

Japan — Chapter 22

IT IS INTERESTING TO NOTE THAT after making the anti-Semitic statement that Jews were responsible for the stockmarket crash (page 209), the Japanese economy began to slowly sink, and it has steadily continued on that course. There has been much Japanese hand-wringing over the fact that Japan's economy has been and still is in 2016, in deflation. Past media reports showed constantly falling sales and decreasing profitability of major Japanese companies and increasing job layoffs. The effect of the downward path of the Japanese economy showed up in the polling booths. In July, 1993 the Liberal Democratic Party lost its majority—for the first time since 1955—after 38 years in power. Kiichi Miyazawa resigned from his posts as prime minister and party president.

New prime ministers have since come and gone, but Japan's economy was still stagnant and battling deflation in 2016.

The economies of each of the G-8 members—Japan, Britain, Canada, France, Germany, Italy, the U.S., and Russia have taken serious nosedives. With the exception of Germany and the U.S., G-8 members have complied with the terms of the Arab economic boycott against Israel in order to court Arab petro-dollars. But the global financial crisis that began in 2008 brought the G-8's whole financial house of cards tumbling down, and with the exception of Germany, which has weathered the storm, each of the other members are still struggling to keep their economy's head above water.

While the economies of the G-8 were really struggling, Israel led the entire world in economic growth. A January 4, 1993 editorial in the *Jerusalem Post* showed that for the corresponding year, Israel's 1992 growth was over three times that of the U.S., more than three and-a-half times that of Japan, and nearly five times that of Germany. Israel now has a little more affluence—rated in 2015 as having the eighteenth highest standard of living among 188 countries, and is number 20 on the purchasing power index.

As it was mentioned on page 122, in August 2015 the U.S. national debt stood at $18.15 trillion and was projected to rise to **103 percent of the GDP** (Gross Domestic Product), but it has since exceeded that figure.

The Japanese national debt exceeded ($10.46 trillion) in 2013, **more than twice Japan's annual GDP**.

In contrast to two of the world's three largest economies and their respective national debts, consider Israel's current fiscal state:

> planned deficit targets, previously **pegged at of 2.5% of GDP** for 2015 and **2% for 2016**, setting both at **2.9%** instead, and planning to gradually **lower it to 1.5% by 2021**. Figures released in January 2016 showed 2015 came in at **2.15% of GDP**, well below the **2.9%** target.

THE OBVIOUS FAILURE OF THE ARAB boycott to strangle Israel economically, together with the universal dip in economies, has caused the lustful eyes of the G-8 countries to turn toward a possible Israeli market. Meeting in Tokyo in July, 2013, they called on the Arab states to end their boycott against Israel. It is now economically "advantageous" to wean themselves from the political path they had so warmly embraced. How great is the magnetic attraction of mammon.

Sins touched upon are:

a) Unprovoked military aggression
b) Extreme cruelty in times of war
c) Allies of those waging war against Israel
d) Anti-Semitism-political, racial and religious
e) Fraudulent, deceitful, and crafty business transactions

The judgments are, therefore: **Defeat with high loss of life**; **Nation conquered and devastated**; **Destruction of nation**; and **Judicial cursing or complete destruction of nation**.

OBVIOUSLY, THE ATOMIC BOMBS DROPPED UPON Japanese cities and its subsequent seven-year occupation by the allied powers, were Divine judgments being satisfied. But fresh judgment is falling because of its anti-Israel policies and greed related anti-Semitism. A catastrophic earthquake (7.8 on the Richter scale) triggered an even more devastating tidal wave— *TIME International*, July 26, 1993, reported a **98 foot (30 meter) high wall of water** which traveled at **310 miles (500 kilometers) per hour**. It bore mute testimony that judgment had begun.

Bearing that in mind we should now turn our attention to the catastrophic magnitude–9.0 earthquake that struck Japan on March 11, 2011, which is considered to be one of the most powerful earthquakes ever recorded anywhere in the world: it moved Japan's main island of Honshu eastward by 8 feet (2.4 meters) and shifted Earth on its axis of rotation, shortening the length of a day by a fraction of second.

The temblor unleashed a savage tsunami which raced outward from the epicenter at speeds of about **500 miles (800 kilometers) per hour** with a wave that reached a height of **133 feet (40.5 meters)**. The tsunami created a level 7 nuclear meltdown at the Fukushima Daiichi Nuclear Power Plant and the release of radioactive materials. About 300 tons of radioactive water continues to leak from the plant every day into the Pacific

Ocean, which slowly moves toward Hawaii and North America where debris continues to wash up on their beaches in 2016, and the sea water contains a small measure of radiation.

The number of confirmed deaths is around 16,000—most died by drowning as a result of the tsunami. More than 2,500 people are still missing. Damages from the earthquake and tsunami are estimated at around $300 billion dollars and in 2015, some 230,000 people who lost their homes were still living in temporary housing.

Adding to all this misery was the November 2015 announcement by Japan's Cabinet Office that, following the economy's contraction during April through June, the contraction of the July through September Q3 period had slid Japan into another economic recession.

The downfall of the Japanese nation might be gradual, or it might be cataclysmic, but it will be certain—*for the* Lord *has a controversy with Japan*.

23

New Zealand

Situated in the South Pacific Ocean, with a divergence of terrain and climatic conditions, New Zealand is without doubt one of the most beautiful and scenic countries of the world. New Zealand became a British colony in 1841, and in her early years had a rich Christian heritage. The first missionary, Samuel Marsden, brought the Gospel to the fierce, semi-cannibalistic northern Maori tribes, and was instrumental in getting them to lay down their arms against the British colonists and accept Queen Victoria's rule. Other missionaries followed Marsden, and New Zealand became what is known as a "Christian nation." The lovely Maori name for New Zealand is *Aotearoa*—"Land of the Long White Cloud." Many New Zealanders affectionately call it, "God's Own."

New Zealand developed an agricultural and dairy industry that had few equals, but was largely dependent upon the British market. Exports, imports, and local manufacturing gave New Zealand one of the highest standards of living in the world. Successive governments, however, both National and Labour, have pursued an extensive welfare system that bred reliance upon government hand-outs. In December, 1989, the *New Zealand Herald* published an article stating that more than 60 percent of all New Zealanders were dependent in some way upon the government for their existence. And the benefits paid just to unwed mothers during a good part of the 1970's, became the nation's largest expense—outstripping the country's oil import bill. The serene, beautiful, paradisaical country of 4.3 million people became a Utopia for many lazy and immoral people—at the expense of the New Zealand taxpayer.

THE SOUTH ISLAND'S PRINCIPAL CITY, CHRISTCHURCH, was founded by God-fearing people who wanted to establish a colony governed by Biblical principles. These "puritan" settlers established a city with tree-lined streets and several large, magnificent parks. Because of the profusion of trees and flowers, Christchurch is known as the "Garden City." But although the parks and trees remain, little evidence is found today of the once almost universal, vibrant faith in God. The focal point of the city, Cathedral Square, which takes its name from an adjacent, majestic 132-year-old Anglican Cathedral, boasted for years a permanent, salaried "wizard" who blasphemed God, Christ, and Christianity, while declaring the blessings of sodomy and other perversions on the very doorstep of New Zealand's preeminent church. He received half of his salary from the Christchurch city council, and the other half from Auckland's city council. However:

Do not be deceived, **God is not mocked**; *for whatever a man sows, that he will also reap* (Galatians 6:7).

The "wizard" and those who funded him poked their tongues out at the LORD, but the Bible tells us two times in the Psalms that:

The fool has said in his heart, "There is no God"

(Psalms 14:1, 53:1).

And they are indeed "fools." They provoked the LORD GOD ALMIGHTY to wrath on September 4, 2010. He struck the haughty Garden City with a magnitude 7.1 earthquake that was widely felt all over the South Island and the southern North Island, and caused considerable damage, especially in Christchurch. The temblor seemed to target "Christian places of worship," and a number of historic stone churches were badly damaged; both the Christchurch (Anglican) and Catholic cathedrals survived, albeit with cracking in their walls. The LORD had caused His voice to be heard:

If a trumpet is blown in a city, *will not the people be afraid?* **If there is calamity in a city, will not the LORD have done it?** (Amos 3:6).

But the people were not afraid, neither did they repent, so the LORD shook the city again on February 22, 2011, with an "unbelievably destructive" 6.3 temblor, which killed 186 people, injured thousands, and caused "significant damage to buildings and infrastructure." Scores of the most badly affected structures in Christchurch were older buildings, including several notable landmarks.

While the temblor was not as powerful as the earthquake on September 4, 2010, the bedrock structure produced exceptionally strong ground motion—three to four times the ground accelerations due to gravity.

The temblor brought down many buildings that had been damaged in September 2010, especially older brick and mortar buildings. Many heritage buildings were heavily damaged, including both the Anglican Christchurch Cathedral—the city's namesake—and the Catholic Cathedral. Among modern buildings irrevocably damaged was Christchurch's tallest building, the Hotel Grand Chancellor. More than half of the buildings in the central business district had to be demolished. Several thousand homes needed to be demolished, and some sections of Christchurch's suburbs will probably never be reoccupied.

New Zealand — Chapter 23

Liquefaction was much more extensive than in the September 2010 earthquake. Some sections of the city were built on a former swamp and the shaking turned water-saturated layers of sand and silt beneath the surface into sludge that squirted upwards through cracks. Properties and streets were buried in thick layers of silt, and water, and sewage from broken pipes flooded streets. House foundations cracked and buckled, wrecking many homes. The toppled bell tower of the Christchurch Cathedral lay on a rock-strewn lawn—a powerful reminder of the scale of devastation. The "wizard" fled the city. The Lord literally put the fear of hell into him.

The cathedral is frozen in its 2011 state as a legal battle works its way through the New Zealand courts over whether the building should be restored or torn down. The church wants to tear it down and rebuild; local activists want it restored.

The dwindling number of Christians in Christchurch were not sufficiently motivated enough to force a cessation of the wickedness that was taking place right outside the iconic Christchurch Cathedral, so the Lord spoke in all too familiar ways:

> *I form the light and create darkness, I make peace and* **create calamity; I, the Lord, do** *all these things* (Isaiah 45:7).

It remains to be seen if the physical shaking will bring forth the repentance necessary for the nation's survival.

In the late 1960's, Britain began its bid to enter the European Economic Community, and advised New Zealand that the traditional market New Zealand had enjoyed for decades would no longer be accessible. Britain became a full member of the EEC in 1971, but the previous two years of heavily reduced imports from New Zealand had sent the New Zealand economy into a tail-spin. Large numbers of farms and businesses went bankrupt. Farmers tried desperately to get out of dairy production and diversify into other types of farming, especially beef, and the government was equally desperate to find new markets. When the country began to show some signs of recovery, the oil crisis in the early 1970's raised the import bill for oil by 123 percent and the economy slid once more.

New Zealand's beef export business had been very small before British entry to the Common Market. Gradually, despite the stringent health requirements of the American FDA (Food and Drug Administration), a market was growing in the U.S. for New Zealand-bred beef. The economy began to level out, that was until New Zealand secured a trial order for a shipment of 3,000 tons of beef to the Soviet Union. But it was not acceptable to the

Nixon administration for New Zealand to sell beef to communists while it was supplying American tables. All New Zealand beef imports to the U.S. were subsequently banned, and the country took another serious plunge into despair.

Slowly, New Zealand found other markets—Arab markets, and the Arab states have remained New Zealand's biggest trading partners until the present day. The Arabs, however, insisted on supplying New Zealand slaughter-houses throughout the country with Muslim slaughtermen to ensure the meat would be killed according to Islamic ritual (*hallal*). After this, mosques had to be built close by so the Muslims could worship. Then, the Arabs insisted that every single animal processed in the slaughter-houses be *hallal* killed. The reason given for this new demand was that their *hallal* meat was made "unclean"—contaminated by the non-ritually killed meat. This demand was also met, and all but two New Zealand slaughter-houses used Muslim *hallal* ritual killing in 1994, but in 2015 all slaughter-houses comply with Muslim demands. Slaughter-houses are operated in shifts, which means Muslims are bowing down over every lamb, sheep, calf, or cow slaughtered in New Zealand—24 hours a day—declaring "Allah is great, Allah is supreme," the ritual prayer before slaughtering an animal.

Many New Zealand slaughter-houses underwent extensive changes in the early 1990s, ostensibly for refurbishing, but in actual fact the changes were made so that the Muslim slaughtermen would face toward Mecca. Muslims see this as fulfillment of the Qur'an (Koran), in which it is written that praises shall ascend to Allah from the ends of the earth (New Zealand is one of the four "corners" of the earth).

For years, the very best of New Zealand lambs have been exported live to Saudi Arabia. The New Zealand stock agents maintained that the lambs were for breeding. But anyone who knows the Middle East, knows that New Zealand lambs could never survive more than a week or ten days in the fierce, dry desert heat. Furthermore, the lambs were not to have their tails docked, nor have any sort of blemish. It took several years before a stock agent admitted to farmers that the lambs were for sacrifice to Allah.

In response, a group of about one hundred New Zealand farmers—all of them committed Christians—refused in the late 1980s and early 1990s to give their sheep over to *hallal* killing. They would not allow their animals to be sacrificed to a foreign god. (For a full expose on Islam and Allah, see my books *When Day and Night Cease* and *Philistine*). This group of farmers found two slaughterhouses owned by the Alliance Meat Company that were willing to kill their lambs in the normal fashion at that time, but the farmers had to wait upon the convenience of the slaughterhouses. (The two

New Zealand — Chapter 23

slaughterhouses have since capitulated to the Muslims.) Furthermore, the Christian farmers all had great difficulty in finding markets for their processed lambs—resistance to buying their produce has come from the local market because of their stand for the LORD. I personally met with these men during trips to New Zealand, and some of them have received serious threats on their lives from the Muslims—for this reason they cannot be identified in print.

God has been faithful to those daring to swim against the stream. Amazing public testimonies are given of constant miracles of God's abundant provision for them and their families. One man testified that in the midst of a drought his farm had six-inch (15 centimeter)-high grass, while his neighbor's adjoining fields had none. Another testified that his ewes were giving birth to twins and even triplets—doubling and tripling his income. When one of the leaders of the group decided to cut his hay, he heard the Lord say, "Don't cut it!" Days passed by, and each morning he would hear, "Don't cut it!" During this period the grass was growing rapidly, but he was getting agitated. In the particular climatic region where he was farming, two weeks without rain was considered to be a long, dry period. Sudden rain would ruin his entire winter feed program, forcing him to buy hay at expensive rates. Finally, after two full weeks, the Lord said, "Cut the hay!" He and his men cut, turned and baled nearly two times the normal crop over the next few days. He had enough for his own farm's requirements, and sufficient to sell and make a good profit. Late one evening, as he sat down to the evening meal after having finished putting the last bales of hay in the barns, he heard the sound of raindrops falling on the roof—God had given them yet another miracle.

In 1988, one man heard the Lord tell him to put the rams into his flocks a number of weeks earlier than usual. He was obedient, but apprehensive. One cold snap, or a period of prolonged rain could spell disaster for the entire flock of new born lambs in the fields. But there was no cold snap and no rain—he actually recorded the highest price ever paid for New Zealand lambs because he was the only farmer with lambs at that time of the year. Later in the season a serious drought struck the country and farmers had to quickly get their lambs to the slaughterhouses because there was no grass for them to eat. Millions of lambs—born at the traditional time—poured into the slaughterhouses like an avalanche, creating such a glut that prices were forced down below anything previously paid for spring lambs.

Each of the leaders of this group of Christian farmers testified to having had their best financial years during the worst years of New Zealand's farming industry. The miracles experienced by the Christian farmers are clear evidence of favor in the midst of God's displeasure with the New Zealand government's policy of Arab appeasement. The situation is reminiscent of the successive plagues that fell upon the Egyptians, while God's people in Goshen were enjoying Divine protection (Exodus 8:22–12:30).

With the economy so dependent upon the Arab states, the New Zealand government must be careful to cultivate Arab friendship. The simplest way to appease the Arab and Muslim nations is to show hostility toward Israel, and not trade with it at all. Consequently, there is no New Zealand consul in Israel, and there are no trade links either.

The New Zealand media is generally anti-Israel, and it is a known fact that those who own the media determine when and what the media will broadcast or publish. While ministering in New Zealand, in 1988, I was informed by the person in charge of incoming news at the government-owned New Zealand Broadcasting Corporation, that news concerning Israel was censored, and that only items that showed Israel in a poor light were allowed to be broadcast.

IN CONTRAST TO THE OFFICIAL POSITION of the government, the true Church in New Zealand is generally very pro-Israel, even if it is small (in 2015 around two percent of New Zealanders have been born again).

The pro-Israel attitude does not hold true for every stream of the New Zealand Church, however. As we said before (see page 151), when Prince Andrew of the British Royal Family married Sarah Ferguson in August 1986 it was requested that no mention of Israel, Jacob, Jerusalem, or Zion be made during the wedding ceremony in Westminster Abbey. Queen Elizabeth is the head of the Anglican Church of England and also of the British Commonwealth, of which New Zealand is a part. The royals, having set the precedent, were soon followed by the New Zealand Anglican Church which removed the words Israel, Jacob, Jerusalem, and Zion from the order of service and prayer books. No doubt the New Zealand government's extreme pro-Arab-anti-Israel stance contributed to this, but the name Israel occurs in the Bible 2,564 times, Jacob 358 times, Jerusalem 812 times and Zion 160 times—a total of 3,894 occurrences. That is a lot of Scripture to lay aside in order to appease the Muslims and their god.

The Arab people, and all other Muslim peoples, are equally as precious in God's eyes as the other races of man. New Zealand was fortunate in being able to find markets among the Arab and Muslim states, but she was foolish to oppose Israel in order to secure a dubious future.

New Zealand — Chapter 23

THE WHINING OF THE AVERAGE NEW Zealander about the high cost of living when he enjoys one of the highest standards of living in the world (New Zealand was rated in fifth place in 2015), must be grating on the ears of God. The pursuit of possessions has turned the hearts of the people away from the One who gave them everything.

When I ministered coast to coast throughout New Zealand in 1988 I was swamped with invitations from churches to address their congregations, yet less than 50 percent of churches gave me an honorarium to offset my expenses, not so much as a single dollar. And in two Christian homes where I was hosted for a meal I saw used teabags being dried out on window sills. When I asked why so many teabags were being dried I was told that they were being sent to the church's missionaries overseas. The people said that used teabags were not subject to a $5 import duty like fresh packets of teabags were. I was horrified! Christians in a land of such plenty would have their missionaries receive used teabags rather than give the missionary $5 to pay the duty. It seemed indicative of the New Zealand church, fortunately there were many exceptions to the rule.

GREED DROVE MANY NEW ZEALANDERS to the banks to borrow large sums of money against their properties for "investment" in the stockmarket. The 1987 stockmarket crash cost New Zealanders billions of dollars—approximately 40 percent of everything invested. Judging by the vast number of "For Sale" signs I saw in New Zealand in 1988, a large number of people were either bankrupt or in deep financial distress. Many properties were being sold by banks, which became the owners after borrowers defaulted on their loans.

The country has an enormous US$67 billion debt (36 percent of the GNP—Gross National Product) due to importing far more than what it can afford. (Compare this to Israel's $6.2 billion debt (2.15 of GDP), bearing in mind that Israel's population is twice that of New Zealand.) The reason for high imports and lower exports is covetousness—living beyond the country's means, and covetousness is *"idolatry"* (Colossians 3:5).

PUBLICIZED AS A MODEL OF INTERRACIAL harmony, parts of Auckland, New Zealand's largest city, have long been hotbeds of hatred and discrimination against the Maori and assorted Polynesian groups. These people live in "ghettos," much the same as the blacks in New York and they have "no go zones" where a *Pakeha* (white person) is not safe. In a front page article in an April, 1990 edition of the *Cedar Rapid s Gazette*, dealing with trends in global violence, New Zealand was said to be (per capita):

the fifth most violent country in the world.

The population of New Zealand has barely increased in more than three decades, despite the immigration of more than one million Asians. Emigration and abortion continually retard population growth.

Black magic and other forms of the occult are widely practiced throughout the country. Even when these abominations were in their infancy in the 1960s, human sacrifice was said to have taken place in a little stone church in East Tamaki, near Auckland.

THE ECONOMIC DISASTERS HAVE BEEN WARNINGS from the LORD, as have been the catastrophic physical disasters, like the earthquakes mentioned earlier and the one which struck Edgecumbe in 1988, and the calamitous Cyclone Bola that struck the same year. The LORD is trying to get New Zealand's attention. The question is: Will it take notice?

The sins mentioned have been:

a) **Murder, perverse and immoral behavior**
b) **Discriminating against strangers** (includes racial discrimination)
c) **Allies of those waging war against Israel**
d) **Homosexuality**
e) **Sodomy** (sexual perversion, including acts with animals)
f) **Anti-Semitism-political, racial and religious**
g) **Rejection of God**
h) **Rejection of God's Salvation**
i) **Refusal to hear and live by God's Word**
j) **Blasphemy**
k) **Coveting** (form of idolatry)
l) **Practicing witchcraft, horoscopes and the occult**
d) **Fraudulent, deceitful, and crafty business transactions**

The judgments are, therefore: **Physical catastrophes and widespread death** (three times); **Destruction of nation** (two times); **Annihilation** (two times); **Judicial cursing or complete destruction of nation**; and **Near annihilation** (three times).

New Zealand is a very young, very beautiful country, but it is already under judgment—the hand of the LORD comes heavily upon it. Without repentance New Zealand has no hope—*for the LORD has a controversy with New Zealand*.

24

Norway

Norway has an infamous demographic history stretching back to the eighth century Norse (Viking) era when they brutally and savagely murdered, looted, pillaged, and raped near and far. Norway's reality has in many ways moved like huge waves; however, it seems that Norway does not learn from its past mistakes.

An oil-rich country that daily extracts countless millions of barrels of the black gold hiding below the Norwegian Continental Shelf. Norway is listed as having the highest standard of living in the world, and constantly tops the "world's highest standard of living" polls. Money, while it cannot buy true happiness, is an important means of achieving high living standards, and it undoubtedly affords many Norwegian people to be miserable in comfort.

Norway, with a population of only 5.1 million, has the world's largest Pension Fund—known as the "Oil Fund"—being made up from some of the excess of its huge oil income and the holding of Europe's largest stock portfolio. The oil came at a price for some of the Deep Sea Divers who died and others who suffer effects from deep water diving without sufficient safety equipment. The Norwegian government denied their responsibility stating that:

> Oil production in the North Sea is driven by strong political and socio-economic interests. The State has a comprehensive social responsibility for the petroleum activities as the property owner of subsea petroleum and, as a result of this, receives significant revenues from this activity. These diver operations have been necessary to carry out this activity, and have contributed to creating enormous values for the Norwegian society. There was little regulation of the diving activity during parts of the pioneer period, and the nature of the activity was extreme and ground-breaking. At the same time, knowledge about diving, including the equipment and methods that were used, was not as good as it is today. Therefore, the Government believes, overall, that the State must assume a political and moral responsibility for the pioneer divers in the North Sea.

For many, however, this state help came tens of thousands of dollars short and thousands of days late. [https://www.regjeringen.no/en/topics/labour/the-working-environment-and-safety/innsikt/the-pioneers-divers/id510905/]

A small minority of Norwegians feel an unavoidable judgment upon their country has begun, and that Norwegians are past the point of hardening their own hearts, that it is the God of Israel, the Almighty One, who is hardening their hearts. Poet, politician, and theologian Elias Blix wrote in the national hymn of Norway (translated):

> If God not will be our builder strong, futility builds our houses,
> If God not defend our towns, our homes, our guardsmen will fall by thousands,
> O God, we beseech thee, watch thou us, and bless us with peace abundant.

Norway has had its share of Christians standing in the gap, praying day in and day out — with a somewhat battered hope for repentance. The next set of crossroads for Norway is less than two years ahead, in the next General election in the Fall of 2017. An astute comment that came in the aftermath of the election of 2015, was:

> Labor has always had a large following. Some choose Labor because they believe Labor represents peace and safety, yet they forget what the Word of God says about the time when people are pursuing peace and safety:
> *For when they say "peace and safety," then sudden destruction will come upon them as labor pains come upon a pregnant woman, and they will not escape* (1Thessalonians 5:3).

It was mentioned on the previous page that Norway has a population of only 5.1 million but has the largest pension fund in the world. It is also a fact that, along with the small population, Norway per capita has the largest Humanist Association in the world. Norwegians are, in the main, wealthy godless liberal-humanists. A 2005 Gallup survey showed that "Norway had become the least religious country in Western Europe."

Apparently, a large and seemingly increasing number of Christians, among them several "Christian leaders" in Norway included simply does not believe God judges nations "in this age of grace." This has led to a major debate around the book *A Breach in the Wall* by Jeremy Hoff (see pages 236 – 238), about God's warning of imminent judgment against Norway as a response to the Oslo Accords.

IN 1993 NORWAY SECRETIVELY SPAWNED THE Oslo Peace Accords — between left-wing Labor politicians in Israel and the Palestine Liberation Organization (PLO) headed by Yasser Arafat, the prince of murderers and the father of international terrorism. In just four years, the Oslo "peace" took

Norway — Chapter 24

more Israeli lives than did 15 years in the state of war. It was the Norwegian government that helped foist the Oslo agreement on Israel and over 2,000 Israelis perished or were maimed by the Palestinian terror which came in the wake of Oslo. The very name "Oslo" has became anathema to most Israelis. Thanks to Oslo, Israel turned over most of the West Bank (Biblical Judea and Samaria) and Gaza to the Palestinian Authority (PA). Israel brought Yasser Arafat, Mahmoud Abbas, and the entire enemy command and control from exile in Tunis and set them up in Ramallah, from where terrorism against Israeli civilians was planned and official incitement to murder is broadcast. In fact, Faisal al-Husseini characterized the Oslo Accords as **Yasser Arafat's "Trojan Horse."** Jeremy Hoff writes on page 53 of *A Breach in the Wall* that "in a 2006 television interview one of the leaders of Fatah [Ziyad Abu Ein] gave credit **to the Oslo Accords for creating the conditions necessary for the boom of Palestinian violence**:"

> **If not for Oslo, there would have been no resistance.** Throughout the occupied territories, we could not move a single pistol from one place to another. **If not for Oslo, the weapons we got through Oslo**, and if not for the "A" areas of the Palestinian Authority, if not for the training, the camps, **the protection provided by Oslo, and if not for the release of Palestinian prisoners through Oslo** — the Palestinian resistance could not have been carried out this great Palestinian *Intifada*, with which we confronted the Israeli occupation.

If not for Oslo at least 1,000 Israelis and 1,600 Palestinians would still be alive today. If not for Oslo terror would never have been granted legitimacy by the international community. Oslo is a four-letter word that grates on Israeli ears like other shocking four-letter words do, but they are gutter-language words, while Oslo is the capital of an anti-Semitic nation.

IN MARCH 2007 RAYMOND JOHANSEN, THE Norwegian deputy foreign minister, became the first European representative to meet Ismail Haniyeh, the prime minister of the new Palestinian Fatah-Hamas unity government in Gaza. Johansen had certainly read Haniyeh's March 17 speech in which he outlined the Fatah-Hamas government program. Haniyeh said: "The government affirms that resistance is a legitimate right of the Palestinian people." And Johansen knew that Haniyeh meant by "resistance"—suicide bombings of cafes and buses, drive-by shootings, rocket launchings. Johansen knew the new government demanded the "right of return" for millions of Palestinian Arab refugees and their descendants to pre-1967 Israel. He knew that meant the end of Israel demographically. Johansen knew that the Fatah-Hamas government was not renouncing violence; that it would not honor previous agreements signed by the PLO, and that it would never recognize the right of a sovereign Jewish state to exist anywhere in the Middle East; yet Johansen rushed to meet with Haniyeh. Johansen was quoted back in March 2001 (by the Norwegian news agency *NTB*) as saying that international law gave the Palestinians the right to fight an "occupier," but he later said that he'd been misquoted.

Sitting down with Hamas terrorist leaders reinforces the Arab belief that Israel can be destroyed. There can be no peace as long as the Arabs believe this and as long as Norway allows the Arabs to fantasize about "the right of return" there can be no end to the Arab-Israeli conflict. This message has failed to reach the consciences of the anti-Semitic Norwegian government. Norway partially funds Hamas (though allegedly they claim, it is impossible to trace their donations back to Norway), this in addition to the funding of a plethora of anti-Israel NGOs (Non-Governmental Organizations). Many of the most virulently anti-Zionist NGOs staffed by Israelis operating in Israel are funded by the Norwegian government.

Norway is one of the largest donors to the Palestinian Authority—in 2014 Norway donated US$150 million. The PA pays millions of dollars annually in salaries to convicted terrorists incarcerated in Israeli prisons, the more Israelis murdered the higher the salary paid to the terrorist. Norway's donor money is, therefore, used to fund terrorism. Questions about this have been submitted to the Norwegian government, but as Hans Olav Syversen of the Christian Democratic Party said in March 2013:

> The answers to Parliament have been based on half-answers and excuses. This is a serious matter. We have clear indications that people convicted of terrorism are actually being rewarded with funding from Norway. How can there be peace and reconciliation if in reality one rewards the opposite?

Former special advisor for the Middle East, Terje Rød-Larsen had a brief career as a minister in the Norwegian government, which was cut short because of his penchant for tax evasion. Rød-Larsen is the one who publicly stated after the death of Yasser Arafat that, "He lied all the time. And he knew it." (*The Atlantic*, 2005).

THE NORWEGIAN LABOR PARTY AND ITS Labor Youth (AUF) have a long and disgraceful record of opposing Israel and bolstering the Palestinians. According to Jeremy Hoff's book *A Breach in the Wall* (p. 67), as far back as 1971, at the AUF's national convention the following resolution was passed by a majority that sided with the Palestinians:

Norway — Chapter 24

The basic prerequisite for a lasting peace [in the Middle East] **is that Israel ceases to exist as a Jewish state**, and that a progressive Palestinian state is established [in its place], wherein all ethnic groups can live together side by side in full equality.

Given that, by Norwegian law, Jews were "excluded from admittance to the realm" from 1687 to 1851 (see page 230) and are barely tolerated today, it is not difficult to understand why AUF is so rabidly hostile to the state of Israel. However, its hostility to Israel and all things moral led up to the massacre on the island of Utoeya on July 22, 2011.

JUDGMENT IS ALSO FALLING ON NORWAY due to the overt anti-Semitism that governs the Norwegian Labor Party as well as it's youth organization, AUF, and the far-left Red Party, which was a merger of the Workers' Communist Party and the Red Electoral Alliance, which is even further to the left than Socialism. Anti-Semitism is ingrained in a large part of the Norwegian populace and Jewish children are targeted at school. An example of this is shown when a 16-year-old Jewish student was branded with a red-hot coin at a school barbecue in June 2012 in Oslo. The Simon Wiesenthal Center reported that the perpetrator of the attack, an ethnic Norwegian student, pressed the hot coin into the back of the victim's neck, resulting in visible burning. School officials did not contact the family after the incident.

The student had reportedly been the target of repeated anti-Semitic bullying and violence because his father is an Israeli. He said he planned to hide his Jewish identity when he transfers to a new school and would not associate with ethnic Norwegians or Muslims, the main sources of the bullying. Some Norwegian "Jewish parents say that their children are still traumatized many years later by the anti-Semitism they experienced in school."

In September 2015 a cartoon published in Norway's third largest newspaper, Dagbladet, portrayed Israel as a nation of murderers equal to North Korea and the Nazis. The strip shows a woman holding up an orange and saying, "These oranges are from Israel. You are supporting murderers." Picking up a box of pasta she sees that it came from North Korea. In the last panel, the woman holds a box of frozen pizza marked with a swastika bearing a "Made in Nazi Germany" label and incorporating the logo of the Nazi SS organization. She says: "And this pizza is from N... What is this store, anyway?"

In August 2015 Norwegian film festival rejected an Israeli documentary on children with disabilities, telling its director that it supports the boycott on the Jewish state and will not screen Israeli movies unless they deal with the Israeli-Palestinian conflict. A letter from the organizers to Roy Zafrani, the Israeli director of "The Other Dreamers" said:

> *I'm sorry but we can't show this film. We support the academic and cultural boycott of Israel so unless the films are about the illegal occupation, or deals with the occupation or the blockade of Gaza, or otherwise about the discrimination of Palestinians, we can't show them.*

With Europe's overt anti-Semitism it is not incredible to understand that an anti-Semitic hit song titled *Allahu Akbar* has shot to the top of streaming charts less than two weeks after terrorists yelled the Islamic phrase while shooting dead victims in the November 13, 2015, Paris attacks. The track, made by DJ Inappropriate, is at No1 on Spotify's Viral Chart, which means it is being widely shared as well as played. The term *'Allahu Akbar'* translates from Arabic as "Allah is the greatest" and has been shouted by Muslim jihadists as a battle cry during acts of terrorism. It was shouted by gunmen as they shot dead 89 concert-goers at the Bataclan theatre in Paris during the November attacks, which killed 130 people in total. According to Spotify's figures, **the song is being most played in Oslo, Norway,** then **Stockholm in Sweden** (a Muslim paradise), then **London**, which is almost 70 percent Muslim.

Several people have put themselves in the gap, praying for Norway and fighting against Norwegian irresponsibility, men of the same ilk as former MP Kåre Kristiansen, who left the Nobel Peace Prize Committee, when it decided to give Yasser Arafat the Peace Prize.

Anti-Semitism remains ripe in Norway. The difference over the years is that today it is being labeled as "anti-Zionism" or "Israel-criticism," which are merely euphemisms for plain, down-to-earth anti-Semitism. Norway's political acceptance of Hamas as a worthy peace partner, the awarding of the Nobel Peace Prize to not only Yasser Arafat, but other people known for their anti-Jewish attitudes, like former U.S. president Jimmy Carter (2002), and the incumbent president, Barack Hussein Obama (2009), when he had only been in office for less than half a year and had done absolutely nothing worthy of the prize.

Geil Lundestad, former director of Norway's Nobel Institute for 25 years, revealed in September 2015, in his then just-published memoir, that he regrets the committee's decision to give the 2009 Nobel Peace award to President Obama.

Norway — Chapter 24

In December 2011, Professor Michael Nobel, grandson of one of Alfred Nobel's two brothers, wrote in an article in *Aftenposten* that he thinks the Nobel committee has consciously disregarded its mission in recent decades and selected winners based on their own preferences, in contravention of Alfred Nobel's will.

FOR NORWAY'S LIBERAL LEFT POLITICS WE need look no further than Labor politician and ideologist Edvard Bull Sr. (Foreign minister for Labor in 1928), who stated In 1923:

> We will secularize the schools, nursing and funeral services, marriage and birth registration. We shall irreconcilably fight the existing official Lutheran church, together with other inane sects. We shall lead ongoing, ruthless church politics, because we believe religion in itself to be a private matter. Children should be turned into socialists and teachers should cooperate in this effort. We will build the socialist schooling system, and we must apply the power of school boards and municipal councils and use our power callously. *We want to obliterate all the barbarism, unhealthy teachings and morals, which children are being taught through religious indoctrination*. School politics is and must remain class politics. [http://www.idag.no/debatt-oppslag.php3?ID=21082 (Norwegian)]

The current law on abortion in Norway was introduced in 1978, being validated from January 1st 1979. This was when Børre Knudsen annulled the public part of his ministry as a priest, yet since 1979 the approximate number of abortions in Norway has been reasonable stable at 16,000 cases a year—fully funded by the public health system.

In the 37 years since this occurred almost 600,000 children have been slaughtered at Norwegian hospitals (medically induced abortions by usage of the "regret, or morning after pill" is not included in these statistics). Norway was among the first countries in the world to introduce these type of abortions, as early as April 1998. The Norwegian government approves of abortion and the blood of the approximately 600,000 Norwegians, murdered while yet unborn, is crying out to God from Norway's soil.

DISCRIMINATION AND BIAS AGAINST FOREIGNERS HAVE a long history in Norway. The discrimination, foremost against the Sami people (traditionally known in English as Lapps or Laplanders, an indigenous people inhabiting the Arctic area of Sápmi), and other migrants. Particular hatred is against the Jews, the chosen people of God. Although there were several men present at the framing of the Norwegian Constitution at Eidsvold in 1814, who had Jewish background, like John Moses from Kristiansand and Wilhelm Frimann Koren Christie, the Framers ended up adopting the following Article into the Constitution:

> "Jesuits and monastic orders must not be tolerated. **Jews are still excluded from admittance to the realm**."

"The Jew's Paragraph," as it was known, had actually been in force since 1687 and withstood several attempts to purge it from the Constitution of 1814 before being finally expunged in 1851. The part about monastic orders remained as it was until 1897, and the portion about Jesuits remained standing until 1956.

DURING WWII, WHEN NORWAY WAS OCCUPIED by Germans and being virtually ruled by them, the Norwegian "Minister-president" Vidkun Quisling reintroduced "The Jew's Paragraph" for the duration of the war. Following the war, among other charges, Quisling was judged for "illegal amendment of the Constitution." Quisling was executed for his crimes against Norway and his name has became synonymous worldwide with traitors and collaborators with an enemy force occupying their country.

IN 1942 THERE WERE SOME 2,100 Jews registered in Norway. In 1946, only 559 remained alive. Many fled to neighboring Sweden. After World War II was over the Norwegian government announced that it would agree to re-absorb within its land, **exactly the same number of Jews as had been living there before 1939**, prior to the community having been murdered in the Holocaust. Precisely **the same number, but not a single Jew more**. This was at a time when tens of thousands of Holocaust survivors were in refugee camps in Germany desperate to get out of Germany and re-build their lives. The Norwegian government had no interest in those "**obstinate survivors of Hitler's death camps**" as Britain's Labour MP called them.

In January 2012, Norway apologized for the first time for the country's complicity in the deportation and deaths of Jews during the Nazi occupation in World War II. In a speech marking International Holocaust Remembrance Day, Prime Minister Jens Stoltenberg said:

> Norwegians carried out the arrests. Norwegians drove the trucks. And it happened in Norway. Today I feel it is fitting to express our deepest apologies that this could happen on Norwegian soil.
>
> It is time for us to acknowledge that Norwegian policemen, civil servants, and other Norwegians took part in the arrest and deportation of Jews.

Norway — Chapter 24

It took 67 years before Norway could "express" regret for its anti-Semitic past. It has yet to express any regret for its virulent anti-Semitic present.

AT THE CLOSE OF WW II NORWAY, by way of a political coup, came under the government of the Labor party, and virtually remained (apart from brief intervals) under its control until the 1980s. While some of the leadership of Labor were known to be on very friendly terms with David Ben-Gurion (Israel's first prime minister) and those like-minded, not the least being Haakon Lie who sold heavy water to Israel in the early 1960s. Labor in Norway, however, experienced a shift in ideals from 1968 through 1972, which has remained in effect until the present day. Israel was not considered friendly anymore. Several politicians like Bjørn Tore Godal, Johan Jørgen Holst (figurehead for the Oslo Accords) then led the party. Holst died suddenly in 1994, only a year after the signing of the Oslo Accords.

The good things done by right thinking Norwegians may alleviate the coming judgment to a certain degree, but it cannot erase it.

Former Norwegian prime minister, and leader of the Christian Democratic Party (KrF) Kjell Magne Bondevik played a leading role in the bombing of Serbia in 1999, and as late as 2012 he denied the release of public documents concerning the bombing of that country.

The same can be said of the 2011-bombing of Libya (initiated by U.S. President Barack Obama without obtaining the approval of Congress), where six Norwegian F-16 war planes dropped nearly 600 bombs over Libya, several in urban areas. The Norwegian attacks were part of a NATO operation, greatly contributed to the Muammar Qaddafi regime's collapse during the fall of 2011, which at the same time opened the country to more extreme, more brutal forces. At the time of writing Libya has become the fall-back capital for ISIL jihadists who are crucifying and beheading opponents and raping the women who refuse to follow its repulsive doctrine.

Norway, continuing its push against the Jewish state was, as early as the 1990s, acting as a willing door-opener for the so-called Palestinian Arabs, by allowing them to open their first "embassy" in Oslo, which is still maintained.

Norway is, despite its small size both in area (number 68 in the world) and in population (number 121 in the world), is number 19 on the world's list of arms and weapons producing countries. Kongsberg-gruppen is the country's largest arms, remote weapons, navigation and positioning and command and control system, producer.

There is also Nammo Gruppen (Norwegian Ammo). Its broad portfolio includes shoulder-launched munitions systems, military and sports ammunition, rocket motors for military and space applications, and environmentally friendly demilitarization services. Nammo has subsidiaries in Finland, Sweden, Germany, USA, Switzerland, and Spain.

THE OFFICIAL AND ORIGINAL BROADCASTER OF Norway, *NRK*, has bloodstained hands when it comes to coverage of Norway. Their coverage of the first Lebanon War was documented by Carl Christian Hauge as being as flawed as news reporting can possibly be (*Mediamakt*, 1983).

The *NRK*s correspondents, headquartered in Amman, Jordan, not Jerusalem, are infamous. Odd Karsten Tveit, Fritz Nilsen, Lars Sigurd Sunnanå, and not forgetting Sidsel Wold, who bears a reputation of infamy—reporting undocumented claims and outright lies to the TV-viewers of Norway. During the Gaza war of 2014, Sidsel Wold repeatedly lied on TV. Sidsel Wold was cornered by a question from a Norwegian journalist who asked her which article and paragraph of "International Law" she refers to when she claims repeatedly on TV that Israel breaks International Law. Her answer was "Yes, that is true. Israel breaks International Law." The journalist re-phrased the question two times, and she claimed "Israel breaks International Law because the United Nations has stated that it does."

Sidsel Wold's infamy, however, doesn't end there. In an interview with Manfred Gerstenfeld in Jerusalem, she managed to (accidentally?) delete her tapes. She received the prize for dishonest journalism from Honest Reporting. [http://honestreporting.com/tag/sidsel-wold/]

Wold also stole sound bytes by Gerstenfeld from other interviews and edited these into something that wasn't even close to being genuine. *TV2*-reporter Fredrik Græsvik, committed a similar sin by cross editing an interview with Gerstenfeld, making Gerstenfeld say, "Gerstenfeld thinks Norwegians are barbarians and unintellectual," when Gerstenfeld actually said: "Norway forbids Jewish ritual slaughter, while killing whales, which is barbarian."

Gerstenfeld is absolutely correct. Norway is not only a paradigm for anti-Semitism, but also has an unenviable reputation for sanctioning cruel blood sports like hunting, and is reviled as one of the last countries that still condone whaling. Yet Norway is the country that banned Jewish ritual slaughter even before the Nazis did in Germany.

Norway is a country that invites rabid anti-Semites like Ilan Pappe to speak at universities but boycotts pro-Israel speakers. A case in point was that of distinguished Harvard law professor Alan Dershowitz who was sponsored on a speaking tour of Norwegian universities by a pro-Israel group. The group offered to have Dershowitz speak without charge to the

Norway — Chapter 24

three major universities in Bergen, Oslo, and Trondheim. Each of the three universities categorically refused to invite him to lecture on "The Case For Peace," on which he has written some half-dozen books. The dean of the law faculty at Bergen University said he would be honored to have him present a lecture "on the O.J. Simpson case," **as long as he was willing to promise not to mention Israel**.

Dershowitz explained in a *Wall Street Journal* article that he was —

the victim of an **unofficial Norwegian university boycott of Israeli universities**. The unofficial boycott is so extensive that it bans not only Israeli academics, but non-Israeli, Jewish academics that are pro-Israel.

Seemingly, every walk in life in Norway feels that it must compete for being the worst anti-Semite in Norway. On November 27, 2008, comedian Otto Jespersen said the following on the country's largest commercial television station. What was worse, however, was that the director of the station defended him:

I would like to take the opportunity to remember all the billions of fleas and lice that lost their lives in German gas chambers, without having done anything wrong other than settling on persons of Jewish background.

A Norwegian diplomat, Trine Lilleng, a first secretary at the Norwegian Embassy in Riyadh, Saudi Arabia, used her Foreign Ministry e-mail account to equate Israel's retaliatory offensive against Hamas in Gaza with the mass murder of 6,000,000 Jews by the Nazis. With her e-mail, she included a juxtaposition of some 40 black-and-white pictures from the Holocaust with color images of Israel's Operation Cast Lead. "The grandchildren of Holocaust survivors from World War II are doing to the Palestinians exactly what was done to them by Nazi Germany," she stated.

The pictures sent as attachments in the e-mail include the famous photograph of a Jewish boy with his hands raised as a German soldier points his gun at him. That image is juxtaposed next to an image of an Israeli soldier aiming his weapon at a Palestinian boy. Another depicts a German soldier firing his weapon, next to an IDF soldier shooting his, while others juxtapose the barbed wire surrounding ghettos and concentration camps to the fence around Gaza, and the West Bank security barrier. The e-mail asks recipients to forward the message to others.

Norwegian physician, Dr. Mads Gilbert, tried to pass himself off as an impartial foreigner, a Good Samaritan who had arrived in Gaza to volunteer his medical skills during Operation Cast Lead. Gilbert, clad in green scrubs, stethoscope hanging around his neck, expressed outrage and called what was happening in Gaza the worst man-made medical disaster he'd ever seen.

Israel claimed that most of those killed were Hamas gunmen. Gilbert, however, asserted that of the hundreds of patients flooding Shifa hospital—under which Hamas had its command center—perhaps two were "militants." He claimed that 25 percent of the dead were innocents, that "801 children were killed or injured."

Dr. Mads Gilbert is no neutral medical man, has been active for over 30 years in "solidarity work with Palestinians." Wikipedia's profile of Gilbert is not that of a humanitarian but that of a political activist with a Marxist agenda. His personal convictions are like those of the Norwegian majority—of the extreme left. In 2001 Gilbert, according to Wikipedia, had the following to say about the terror attacks on 9/11 that killed some 3,000 people:

Question: So do you support this terrorist attack on the US?
Answer: "Terror is a bad weapon but my answer is yes."

CHEATING, SWINDLING, AND FRAUD IS RAMPANT in Norway. The notion put forward in the movie Wall Street that "Greed, for lack of a better word, is good!" is a reliable description of Norway. Most Norwegians have grown accustomed to greed, due to petroleum riches, but certain Norwegians traveled to Arab oil producing nations and convinced them that the price of US$1 was "far too low" for a barrel of oil (1972–1973). The price consequently exploded and made Norway rich, until recently. One barrel of oil has since fallen from approximately US$140 to a little over US$20 at the time of writing.

Norway's income has plummeted and the Norwegian Kroner has lost a large part of its value against the US Dollar. However, according to the Norwegian newspapers Norwegian politicians and bureaucrats remain super-rich and super-greedy.

In the first years after 2000, several municipalities gambled with taxpayer's money in eagerness to make their municipalities rich. They ended up leading their respective municipalities into deep debt and several municipalities are still suffering from these losses, but most of the politicians responsible for the mismanagement still remain in their high-paying jobs.

NORWAY WAS ONE OF THE FIRST countries in the world to open its doors to homosexual cohabitation, and later for "homosexual marriage." The Bible

(Leviticus 18:22) explicitly forbids homosexuality and zoophilia (sex with animals). But the leadership of the public church—the College of Bishops, the Church of Norway, the Lutheran Church—began early to accept all of the above. In 2005 only one of 11 bishops was explicitly against "homosexual marriage." After some castling the number of bishops changed around, only to get back to square one. At present still only one of the bishops is against "homosexual marriage."

A majority (eight) of Bishops stated around 2000:

> Presently homosexual cohabitation exists among Christians. Although they refuse the correction of the church, they too have full rights to understanding within the Christian fellowship. They ought to be included in the Church.

Zoophilia (bestiality) is not only a stain on humankind, but clearly and explicitly condemned in God's Word (Deuteronomy 27:16–23; Exodus 22:19). God's Word does not differentiate between homosexuality, incest and zoophilia (Leviticus 18:22 – 23; 20:15). Yet Norwegian politicians blindly accept homosexuality by pound, and invalidate the institution of marriage by distinguishing.

Prostitution is often labeled "the world's oldest profession," but there is little difference in age when talking about either of the aforementioned perversions, incest included, and Norway is seeing an increase in such incestuous behavior in recent years.

In the case of the "Lommemannen" (Pocket guy) a Norwegian businessman, committed between 1976 and 2008 at least 160 acts of pederasty against boys aged between six and 12 years. Since the Internet became public via the World Wide Web in the middle of the 1990's pornography has exploded into formerly unknown areas and quantities. Norway is not innocent in the spread of such immorality, and a number of Norwegians have created a name for themselves within the "industry."

SEEMINGLY ACCEPTABLE SINS IN NORWAY ARE prostitution, divorce, and sexual immorality. Oslo Municipality owns and finances PRO-senteret, which is supposedly an organization that works to alleviate and help both male and female prostitutes with their problems. Prostitution in Norway is forbidden by law, but the ban only applies to the "customers," and this ban also applies to Norwegians when traveling abroad.

Cohabitation outside of wedlock was introduced in Norway in the 1960's called "Paperless Marriage," which was later changed to "*samboerskap*" (cohabitation). A number of professing Christians consider cohabitation acceptable, and are themselves living together without being married.

Religious sins are equally conspicuous in Norway. Schools in Norway do not allow any form of creationism to be taught. Private schools are also forced to present the theory of evolution as accepted truth.

The Politically Correct whip has long been used in Norway. By 2013 the percentage of Norwegians that are members of the Church of Norway is 82, but perhaps only 12 percent are active attendees. The general election of 2015 also included Church Election, where the homosexual lobby "Open Church" led a campaign to get the Church to open itself for acceptance of a homosexual marriage liturgy. More than 30 percent of the electorate participated, compared to between two and five percent ten years previously. The number of members in Pentecostal churches is either stagnating or suffering from castling to other churches.

From 1741 through 1842, it was not allowed for anyone who was not ordained to preach the gospel without a special permit from the local vicar or pastor. Hans Nielsen Hauge spent close to eleven years in prison for disobeying this law, and died as a result of the diseases he got contracted from cold prison cells.

In 1953, theologian and preacher Ole Hallesby spoke on direct broadcast in *NRK* radio, saying: "How can you go to sleep this night, not knowing whether you will awake in your bed tomorrow – or in hell?" This led to repressive regulations demanding that anyone who will speak devotionals on *NRK* radio must present a manuscript ahead for censorship.

There are virtually no towns in Norway where one cannot find shops selling occult goods—crystal, jewelry, tarot cards, books by Aleister Crowley, etc. The growth in number of sects and cults preaching occult messages is mushrooming.

Regulations against blasphemy was for most of their duration counted as a "sleeping regulation," and was revoked entirely a few years ago.

It is now time to turn our attention to the events of July 22, 2011, events that shocked not only the blue-eyed people of Norway, but also many in the Western world. It has been described as a fire bell in the night, a true wakeup call to a sleeping nation. The events were the handiwork of a single homegrown terrorist—Anders Behring Breivik, a deluded right-

Norway — Chapter 24

wing extremist. On the above date Breivik detonated a 2,100 pound (952.5 kilograms) fertilizer car-bomb in the heart of Norway's government complex in Oslo. The destruction and carnage was by no means on the scale of the 1995 Oklahoma City bombing—loss of life in Oslo was, in relation to the explosion, small at eight persons, but it was the beginning of a nightmare for Norway.

The car-bomb was merely a diversion planned by Breivik. Less than two hours after the massive blast Breivik had made his way to the privately owned island of Utoeya, belonging to the Labor Party Youth organization (AUF), which was then holding its summer camp, and which was Breivik's real target. Once on the island, Anders Behring Breivik proceeded according to his predetermined plan: disguised as a police officer he gathered the holiday makers around him in a circle and gunned down 69 children of the ruling elite before being arrested by a police SWAT team. It is interesting that Breivik killed no one under the age of 14 years, he killed the offspring of Norway's ruling class which supported the genocidal Hamas terror organization against Israel in Operation Cast Lead. Breivik's murderous rampage was the deadliest attack by a solo gunman in world history.

NORWAY'S HISTORY OF ANTI-SEMITISM AND anti-Israelism has been spawned by Socialism and Humanism and the vanguard of this has been the Labor Party and the AUF. *Almighty God, the Holy One of Israel*, had His hand in the events of 22/7. Reading *A Breach in the Wall,* which contains all the facts and exact timing of the events, is like reading a Marx Brother's movie script. Hoff opines (correctly) that the level of confusion and ineptitude by the Norwegian security forces goes "beyond spontaneous incompetence." One needs to read the book in order to understand this.

For years the island of Utoeya has been used as a pro-Palestinian venue for anti-Israel gatherings and resolutions, and as a platform for calling for "unilateral" economic and academic boycotts of Israel. Norwegian politicians are complicit in what Utoeya is used for and at least one terrorist has been a guest on the island. The radical Rogaland chapter of AUF even divided the island into Palestinian and Israel camps in July 2010, establishing borders with border guards.

Some Norwegians, being less obtuse than the great majority, can see the links between the Utoeya massacre and the treatment handed out to Israel by Norway. Hoff points out that on January 2012 a political scientist by the name of Per Haakonsen gave a paralyzing speech that was carried by the *Dagen* newspaper of which an excerpt is reproduced below:

The Utoeya massacre can be seen in the light of the *increasingly inflamed relations between Israel and Norway,* and the diplomatic controversies that have occurred in recent times. On July 21st, the Foreign Minister came to Utoeya and allowed himself to be photographed in front of a banner with the text "**Boycott Israel**." In his speech, the Foreign Minister gave his full support for the Palestinians getting their own state, stating that the occupation must end and the wall be demolished.

The "wall" referred to is part of a barrier built to stop Palestinian suicide bombers and other terrorists from freely entering Israel proper. Only part of the barrier—bordering the most frequently used crossing points for Palestinian terrorists—consists of prefabricated concrete sections, the greater part of the barrier is chain-link fencing. But Norway's Foreign Minister, on the day before the massacre on Utoeya island, would have this security fence, the so-called "apartheid wall," removed in order to allow suicide bombers to have unfettered access to Israeli civilian targets.

THE UTOEYA MASSACRE STUNNED NORWAY; HOWEVER, the widespread and popular support for Palestinian terrorists in Norway shows that for the majority of Norwegians, their opposition to terrorism is less than total.

Most Norwegians think that the Palestinians' resistance to the so-called Israeli "occupation" is justified, thus lack of sympathy for Israeli victims of Palestinian terrorism is unlikely to change even in the days following Breivik's attack on Norwegians. There is an academic and political climate of hatred towards Israel and Jews, its stench pervades almost the whole of Norwegian society. This climate is not a modern development; it has been a cornerstone of Norwegian culture. Harvard Professor Alan Dershowitz said:

> I know of no reasonable person who has tried to justify the terrorist attacks against Norway. Yet there are many Norwegians who not only justify terrorist attacks against Israel, but praise them, support them, help finance them and legitimate them.

As it has been said earlier, Norway banned kosher ritual slaughter in 1929—three years before an almost identical ban was instituted in Nazi Germany. And whereas the ban on kosher ritual slaughter was lifted in post-Nazi Germany, it has never been repealed in Norway. Norway's prohibition on Jewish ritual slaughter makes the Jewish religion the only religion that cannot be freely practiced in Norway.

IN THE DAYS FOLLOWING THE NAZI invasion, the governing body of Norway founded and joined the Norwegian Nazi Party. It would also seem that sympathy for Nazi collaborators is just as strong in Norway today.

Norway — Chapter 24

Manfred Gerstenfeld noted, in a report on the rise in Norwegian anti-Semitic attacks during 2009, that two years ago the Norwegian government allocated more than US$20 million in taxpayer money to commemorate the 150th birthday of Norwegian novelist Knut Hamsun, the 1920 Nobel laureate for literature. The *New York Times* reported, in February 2009, that Norway's Queen Sonja opened the year-long, publicly financed commemoration, called "Hamsun 2009."

While Hamsun may have been a good writer, he is really remembered for being an overt Nazi. Hamsun even gave his Nobel prize to Josef Goebbels, the Nazi propaganda chief. During a wartime visit to Germany, Hamsun met with Adolf Hitler at Hitler's Bavarian mountain home.

NORWEGIAN ANTI-SEMITISM DOES NOT COME from the grassroots, but from the Norwegian leadership—from politicians, organization leaders, church leaders, and senior journalists. It does not come from Muslims, but from the "Christian" majority. Norway adamantly claims that anti-Semitism and anti-Israelism are unrelated, but Norway has shown the world that its elite anti-Semitism merges seamlessly with its anti-Israelism. For this it must pay a price, and Breivik's massacring of 77 members of Norwegian society is but a down payment.

According to God's Word, a few of the sins of which Norway is guilty are:

a) Rejection of God
b) Rejection of God's Salvation
c) Suppressing or Hindering the preaching of the Gospel
d) Refusal to hear and live by God's Word
e) Practicing witchcraft, horoscopes and the occult
f) **Coveting** (form of idolatry)
g) Blasphemy
h) **Slavery and Oppression** (Sami people)
i) **Discriminating against strangers** (includes racial discrimination)
j) Murder, abortion, perverse and immoral behavior
k) Breaking political agreements
l) Pride in National Security
m) Using power and wealth to make other nations subservient
n) Allies of those waging war against Israel
o) Homosexuality
p) **Sodomy** (sexual perversion, including acts with animals)
q) Incest

r) Adultery, divorce and sexual lusts

The judgments are therefore:

Physical catastrophes and widespread death (6 times); **Destruction of the nation** (7 times); **Near Annihilation** (5 times); **Annihilation** (3 times); **Defeat with high loss of life** (2 times); **Judicial cursing or complete destruction of nation**; and **Accelerated destruction of nation**.

Time is running out for Norway. The message from the LORD is "*Repent or Perish!*" *For the LORD has a controversy with Norway.*

I am indebted to Lars-Toralf Storstrand for writing and supplying a very large part of the content for the chapter on Norway. As a Norwegian media man, Lars keeps abreast of what goes on in his country and graciously translated everything into English for me.
    I am also deeply indebted to Jeremy Hoff, another native Norwegian, who kindly sent me a copy of his book, *A Breach In The Wall*. Hoff's Norwegian readers owe him a debt of gratitude for clearly and accurately showing the nation's danger as its humanistic and anti-Israel policies causes the sleepwalking nation to stagger blindly toward the edge of what could be catastrophic destruction, of which 7/22/2011 was but a foretaste. I have, with permission, used various segments of information contained in *A Breach In The Wall*; however, it was simply not possible to include the multitude of documented facts contained in Hoff's spell-binding volume within a few pages of this book. Interested readers should go to: ***www.a-breach-in-the-wall.com***.

25

Rome

Rome today is a historical city and a mecca for tourists, but in antiquity it was much more than a city; it was a great and powerful empire whose seat of government lay in its bosom. Like other empires that came against Israel, Rome sealed its fate when it took the sword against the people of God. Slowly, but surely, she declined—torn apart by strife and gross immorality and later vanquished and sacked by the Huns and Vandals. Rome wasted away, leaving for posterity only crumbling structures as monuments to its faded glory.

EVANGELICAL CHRISTIANITY BEGAN IN ROMAN-OCCUPIED Jerusalem, just 47 days after the resurrection of Jesus in 28 or 29 AD. Rome became history's cruelest persecutor of the Christian Church. The tortures, the barbarities, and the ignominies to which the Christians were subjected, almost defy description—they were among the most heinous in human history. The Christians, however, won the day, and a divided, disintegrating Roman empire under Constantine, accepted Christianity around the year 320 AD.

The early Christian Church was entirely made up of Jews who believed Jesus (Yeshua) to be the Messiah and King of Israel. The center of early Christianity was Jerusalem, and the first Bishop was James—the brother of our Lord. There were fifteen consecutive Jewish bishops of Jerusalem from the time of James until 135 AD, when the Romans banished Jews from Jerusalem and her environs.

The historical account set down by Eusebius (260 – 340 AD) in his *Ecclesiastical History*, the Church's most important historical narrative, tells us that the bishops of Rome had "no pre-eminence above other bishops." We can safely assume, despite the scanty evidence offered by the Roman Catholic Church, that the bishops of Rome—the Popes—usurped the headship of the Church.

The Roman Church fell into apostasy, and the veneration of Mary, the mother of Jesus, passed from respect to idolatry, and praying to her as a mediator between God and man became the norm. In direct contravention of New Testament teachings, praying to saints was encouraged, and priests were called "Father" and forbidden to marry. The bishops of Rome took exclusively to themselves the title of "Pope," literally meaning "Father," but more correctly "Holy Father."

Just as the Romans had been the worst persecutors of the early Church, so the adherents of an apostate Roman Church followed in their footsteps. They tortured and killed tens of thousands of Christians who rejected the idolatry, apostasy and hypocrisy of the Roman Catholic (Universal) Church. In the sixteenth century a Christian, John Fox, took upon himself the long and arduous task of chronicling some of the atrocities of the Roman Church in his *History of the Acts and Monuments of the Church*. This book became a Christian classic and is known to Christians today as *Fox's Book of Martyrs*. The corruption within the Roman Church has a long history. Martin Luther's recollections of his visit to Rome in 1510 are recorded in D' Aubigne's (1843) *History of the Reformation*:

> It is incredible what sins and atrocities are committed in Rome; they must be seen and heard to be believed. So that it is usual to say: "If there be a hell, Rome is built above it; it is an abyss from which all sins proceed."

Nicolo Machiavelli (1469 – 1527), one of the most profound geniuses of Italy, and himself a Roman Catholic, is also quoted in *History of the Reformation*:

> The greatest symptom of the approaching ruin of Christianity is, that the nearer we approach the capital of Christendom, the less do we find the Christian spirit of the people. The scandalous example and crimes of the court of Rome have caused Italy to lose every principle of piety and every religious sentiment.

PRIDE, CORRUPTION, APOSTASY, IDOLATRY AND HYPOCRISY have been a hallmark of the Roman Church, as have been the homosexual sins of the priests. The forbidding of marriage has been the cause of much of the acts of sodomy committed by priests with parishioners or children. The sodomizing of young boys is still an ongoing illness affecting many Catholic priests at the time of writing in 2016. The effects of sexual abuse by a priest is devastating. (I can personally testify to this because in 1953 at 13-years of age I was repeatedly sexually abused by a priest from Rio de Janeiro.) Some boys never recover and this is made clear in the following excerpt from the September 24, 2015, *LA Times* article titled, ABUSE VICTIMS SAY CATHOLIC CHURCH MUST DO MORE TO ATONE FOR PREDATORY PRIESTS:

> Each morning when he wakes and walks to his shower, Mark Rozzi is reminded of a priest from his childhood, and the nightmare that unfolded in the rectory back in 1983.

Rome — Chapter 25

He was a 13-year-old student and altar boy at Holy Guardian Angels Catholic Church and school in his hometown of Reading, about 65 miles north of Philadelphia, when he was raped in the shower by the Rev. Edward Graff.

Rozzi said he managed to get away and told his parents, who complained to the principal, but Graff was never prosecuted. Instead, like so many other priests accused of abuse, he was transferred to other churches, Rozzi said. Eventually, the priest was arrested in Texas and died while in custody before trial.

Rozzi later discovered that several of his friends had been abused by Graff as well; one struggled for years with mental illness and unemployment until he committed suicide this year, on Good Friday.

"I have seen my friends kill themselves, my friends become alcoholics and drug addicts, and then the church make a mockery of us," he said.

Worldwide, the financial backlash resulting from priests' acts of sodomy is draining the Roman church's coffers. The *LA Times* article reported that:

> The Los Angeles Archdiocese agreed in **2007** to pay **more than 500 abuse victims $660 million**. Later settlements pushed the archdiocese's tab to **more than $740 million**.

And this is just the Los Angeles Archdiocese in the U.S. The costs of payouts to victims of sexual abuse by the Roman Catholic clergy worldwide runs into billions of dollars.

The *LA Times* article also reported:

> victims say the Roman Catholic Church in the United States continues to fight proposed laws that would allow the prosecution of crimes committed long ago.

Sex escapades involving Catholic clergy seem not to have lessened over time in either frequency or depravity—they appear to have gotten worse. In December 2015 a scorned ex-girlfriend of an S&M "master" to a Catholic priest revealed the details of romps funded with cash taken from the poor box. She told how the Rev. Peter Miqueli of the Bronx wore a locked chastity belt, along with a dog collar, during sessions with his lover. Apparently, Miqueli also had a fantasy of being humiliated in front of a "nice Jewish girl."

Also in December, Miqueli's parishioners filed a lawsuit claiming the pastor had stolen at least $1,000,000 in church funds so he could enjoy his **$1,000-per-session** "homosexual sex master." The lawsuit also claimed Miqueli took trips to Italy with money taken from collection plates.

JUST AS THE BISHOPS OF ROME usurped the headship of the early Church and took for themselves the title of "Holy Father" in contravention of holy Scripture, so they also carved out Vatican City in 1929, and made an independent Roman Catholic state to which countries must establish diplomatic relations. Vatican City lies within the city of Rome, occupies 526,592 square yards (440,298 square meters), and once had a population of around 1,000 persons, but this dropped to around 890 in 2001, and in 2012 the population stood at 451.

The Catholic enclave has its own passports, police force, Vatican lira currency that depicts the Pope; and bank—the Institute for Works of Religion (IOR). According to *Grolier's Encyclopedia*, this bank was "implicated in the questionable dealings and collapse of Italy's largest private banking institution, Banco Ambrosiano." There have also been accusations of other "questionable dealings," including the laundering of Mafia money by members of the Vatican itself.

On November 3, 2015, *Reuters* reported that:

> financial investigators suspect a department of the Vatican which oversees real estate and investments was used in the past for possible money laundering, insider trading and market manipulation.
>
> The information in the confidential document, which covers the period from 2000 to 2011, had been passed on to Italian and Swiss investigators for their checks because some activity tied to the accounts allegedly took place in these countries.

UNTIL THE 1960S, WHEN THE BAN on personal reading of the Scriptures was lifted, Catholics had little chance of finding salvation because the Mass was conducted throughout the world in Latin—an ancient language which few understood. But it would neither be true, nor fair, to say that there are not real believers within the modern Roman Church. I am personally acquainted with a Catholic priest who publicly stated, in the presence of other priests and nuns, that the adoration of Mary is totally and utterly wrong. I have also been acquainted in the past with some delightful Catholics who came to faith, but each opted to remain in the Roman Church and have since fallen away. The much publicized "charismatic renewal" within the Roman Church should be seriously questioned, however, as messages from Mary are prevalent in many of the meetings.

ROME AS A NATION COLLAPSED, AND Rome as a wealthy, religious empire is also collapsing. The number of Roman Catholic adherents is shrinking by millions each year, and much of the Roman Church is in financial straits. The Vatican has consistently taken the side of the Arabs against Israel, and a 45-year opposition to the recognition of the Jewish state was ended only on December 30, 1993, when formal diplomatic relations were established as part of the Vatican's Christian-Jewish reconciliation effort. On June 26, 2015, the Vatican formerly signed an accord recognizing a sovereign state of Palestine, when in fact no such state exists. It was an overt display of the Vatican's pro-Palestinian, anti-Israel stance, which can only hasten the Roman Church's demise.

Sins committed are:

a) Murder, perverse and immoral behavior
b) Allies of those waging war against Israel
c) Homosexuality
d) Anti-Semitism—political, racial and religious
e) Refusal to hear and live by God's Word
f) Suppressing or Hindering the preaching of the Gospel
g) Fraudulent, deceitful and crafty business transactions

The judgments are, therefore: **Physical catastrophes and widespread death**; **Destruction of nation** (two times); **Annihilation**; **Judicial cursing or complete destruction of nation**; **Near annihilation** (two times); and **Acceleration of the destruction of nation**.

THE ROMAN CHURCH BECAME PROUD BEFORE it became an institution. Its apostasy and idolatry have kept millions in the grip of Satan and away from the *"Light of the world"* (John 8:12). The loss of all these souls must be accounted for—just as the blood of the Protestant martyrs must be. Most, if not all, major commentators agree that the number 666 in Revelation Chapter 13 refers directly to Rome (see, for example, Albert Barnes' *Notes on the New Testament*, vol. 14, pp. 334–338). Those that have had greater light must bear a greater judgment. And *the LORD has a serious controversy with the Church of Rome.*

26

Syria

Syria is a modern state in an ancient land. The contemporary boundaries were drawn by Britain and France during World War I through the secret convention that dismantled the Ottoman Empire, known as the Sykes-Picot Agreement. However, the name Syria has been applied to the larger Mediterranean coastal area for centuries. The historic region known as "greater Syria" comprised present-day Syria, Lebanon, Israel, and Jordan. This area was successively ruled by Egyptians, Hittites, Assyrians, Persians, Greeks, and Romans. After the breakup of the Roman empire in the fifth century, Syria became part of the Byzantine empire, which fell to the Muslims in the seventh century.

Christians often confuse Assyria and Syria and some teach that Syria is the modern counterpart of Assyria, but this is not true. The Assyrians were from a more northern location, and their capital was Nineveh, whose ruins are in present-day Iraq. The capital of Syria is Damascus, which is thought to be the world's oldest continuously inhabited city.

THE FIRST BIBLICAL ACCOUNT OF WAR between Israel and Syria is recorded in the days of King David:

> *David killed twenty-two thousand of the Syrians. Then David put garrisons in Syria of Damascus; and the Syrians became David's servants, and brought tribute* (2Samuel 8:5,6)

Since the days of King David there have been numerous military conflicts between Israel and Syria. In the 67 years since Israel's declaration of statehood on May 14, 1948, she has been embroiled in four major wars with Syria, and has emerged victorious on each occasion. Despite the defeats inflicted by Israel and the terrible losses of men and equipment, Syria has continued to rattle her sabers. The *Bangkok Post*, March 10, 1990, carried a front page article under the headline: **"SYRIA: WAR AGAINST ISRAEL TO LAST FOREVER."** The article began:

> President Hafez al-Assad made a bitter anti-Israel speech on Thursday, saying his holy war against the Jewish state would last "as long as time."

A super-dovish Israeli government took office in 1992, until that time Israeli governments held no illusions about Syria's aspirations to conquer Israel. Another *Bangkok Post* article of February 27, 1991, quoted Yitzhak Shamir, the former Prime Minister of Israel as saying: "Assad is Israel's 'real enemy.'" Arab people have an inherent sadistic streak in their natures, but it is the Syrians who are regarded as Israel's most savage enemy. In conjunction with the Egyptians, Syria launched a surprise attack in 1973, on Yom Kippur (the Day of Atonement), the holiest day of the Jewish year. Most soldiers were home for the high holy-day, and those that were left on the Golan Heights fought almost to the last man. After the Israelis had fought their way back to the top of the Golan plateau, they found many of their fallen Israeli comrades had been shot through the back of the head and with their male member cut off and stuck in their mouths. Just prior to the Gulf War in 1991, while America turned a convenient blind-eye, the Syrians invaded the Christian enclave in Beirut, Lebanon, and virtually wiped it out. Around 600 Christian officers were found bound hand and foot—and shot through the back of the head.

In 1982, President Hafez al-Assad personally ordered the slaughter of some 20,000 Syrians in the city of Hama, during a rebellion by the Muslim Brotherhood. Amnesty International, in its 1983 Report, said the Syrian army came to the city and opened fire with tanks and artillery causing about 2,000 fatalities. The report went on to say that after the shelling, soldiers systematically sealed the houses—with the occupants still inside—and pumped in cyanide gas, killing another 18,000 people. The city was then bulldozed under a pile of earth. A man who escaped miraculously survived to tell the tale.

THERE WAS MUCH IN THE NEWS at the time of writing the first edition of this book (1993) concerning the Middle East "peace process." Articles had been published all over the world stating that president Hafez al-Assad has "changed," and that many left wing Israeli cabinet ministers also believed this. But, *"can the Ethiopian change his skin or the leopard its spots?"* (Jeremiah 13:23). Perhaps an excerpt from an article in the *Jerusalem Post*, July 30, 1993, will clarify al-Assad's intentions:

> Assad has not abandoned the vision of Greater Syria; he is trying to realize it through the political process. It is no coincidence that, precisely on the eve of the crisis with Lebanon, Syria reiterated its age-old stand: Lebanon is Syrian territory.

Syria — Chapter 26

The reason for al-Assad's supposed "change of heart" is that he hopes the United States will pressure Israel into giving up the Golan Heights, captured in the 1967 Six-Day War. For 20 years Syria fired artillery shells into Israeli *kibbutzim* and *moshavim* below the Golan plateau. Syria had 100,000 troops stationed along a wide front on the strategic plateau during the Six-Day War. On the fifth day of the war, June 9, 1967, Israel stormed the Heights and thrashed the Syrians in 12 hours. Both America and Russia intervened and a ceasefire became effective at 6:00 p.m. the following day. Now Syria wants the Golan back. But the more territory Israel is forced to give up, the more likelihood there is for Syrian victory over parts of Israel, for al-Assad has said, "War is inevitable."

The US allowed al-Assad to realize his territorial ambitions in Lebanon, and he hopes that the US would help him realize his ambition to conquer Israel also. History has proved time and again that signed peace agreements are mere scraps of paper—effective until one party tears their piece up. In war, all is fair—there can never be too much deceit. The Syrians maintain their state of war against Israel, and they are masters of deceit.

The LORD swore an oath to Abraham and the Jewish people:

To your descendants I have given this land, from the river of Egypt to the great river, the river Euphrates (Genesis 15:18).

In 1948, 1967, and 1973 the Arabs launched wars of annihilation against Israel, but each time Israel came out victorious and extended her boundaries. Since the 1948 War of Independence, Israel's southern boundary has been the river of Egypt, just above the Sinai desert. In 1967, Israel captured the Biblical heartland—the Old City of Jerusalem, Judea, and Samaria—as well as the Gaza Strip and the Golan Heights. All that stops the Jewish state from extending to the great river, the river Euphrates, is a large piece of Syrian territory. Israel desires to live peacefully on any land that it holds: there is little inclination to possess all of its God-given heritage. Most Israelis are non-religious—disinterested in God and Biblical boundaries. But indications are that Syria will attack when she feels the time is right, and this will cause more of the Promised Land to fall into Israeli hands.

AS THE OLDEST CONTINUOUSLY INHABITED CITY in the world, Damascus has been conquered, sacked and possessed several times, but has never been destroyed. The Bible, however, says that the city will be destroyed:

Behold, Damascus will cease from being a city, and it will be a ruinous heap (Isaiah 17:1).

Obviously, the future for Damascus is bleak. Her leaders continually threaten Israel with more wars, but as Leonard Spector of the Carnegie Endowment put it, Israel has the ability "to level every urban center in the Middle East." If Syria fulfills her ambition to make war on Israel, Damascus could become a ruinous heap, and Israel will have fulfilled yet another Biblical prophecy.

Syria has been one of Israel's most implacable enemies. Three times she has been directly responsible for initiating all-out-war against Israel. Each time Syria has been humiliated and lost territory. Several times she has encouraged others to wage war against Israel, and has cooperated with them in their efforts to harass or destroy the Jewish state.

According to Benjamin Netanyahu, Israel's Prime Minister, "Syria has the fifth largest army in the world." This formidable array of men, machines and missiles waits for the opportune moment to launch another attack against God's people. Another attack will mean yet another defeat

Sins mentioned or alluded to are:

a) Murder, perverse and immoral behavior
b) Unprovoked military aggression
c) Waging war against Israel
d) Allies of those waging war against Israel
e) Rejoicing at another nation's misfortunes (especially Israel's)
f) Appropriating Israel's land
g) Extreme cruelty in times of war
h) Anti-Semitism-political, racial and religious

The judgments are, therefore: **Physical catastrophes and widespread death; Defeat with high loss of life; Destruction of nation** (four times); **Near annihilation; Nation conquered and devastated;** and **Judicial cursing or complete destruction of nation.**

ALMOST ALL OF THE ABOVE CHAPTER WAS WRITTEN FOR THE FIRST EDITION OF *SAGA* IN 1993. Bearing in mind the judgments listed above at that time we should consider Syria's proven history of the past 22 years to see the accuracy of those judgments, which indicates the certainty of them continuing to fall, but perhaps on a more catastrophic level.

IN APRIL 2000 ISRAEL'S INTELLIGENCE SERVICE made it public that it had obtained a sample of Hafez al-Assad's body waste, that he had cancer, and that he was not expected to live longer than a few months. Hafez al-Assad died on 10 June 2000.

Syria — Chapter 26

Hafez had been grooming his eldest son Bassel to succeed him, but Bassel was killed in a car accident in January 1994 when he drove in fog at high speed and hit a roundabout with his chauffeur in the rear seat; he was not wearing a seatbelt. Following the death of Bassel, his brother Bashar, who was studying medicine in the UK and had no political aspirations, was made heir-apparent by Hafez and began to be groomed to take control by immersing him in the military and security apparatus.

After Hafez al-Assad died Bashar became president 10 days later via an unopposed referendum and was reconfirmed in 2007 in another unopposed referendum that accorded him 97.6 percent of the vote.

IN MARCH 2007, ISRAELI MOSSAD AGENTS broke into the Vienna home of Ibrahim Othman, Syria's Atomic Agency director, where they found key information and pictures taken inside a nuclear reactor near al-Kibar in Syria. In September 2007, in what was named Operation Orchard, eight Israeli fighter jets dropped 17 tons of explosives on the Syrian site, destroying it completely. The operation was in accordance with a doctrine established by prime minister Menachem Begin in 1981 when it bombed Iraq's Osiraq nuclear reactor. Israel's unshakable policy is to never allow enemy countries to obtain nuclear weapons. Israel has never publicly claimed that it carried out the strike, and Syria has never acknowledged that it even had a reactor let alone that it was destroyed. Iran should take note of Israel's policy because its nuclear program is probably next in line for the chopping block.

AS IT WAS MENTIONED EARLIER, SYRIA considers Lebanon part of Greater Syria and has wielded a great deal of power over the Lebanese puppet governments. Syria slowly increased its troop numbers in Lebanon up to 40,000 and for all intents and purposes entirely controlled Lebanon. Former Lebanese prime minister Rafic Hariri stood against the Syrian presence and on February 14, 2005, Hariri and 21 others of his bodyguards and friends died in a massive bomb explosion from 2,200 pounds (1,000 kilograms) of TNT against his motorcade in Beirut. Syria was widely blamed by the international community for the assassination and the fallout from its pressure caused Syria to withdraw its troops from Lebanon.

Syria's allies and patrons are Russia and Iran, which both arm al-Assad with weapons and missiles, as well as providing training for Syrian troops. Since the formation of the Iranian-funded Hizb'allah (the Lebanese terror organization) in 1982, which has since become a serious military threat to Israel, Syria has systematically delivered weapons to Hizb'allah. Israel has boarded several ships at sea and seized them and their cargoes of weapons. Israeli air attacks on convoys transporting, or being readied to transport weapons to Hizb'allah occur frequently, which incurs the wrath of both the al-Assad's and Hizb'allah. However, responses to Israel's destruction of Hizb'allah's weapons stockpiles and convoys have thus far been limited.

BASHAR AL-ASSAD MADE A STRATEGIC mistake in January 2011 when he used his military against protesters calling for political reforms and the reinstatement of civil rights. The demonstrations, originally called the "Damascus Spring," grew both in size and frequency and soon morphed into a civil war that has taken the lives of hundreds of thousands of soldiers, rebels, and civilians. Bashar al-Assad is known for his cruelty toward those opposing his regime and has allowed his military to use chemical weapons against both soldiers and civilians, and has dropped barrel bombs on civilian enclaves, which have taken a high toll on civilian lives.

According to the UNHRC the number of refugees that have fled Syria passed the four million mark in December 2015—the biggest refugee population from a single conflict in half a century. It is estimated that an additional 7.6 million people are displaced inside Syria—many of them in extreme circumstances and in locations difficult to reach with humanitarian aid.

SYRIA'S CONFLICT HAS DEVOLVED FROM PEACEFUL protests against the government in 2011 to a violent insurgency that has drawn in numerous other countries and groups. It is partly a civil war of government against people; partly a religious war pitting al-Assad's minority Alawite sect aligned with Shiite fighters from Iran and Hizb'allah in Lebanon, against Sunni rebel groups; and increasingly a proxy war today featuring Russia and Iran against the U.S. and its allies. Many of the Islamic jihadist groups have merged together since the beginning of the war, which has greatly reduced the more than 1,200 groups that were at one time fighting al-Assad and each other.

For four bitter years, the Syrian civil war has been raging less than a mile (kilometer) from Israel's borders. Apart from the occasional Israeli returns of fire from Syrian forces and bombing runs against weapons bound for Hizb'allah in Lebanon, Israel has thus far avoided being dragged into the war. However, Israel (!) has, at great personal and financial cost, clandestinely treated some 2,000 injured fighters from the Syrian conflict, irrespective of which group they belong to. Israeli commandos receive messages from the border with Syria and travel to the border, enter Syrian territory, and evacuate the waiting wounded. After receiving treatment from Israeli medics at the border the wounded are sent right back into the fighting. Heavily

Syria — Chapter 26

wounded fighters and civilians are taken to the nearest Israeli hospital and there receive treatment until sufficiently strong enough to be returned to the border again. By treating the Syrian wounded Israel is carefully keeping aloof from the actual fighting, while at the same time hoping to turn the hearts of the Syrians away from the hatred held for Israelis since time immemorial.

SYRIAN FORCES CURRENTLY ONLY OPERATE IN al-Assad's stronghold in western Syria, having lost most of the country to rebel groups, but at the time of writing they are regaining territory with the help of heavy Russian air support.

Iran officially denies that it has combat troops engaged in Syria, but numbers of Iranian troops have been killed in action in Syria since January 2013. Iran's supply of weapons and cash to al-Assad is the only reason al-Assad had not been overrun. Iran is the foremost of the enemies of Israel and its deep involvement in Syria is causing deep concern in Israel.

Next to Iran on Israel's list of deadly enemies is the Iranian-funded **Hizb'allah**, which has formidable capabilities, and has thousands of troops fighting on al-Assad's behalf, obtaining valuable combat experience that will eventually be used against Israel.

Russia is on friendly terms with Israel, but in September 2015 it decided to go beyond supplying weapons and aircraft to prop up its ally al-Assad. It moved troops and military equipment into Syria as well as using its fighter jets and attack helicopters to bomb al-Assad's opposition. Russia has been primarily targeting the "moderate" rebel opposition, because it has taken territory from al-Assad's troops. Russia's priority is to prop up al-Assad at all costs. Syria is Russia's only real foothold into the Middle East and therefore cannot allow al-Assad's regime to completely collapse. A statement from Hizb'allah on January 11, 2016, reported in the *Daily Beast*, says that the terror group is now receiving "long-range missiles, laser-guided rockets and other sophisticated weaponry directly from Russia in Syria, and is free to use that weaponry against Israel if it so chooses." Hizb'allah claims that by standing with Russia in its fight to prop up al-Assad, it has become an "ally" of Russia and that Russia is arming the group in its fight against al-Assad. This new development, if true, will pose a new and dangerous situation for Israel.

The brutal **ISIL** (Islamic State in Iraq and the Levant) jihadist group—also known by the acronyms IS, ISIS, and Daesh—has of late become the West's number one enemy following the November Paris attacks, which it funded and orchestrated. ISIL controls large areas of both Syria and Iraq and in June 2014 established a Muslim Caliphate with its headquarters in the city of Raqqa in northern Syria, from which Islam is meant to conquer and rule the world.

Saudi Arabia is the principal financial backer of the Sunni militias who are fighting al-Assad, which include Islamist rebels linked to al-Qaeda.

Iran has mobilized a **network of Shia militias** in Syria, which analysts believe serves as Iran's "Foreign Legion," fighting the Sunni networks of ISIL and al-Qaeda. This network includes Shia **fighters from Afghanistan and Pakistan**.

Various al-Qaeda affiliate groups are battling Assad in Syria, including the feared and cruel **al-Nusra Front**, also known as the Syrian Al Qaeda.

The **Kurds** have been fighting for an independent Kurdistan for decades, and is currently engaged in a bloody war with ISIL and have proven themselves to be the most effective fighting force against ISIL.

At the time of writing **Turkey** is being accused (with good reason) of helping ISIL with weapons and of buying its oil (see following chapter). Turkey has conducted airstrikes in Syria, but the strikes have mostly be against the Kurds fighting ISIS.

A range of what are called "moderate" militias opposed to Assad are referred to generally as the **Free Syrian Army** and their numbers are estimated to be at about 70,000, but they do not share a unified central command and operate in different parts of the country.

U.S. President Barack Obama chickened out and failed to attack al-Assad's forces when they crossed Obama's "red line" of using chemical weapons in 2014. The U.S. has, however, conducted air operations against ISIL, the al-Nusra Front and other jihadi groups, but it was reported on September 22, 2015, that Division 30, a **Pentagon-trained** rebel force in Syria, handed their weapons—"a very large amount of ammunition and medium weaponry and a number of pick-ups"—over to the al-Qaeda affiliated al-Nusra Front immediately after re-entering the country. Russia mocks the U.S., accusing it of "imitating a fight against ISIL."

Following the Paris terror attacks, **France** has played a leading role in rallying support for Western strikes on ISIL, and has significantly stepped up its own air operations.

Britain's RAF has been carrying out fierce air assaults on ISIL in Syria since December 2015.

Due to all the political jockeying by international coalition powers in Syria, hundreds, if not thousands, of Syrians are being denied humanitarian aid. According to the *New York Times* (January 10, 2016) the Syrians in Madaya for example, are starving and dehydrated. They are fenced in by rebel groups with barbed wire, land mines, and snipers, and encircled by

Syria — Chapter 26

pro al-Assad's forces. They have been reduced to making soups of grass, spices, and olive leaves, and eat their donkeys and cats to remain alive.

THE REGIME OF BASHAR AL-ASSAD, a member of an Alawite clan, supported by its two major allies Iran and Hizb'allah, controls only 20 percent of Syria at the time of writing. The years-long civil war has shattered the al-Assad dream of a Greater Syria and reduced it to a virtual fiefdom that includes the capital, Damascus, the coastal strip, which is predominantly populated by Alawites (an ethnic sect of Shi'ite Islam), as well as a small strip in the south adjoining the border with Jordan. With the extensive Russian involvement, the focus of the regime and its Iranian-Russian-Hizb'allah allies allows al-Assad to consolidate the control of his territory and possibly to slowly regain small areas of lost land. Nevertheless, military intelligence estimates, as well as Western intelligence analysis, are that the Russian involvement will only prolong the war and not help to end it.

A perfect storm is brewing in Syria, a storm in which Russia and Iran are reportedly increasing their support for Bashar al-Assad's regime, while Western countries deliberate increasing their involvement in the war-torn country. The fact that Iran, Hizb'allah, and Russia are willing to escalate the conflict by putting troops on the ground and increasing arms shipments means that al-Assad's position in power is assured for the near future. However, the country that was once called Syria will never be the same again. When the fighting ends and the dust settles, what had formerly been a powerful Arab country will be a smattering of small states run by Islamic jihadists who will incessantly attempt to make their particular piece bigger by warring against the neighbors.

Syria was a proud country that was once held in esteem by the Arab world. Today, Syria is ravaged by war, torn and shattered like no other country, broken into so many pieces that, like Humpty Dumpty, it can never be put back together again. Its people have fled and most will never, ever return. On page 250, the judgments of: **Physical catastrophes and widespread death**; **Defeat with high loss of life**; **Destruction of nation**; **Near annihilation**; **Nation conquered and devastated**; and **Judicial cursing or complete destruction of nation** were *forecast 22 years ago*. These judgments have fallen upon Syria, but there is yet more to come *for the* LORD *has a controversy with Syria.*

27

Turkey

Turkey is an ancient civilization, inhabited since the paleolithic age. Turkey, however, is perhaps best remembered for being the seat of the large and powerful Ottoman Empire (often called the Turkish Empire), one of the largest imperial projects in human history, ruling vast Muslim territories in North Africa, the Balkans, and the Middle East for over 500 years. World War I effectively broke up the Empire and victorious allied powers received mandates to rule its provinces in line with the secret 1916 Sykes-Picot Treaty made between Britain and France (see pages 172 and 247). The Syrian Mandate was given to France and Britain was handed the Mandate for Palestine.

Modern Turkey was founded in 1923 by Mustafa Kemal Atatürk who established it as a strictly secular society. Whenever Islamists began to take hold of power the Turkish military would step in and prevent Islam from holding sway over the people, and thus it was until the year 2010.

TURKEY HAS A HISTORY OF ATROCITIES against its minorities. There has been no small amount of condemnation of Turkey for its slaughtering of some 1.5 million Armenians during the World War I era. The vast majority of historians say that the massacres of the Armenian people clearly constituted genocide, but most Western nations keep their eyes fixed on commercial activity with Turkey and dodge labeling the slaughtering of the Armenians as genocide. Israel has followed suit and avoided the issue because it wants to keep relations open with Turkey; however, the 2010 *Mavi Marmara* incident that torpedoed Israel-Turkey relations might bring an about-turn. Already, the Jewish public policy umbrella (JCPA) called on the U.S. government to recognize the massacres of Armenians as a genocide, a reversal of years of the Jewish community treading delicately around the issue.

KURDS IN TURKEY NUMBER AROUND 15 million persons and make up the largest ethnic minority in the country. The Kurds speak an Indo-European language and live in all areas of Turkey, but are primarily concentrated in the east and the southeast of the country—the Kurdistan region. Massacres of Kurds by Turkish troops have periodically occurred since the establishment of the Republic of Turkey in 1923, massacres such as the Zilan massacre in

1930, in which between 15,000 – 40,000 Kurds were killed, and the Dersim massacre of 1937 – 1938, in which some 80,000 Kurds were killed.

In an attempt to deny their existence, the words "Kurds," "Kurdistan," or "Kurdish" were banned by the Turkish government. Following the third military coup in 1980, the Kurdish language was officially prohibited in both public and private life. Many people who spoke, published, or sang in Kurdish were arrested and imprisoned. Since the ban was lifted in 1991, the Kurds of Turkey have sought to have Kurdish included as a language of instruction in public schools as well as being taught as a subject.

ON JULY 20, 1974, TURKEY LAUNCHED an invasion of the Greek-Cypriot island country of Cyprus. The invasion followed the July 15, 1974, deposing of the Cypriot president Archbishop Makarios III when sections of the Cypriot National Guard, led by its Greek officers, overthrew the government. The small ethnic-Turk population was being allocated government positions out of all proportion to the size of its ethnicity, drawing the ire of both the Cypriot and Greek ethnic populations, which comprised a majority 82 percent of the population. After Makarios was deposed the Hellenic Republic of Cyprus was declared, and Turkey resorted to war five days later.

In July 1974, 40,000 Turkish forces invaded Cyprus, and with an additional 12,500 Turkish Cypriot troops, captured three percent of the island before a cease-fire was declared. The Greek military junta with only 12,000 troops at its disposal collapsed and was replaced by a democratic government. In August 1974, however, a second Turkish invasion resulted in the capture of approximately 40 percent of the island and the ceasefire line from August 1974 became the UN Buffer Zone in Cyprus. Over a quarter of the population of Cyprus—one-third of the Greek Cypriot population— was expelled from the Turkish-occupied northern part of the island where Greek Cypriots constituted 80 percent of the population. (A Greek-Cypriot family hosted the author on the island in 1984. They recounted how they lost their home, its contents, and their bakery business in the northern part of the island when the Turks drove them out.) A little over a year later some 60,000 Turkish Cypriots, constituting half of the Turkish Cypriot population, were displaced from the south to the north. The Turkish invasion ended in the partition of Cyprus along the UN-monitored Buffer Zone, which still divides Cyprus. In 1983 the Turkish Republic of Northern Cyprus (TRNC) declared independence, but Turkey is the only country recognizing it. The international community considers the TRNC's territory to be Turkish-occupied territory of the Republic of Cyprus. Turkey's occupation is held to be illegal under international law, which constitutes illegal occupation of EU territory since Cyprus became a member on May 1, 2004 and EU legislation is suspended in the territory occupied by Turkey. A good half of the world gnashes its teeth at tiny Israel over land it captured in wars of self defense — wars that were forced upon it — but it turns blind eyes to a powerful Turkey that seized almost half of an entire country through unbridled, unprovoked military aggression.

IN JULY 2015 IT WAS REVEALED by a courier who worked for an Iranian businessman that Turkish President Recep Tayyip Erdoğan and a family member were involved in the complex graft operation. The Turkish government bought oil and natural gas from Iran in exchange for as much as $20 billion in gold, in a scheme designed to evade international sanctions. A *quid pro quo* agreement allowed Turkey, an energy-starved country, to, in violation of UN sanctions, obtain Iranian oil and gas. To avoid detection, the cash was apparently deposited in a Halkbank account in Turkey. The money was then converted to gold and transferred to Tehran, reportedly through the Dubai free-trade zone.

IN THE 1990s AND EARLY 2000s Israel enjoyed good diplomatic and commercial relations with Turkey, even to the extent of being able to use Turkey's open airspace to train IAF pilots. With the rising fortunes of Recep Tayyip Erdoğan and his Justice and Development party (AKP), relations with Israel began to cool, then slowly got frosty. Relations went into deepfreeze following the Turkish-owned ship *Mavi Marmara* attempting to break Israel's sea blockade of the Gaza Strip in May 2010, in which 10 Turkish nationals lost their lives. Israel's blockade was and is ruled legal under international law and was established in order to prevent the smuggling of weapons and explosives into the Strip for use by Hamas terrorists against Israel.

The *Mavi Marmara* was one of six ships that made up the fleet called the "Gaza Freedom Flotilla." After refusing to alter course and head for an Israeli port, where its cargo would be inspected before being transferred by truck into Gaza, it was boarded by Israeli commandos armed with paintball guns. The other five ships offered only passive resistance, but some 40 activists from among the 590 passengers on board the *Mavi Marmara* attacked the Israeli commandos with chains, iron bars, and knives, injuring a number of commandos, one seriously. Shots were also fired at the Israelis, who were forced to use their personal sidearms in self defense. The Turks were members of the Foundation for Human Rights and Freedoms (IHH), a radical Islamic group which, the *New York Times*, in a June 11, 2010, editorial, said, "At least some of the activists on the lead ship, the *Mavi Marmara*, were seeking a confrontation – and got one."

Israel had asked the then Turkish Prime Minister Recep Tayyip Erdoğan to prevent the ship from sailing, but he said that he could not interfere because the ship was undertaking a private journey. Erdoğan, a hardline Islamist, obviously preferred picking a fight with Israel, and from that day until the present time the fight is ongoing. Erdoğan demanded an apology from Israel for killing eight Turkish citizens and one Turkish-American (another Turk who had been in a coma died four years later). Erdoğan demanded millions of dollars in compensation for the families of those killed, together with a complete end to Israel's land and sea blockade of Gaza.

President Barack Obama engineered a telephone call between Israeli Prime Minister Netanyahu and Erdoğan, in which Netanyahu "apologized" if there had been "operational failures" on Israel's part during the interception of the *Mavi Marmara*. Until Obama called Erdoğan and handed Netanyahu his phone and saying, "Be nice," Israel had been adamant that it would not apologize for defending itself. In a bid to restore relations Israel has since offered a $20 million compensation package providing Turkey agrees to drop international criminal charges against the ministers and IDF officers who oversaw the interception of the *Mavi Marmara*—not much progress has been made with the Turks since the offer was made in February 2013. Israel believes Erdoğan simply wants to humiliate Israel internationally.

THE TURKISH AKP PARTY WAS FOUNDED by Recep Tayyip Erdoğan in 2001 and he has been its longtime leader. AKP is an Islamic party with an ideology mirroring that of the Muslim Brotherhood, of which Hamas is an offshoot.

Erdoğan served as Turkey's Prime Minister from 2003 to 2014 and became President of Turkey in August 2014. He partly designed and built himself (in breach of court orders) a presidential palace in protected forest land at a cost far in excess of $600 million. Additional to this is the cost of thousands of imported Italian trees at a median price of $6,875 each. Erdoğan has since installed himself into *Ak Saray* (White Palace), which is the biggest residential palace in the world, boasting 1,000 rooms and has a floor area of 3.1 million square feet (288,000 square meters).The White Palace is larger than either the White House or the Kremlin and is four times the size of Versailles, allowing Erdoğan to surpass the residential grandeur of Louis XIV of France. The monthly electricity bill—paid for by Turkish taxpayers—is expected to be in the vicinity of $313,000. Erdoğan has also spent $174.25 million on a new presidential jet designed to his own specifications.

President Recep Tayyip Erdoğan seeks to change Turkey's constitution to allow him autocratic rule, which would effectually make him Sultan of Turkey.

Erdoğan, now president, suffered a stinging electoral defeat in the June 2015 general elections which left his party without a majority in Parliament and which seemingly dashed his hopes of getting the supermajority required to change the constitution and establish an executive presidency whereby he could run the country from the presidency. AKP's denial of an outright majority in June was due to a rise in votes for the pro-Kurdish Peoples' Democratic party (HDP). Denied the majority he sought meant Erdoğan needed to form a coalition government. Erdoğan covertly prevented any coalition from being formed, and in a calculated strategy initiated military operations against the separatist Kurdistan Workers' Party (PKK) in order to turn voters away from the pro-Kurdish HDP. War with the Kurds was simply being used as a tool to reverse the Erdoğan election defeat. He called snap elections in November 2015 and the AKP was returned to power, although Erdoğan still did not obtain the desired supermajority.

DURING ERDOĞAN'S YEARS AT TURKEY'S HELM he has consistently steered a course of slow, but systematic Islamification of the country. Women must now wear the hijab (headscarf) and Islamic studies have become mandatory in all schools. Areas for prayer have had to be built in both existing and new workplaces and shopping malls, and the construction of mosques has been intensified.

Erdoğan, being a hardline Islamist, is a ardent supporter of the Hamas terror organization, but he rejects the notion that it a terrorist group. Turkey, under the country's Directorate of Religious Affairs, has begun the rebuilding of nine mosques in Gaza that were destroyed in Operation Protective Edge, the 2014 war between Israel and Hamas in which around 5,000 rockets and mortars were fired into Israel's civilian centers.

Turkey plays host to Hamas politburo leader Khaled Mashaal who lives in exile in Qatar. Mashaal arrived in Turkey in September 2015 at the head of a delegation from the Hamas terror group and attended the conference of the ruling AKP in Ankara. The delegation included Jihad Yarmur, a member of the Hamas cell that kidnapped and murdered an IDF soldier, and who was released from an Israeli prison in 2011 as one of the 1,027 Palestinian terrorists exchanged for a single kidnapped soldier, Gilad Shalit.

Mashaal has met with Turkish President Recep Tayyip Erdoğan at least twice in the past year; and Israel blames Turkey for the 2015 flare up in Palestinian terrorism because it houses Saleh al-Arouri, a senior Hamas terrorist. Israel says Saleh al-Arouri is in charge of training terror cells in the West Bank and is remotely organizing Palestinian violence. Saleh al-Arouri was behind the kidnapping and murder of three Israeli teenagers—Gilad Sha'er, aged 16 years, Naftali Fraenkel, also aged 16, and Eyal Yifrach, aged 19 years—in June 2014, which sparked the 2014 Gaza War, officially known as Operation Protective Edge. Seventy-one Israelis, including a four-year-old boy, were killed along with some 2,200 Gazans, of which over 50 percent were terrorists.

On June 10, 2015, the Israeli Hebrew daily *Ha'aretz* reported that Erdoğan had asked a senior member of Hamas's military wing based in Turkey "to cut back on his anti-Israel terrorist activity, due to fears that the U.S. will accuse Turkey of abetting terror." The request was transmitted to Saleh al-Aruri by Turkish intelligence, which is well aware of his activities. Israel deported al-Aruri from the West Bank in 2010.

At the time of writing al-Aruri, from his base in Turkey, commands Hamas's West Bank division, meaning he is responsible for building the organization's terror infrastructure in the West Bank (Biblical Judea and Samaria). His responsibilities include recruiting operatives, transferring money to them and giving them general instructions. Other Hamas operatives from the West Bank also live in Turkey, and Israeli defense officials recently said Hamas was running terrorist training camps in the country, while Turkish authorities turned a blind eye. This accusation apparently spurred the U.S. to demand explanations from Turkey, and in response, Ankara asked al-Aruri to lower the profile of his activities.

CRITICISM OF ERDOĞAN HOLDS ITS OWN perils; political opponents can end up in prison on trumped-up charges. Those daring enough to criticize him through print or electronic media find their newspapers or broadcasting studios fined and shuttered. Erdoğan silences every critical voice and over 300 journalists have lost their jobs since 2013. Confronted with widespread protests that began in May 2013, then Prime Minister Recep Tayyip Erdoğan ordered an extreme police crackdown and labeled the demonstrators as traitors and spies. And faced with a corruption inquiry focused on his inner political circle, he responded by purging the police and judiciary. Local media reported that Erdoğan's government removed a total of 560 police officers. It was the latest twist in a vast corruption scandal that ensnared Erdoğan's key allies. The officers, including the powerful Istanbul police chief, were sacked by a government decree published at midnight and included chiefs of the financial crimes, anti-smuggling, cyber crime, and organized crime units.

It was said earlier that Erdoğan has steered a course of slow, but systematic Islamification of Turkey. In fact Erdoğan has transformed Turkey from a secular state into an Islamist state. To ensure the military did not step in and slow the halt of his Islamization as it had done in years past, Erdoğan stomped on the army as he later did with the police and judiciary. The army issued a statement of its interests in which it said that:

> the army is a party to arguments regarding secularism; that Islamism ran counter to the secular nature of Turkey, and to the legacy of Mustafa Kemal Atatürk.

The Army's statement ended with a clear warning that the Turkish Armed Forces (TAF) stood ready to intervene if the secular nature of the Turkish Constitution is compromised, stating:

> the Turkish Armed Forces maintain their sound determination to carry out their duties stemming from laws to protect the unchangeable characteristics of the Republic of Turkey. Their loyalty to this determination is absolute.

Over 100 people, including several generals, have been detained or questioned with respect to having ties to members of the country's military and security forces, which is accused of terrorism in Turkey. These accusations are reported in the counter-secular and Islamist media even while the trials are taking place. In February 2010 more than 40 officers were arrested and then formally charged with attempting to overthrow the government with respect to a planned coup attempt to overthrow Erdoğan and the AKP. They include four admirals, a general and two colonels, some of them retired, including former commanders of the Turkish navy and air force. The *Washington Post* reported in April 2010 that the military's power had decreased.

On the eve of the Supreme Military Council of August 2011, the Chief of the General Staff, along with the Army, Navy, and Air Force commanders, requested their retirement, in protest of the mass arrests which they perceived as a deliberate and planned attack against the Kemalist and secular-minded officers of the Turkish Armed Forces by the Islamists in Turkey, who began to control key positions in the Turkish government, judiciary and police. There was a swift replacement of the force commanders in the Supreme Military Council meeting which cemented Erdoğan's firm control over the appointment of top-level commanders.

IT WAS STATED EARLIER THAT ERDOĞAN initiated military strikes against the separatist PKK following the electoral loss of his majority in the June 2015 general elections. The strikes against the PKK were sold to the Turkish public as being predominantly strikes against ISIL in Syria, but in fact the strikes have been primarily against Kurdish forces who have been the only fighters effectively dealing with ISIL in Iraq and Syria. Erdoğan has a problem with the Kurds, and at the time of writing the Kurdish Peshmerga forces have been routing ISIL fighters in a number of areas in Syria and now control more than half of Syria's 560 mile (900 kilometer) border with Turkey. Apparently, Erdoğan is afraid the PKK forces in Iraq will join with their Peshmerga brethren fighting in Syria, turn against Turkish troops and join the area captured from ISIL in Syria with the area of Iraq under Kurdish control, thus establishing a large independent Kurdistan. With a world Kurdish population of around 30 million (all but 1.5 million living in proximity to each other in the Middle East) it is past time that a sovereign, independent Kurdistan came into being. Thus Erdoğan is attempting to prevent this from happening by bombing the Kurds fighting ISIL in both Syria and Iraq.

RUSSIA ENTERED THE SYRIAN WAR ON behalf of its ally Bashar al-Assad and is bombing virtually everyone who is fighting al-Assad's troops. Erdoğan, however, in a mindless move, warned Russia that its jets would be shot down if they encroached—however inadvertently—into Turkish airspace. On November 24, 2015, Turkish fighter jets shot down a Russian Sukhoi SU-24 bomber with a surface-to-surface missile as it operated along the Syrian border with Turkey. Russian President Vladimir Putin called it "a stab in the back" and his rage is unquenchable at this time.

Russian radar images show the Russian bomber to have been in Syrian airspace when it was shot down. One Russian pilot died and a Russian rescue helicopter engineer was shot dead by Turkmen (Syrians with Turkish ancestry) as they rescued the surviving pilot. Putin ordered upgraded SU-34 fighter planes and warships brought into the area and every Russian bomber now has an escort of fighter-jets on their missions. Putin also had Russia's state-of-the-art S-400 air defense missile system brought into active service in Syria. The S-400 is the most sophisticated ground-to-air defense system in the world and is able to bring down multiple aircraft with a single missile—up to 250 miles (400 kilometers) away. The Russian president has not only slapped various sanctions on Turkey, but Syrian rebels reported that Russian bombers were pounding areas in Syria's Latakia province, on Turkey's border, unleashing a wave of airstrikes on mountains near where the SU-24 warplane was shot down. A spokesman for a rebel brigade in the region, said the Russians were taking "revenge" for its plane being downed by Turkey, a key backer of the rebels in the area.

Turkey — Chapter 27

Russia is also humiliating Erdoğan by targeting the Turkish economy in retaliation for downing the warplane. Putin is holding up truck convoys transporting Turkish foodstuffs into Russia at the border crossings while Russian inspectors slowly and tediously inspect everything. Russia has rejected tons of fruit and vegetable and has put out feelers to other countries with a view to curtailing Turkish exports of food foodstuffs.

On November 25 President Putin said, in reference to the downing of a multi-million dollar jet bomber by an ally:

> The problem is not the tragedy we witnessed yesterday. The problem is much deeper. We observe ... that the current Turkish leadership over a significant number of years has been pursuing a deliberate policy of supporting the Islamization of their country. Only Allah knows why they did it. I guess Allah decided to punish the ruling clique in Turkey by stripping it of its sanity.

Due to the brouhaha over the downing of the Russian jet bomber, NATO, of which Turkey is a member, has taken over the patrolling of the borders to limit "incidents" between allies. Turkey's action against the Russian plane was called "stupid" and Erdoğan was asked why his planes could not just have "escorted" the friendly plane back across the border if it inadvertently strayed into Turkish airspace. (Turkey has for years prevented Israel from becoming a member of NATO).

EARLIER, PUTIN ACCUSED TURKISH PRESIDENT RECEP Tayyip Erdoğan and his country's government of both propping up and enabling ISIL by buying its oil which is smuggled in from Syria. Erdoğan was beside himself and spluttered that he would resign if there was any truth to the accusations. Putin, however, later repeated his accusations and said Russia has received additional intelligence confirming that oil from deposits controlled by Islamic State is moved through Turkey on an industrial scale. Putin went further:

> We have every reason to believe that the decision to down our plane was guided by a desire to ensure security of this oil's delivery routes to ports where they are shipped in tankers.

Apparently, where there is smoke there is fire: On December 20, 2015, the Norwegian daily *Klassekampen* published a leaked report on illegal oil sales by ISIL, which was ordered to be compiled by Norway. The report revealed that most of the ISIL-smuggled oil has been destined for Turkey, where it is transported by tankers via smuggling routes across the border and sold off at bargain low prices.

It was mentioned before that the Kurdish Peshmerga forces are a powerful fighting force against ISIL. And in the summer of 2015 the Kurds overran the ISIL-held town of Tel Abyad and subsequently took possession of ISIL records. Kurdish commanders seized seven passenger manifests from December 2014 to March 2015, which showed ISIL ran a sophisticated immigration operation through a Syrian border town with Turkey, until its defeat by Kurds during the summer. The documents carry the stamps of ISIL's "*department of immigration*" and "*department of transport*." They show that buses passed through the town having submitted the names, dates of births, ID numbers and even birthplace of travelers.

It is almost inconceivable that an operation of such scope could have been kept under wraps without the acquiescence of Turkish officials. The passenger manifests, countersigned by travel agents in Mosul, Iraq, and Raqqa, Syria, overtly suggest that there was a period of formalized passage on the Syrian side of the border. The border crossing remained open until Kurdish forces took control of the town in June 2015, at which point Turkey promptly sealed it. David Phillips, a Columbia University academic and the author of two recent research papers into links between Turkey and ISIL, told the *Guardian* that the country "knows the movements of all persons and can control the flow across the border if it chooses."

Even more damning for Turkey was a December 28, 2015, article in *RT* which claimed Turkey is training ISIL terrorists in a camp disguised as a training ground for the Western-backed Free Syrian Army. Captured by Kurdish fighters in Northern Syria in November 2015, Abdurrahman Abdulhadi, a 20-year-old Syrian national said he was trained in Turkey before receiving his first assignment with ISIL in Syria. Another jihadist captured by the Kurds in June 2015 is 24-year-old Mahmud Ghazi Tatar, who told *RT* that he joined ISIL from the Turkish city of Adiyaman and, together with other recruits, he was transported over the border into Syria where he received terrorist training. "At the training camp in May 2015, our commander told us that the group sells fuel to Turkey and that the income covers ISIL's costs." Tatar said the "oil trucks crossing into Turkey every day carry crude oil, as well as petrol."

A video was also made in Syria, just over the Turkish border, of a Turkish military vehicle loaded with weapons for ISIL—the "smugglers" were non other than members of the official Turkish Intelligence. The video was quickly pulled from the internet and the people involved in the uploading of it were arrested and imprisoned as "traitors." Obviously, Turkey is undermining coalition efforts against ISIL in every which way.

Turkey — Chapter 27

Diplomats said the U.S. and European allies are pressuring Erdoğan to do more against ISIL in Syria—including sealing a section of Turkey's border crossed by ISIL fighters and oil smugglers—while avoiding further incidents with Russia and to restart a peace process with the Kurds in southeastern Turkey. Turkey's porous border has been the transit point for thousands of jihadists from Western countries to enter Syria and join the fighting.

TURKISH MILITARY SET UP A "TRAINING camp" in Iraq, but the Iraqi government repeatedly demanded a full withdrawal of Turkish troops from its territory, saying that Turkey must respect Iraqi sovereignty. Turkey, however, refused to withdraw its troops saying that "it is out of the question." Iraq experts say that Turkey's real purpose for being in Iraq is to fight the Kurdish PKK and that Turkey aims to split Iraq into three independent areas. There would be a government, but they would remain divided, which is in line with Turkish interests. Iraq has its hands full with fighting ISIL and is making headway against it, but it does not have the manpower to engage Turkish militarily as well.

On December 18, 2015, Iraq took the issue to the United Nations, demanding that Turkey withdraws its troops from northern Iraq immediately. Turkey countered by saying that Iraq's demand serves no other purpose than to undermine the "solidarity of the international community against ISIL." The UN Security Council, however, ordered Turkey to withdraw its troops.

ERDOĞAN'S BELLIGERENCE TOWARD ISRAEL SINCE THE *Mavi Marmara* incident allowed Israel to deepen diplomatic and business relationships with Greece and Cyprus, traditional enemies of Turkey. Relations and commercial ties between the three have blossomed. Israel is also helping Cyprus locate and drill its offshore gas fields, much to the chagrin of Erdoğan who claims the waters around Cyprus belong not only to Cyprus but to Turkey also.

Turkey's shooting down of the Russian bomber in November 2015 is reaping an unexpected but very fruitful harvest for Israel. Erdoğan is feeling increasingly isolated both in the region and internationally, and has begun trying to soothe Israel's ruffled feathers by speaking about rapprochement with Israel after years of harsh rhetoric and actions. Erdoğan's charm offensive has nothing to do with a change of heart, but everything to do with the crisis with Russia.

Erdoğan must have thought about offsetting the potential loss of Russian energy—more than half of Turkey's gas and 10 percent of its oil come from Russia, and Israel has recently tapped into some of the largest fields of natural gas in the world. Suddenly, the ruling Islamist AKP allowed the first ever public Hanukkah event to take place in Turkey on December 13, 2015, in Istanbul. Erdoğan followed that up the following day by speaking positively of normalizing relations with Israel; he said, "the entire region would have much to gain from normalized ties."

On December 17, 2015, Israelis awoke to headlines that screamed: **ISRAEL AND TURKEY ON VERGE OF DRAMATIC REVIVAL OF TIES**. Apparently, secret talks were held in Switzerland between high-ranking Israel leaders and the director general of the Turkish Foreign Ministry. According to an Israeli official of the Prime Minister's Office, the as yet unsigned agreement provides for:

> both countries to return their ambassadors; a cancellation of pending lawsuits against IDF soldiers; the establishment by Israel of a fund for the welfare of victims of the 2010 *Mavi Marmara* incident; a Turkish commitment not to tolerate any "terrorist activities" on its sovereign territory; Turkey barring from its soil Salah al-Arouri, the Hamas operative who orchestrated the kidnapping and killing of three Israeli teens in the West Bank in June 2014; Turkey allowing Israel to lay down a gas pipeline on its soil; and the opening of immediate negotiations on the sale of natural gas from Israel to Turkey.

On December 19, 2015, the Turkish *Today's Zaman* quoted former foreign minister Hikmet Cetin, of the Kemalist opposition Republican People's Party, as welcoming the deal, and saying it came five years too late. Cetin was quoted as saying:

> We started off with a "Zero problems with neighbors." Now we have no neighbors left. Turkey is isolated in the region. However, even if Turkey were not so isolated, I would still have welcomed the news as Turkey needs good relations with Israel.

The former foreign minister also said:

> the *Marmara* incident was an unfortunate event, but **the ship should have heeded warnings and never set sail in the first place**.

Not everyone in Turkey agreed with Cetin: *Today's Zaman* also quoted the Foundation for Human Rights and Freedoms (IHH), the radical Islamic group that organized the *Mavi Marmara* voyage to Gaza, as severely criticizing the deal, saying that it served neither the interests of Turkey nor the Palestinians.

> An agreement with Israel, especially one that is detrimental to the *Mavi Marmara*, will negatively affect both Turkey and Gaza.

Turkey — Chapter 27

DESPITE THE DRUM ROLLS ABOUT RENEWING relations with Israel, Turkish President Recep Tayyip Erdoğan met again with the Hamas kingpin, Khaled Mashaal, on December 19, 2015, in Istanbul. A Hamas source told *Kol Yisrael* that Erdoğan made no mention of a change in Turkey's stance toward Hamas; however, Israeli media reports that Salah al-Arouri has since left the country, albeit his Hamas-controlled office continues to operate.

Not everyone in Israel is happy about a possible rapprochement with Turkey. Giving in to Erdoğan's demands has been likened to making a pact with the devil.

THERE MAY BE A POLITICAL RAPPROCHEMENT between Turkey and Israel, but the ball is still in play. If it happens it would only be because Turkey shot down a Russian bomber that apparently strayed into Turkish airspace for a matter of seconds. And if Russia and Turkey settle their differences Erdoğan may again vent his anti-Israel rage upon the Jewish state again. Empires have risen and fallen because of a single short-lived moment of time when someone miscalculated its possible fallout.

Sins of Turkey touched upon are:

a) Unprovoked military aggression
b) Murder, perverse and immoral behavior
c) Military aggression to enlarge territory
d) Extreme cruelty in times of war
e) Discriminating against strangers (includes racial discrimination)
f) Pride in national security
g) Breaking of political agreements
h) Fraudulent, deceitful and crafty business transactions
i) Allies of those waging war against Israel
j) Anti-Semitism-political, racial and religious
k) Rejection of God
l) Extreme cruelty in times of war
m) Rejoicing at another nation's misfortunes (especially Israel's)
n) Suppressing or Hindering the preaching of the Gospel
o) Refusal to hear and live by God's Word
p) Slavery and Oppression
q) Using power and wealth to make lesser nations subservient

The judgments are, therefore: **Defeat with high loss of life**; **Physical catastrophes and widespread death** (three times); **Destruction of nation** (seven times); **Acceleration of nation's destruction; Judicial cursing or complete destruction of nation; Near annihilation** (three times); and Nation conquered and devastated.

Turkey has a history of murder, oppression, and cruelty—for this the old Turkish (Ottoman) empire paid a heavy price. Modern Turkey has resorted to its former ways, and also plays with fire regarding God's people, Israel. A hundred years of sin must and will be wiped away—*for the* L*ORD* *has a NEW controversy with Turkey.*

28

Armageddon

We have dealt briefly with a few sins of a few nations. The dilemma faced by the writer of the book to the Hebrews (Hebrews 11:32) accosts me also: *"And what more shall I say? For the time would fail me to tell of"* the sins of other nations which could and should be in this book. Time would fail me to tell of Spain's memorable year of 1492, when Columbus "sailed the ocean blue" and discovered the Americas—that same memorable year of tragedy in Jewish history. After having lived in Spain for over 1,500 years, all Jews were expelled on pain of death—they were allowed to take little else than the clothes they wore, and Spain began her journey downward from being a great world power. Time would fail me to tell of Pakistan's bitter hatred of the Jewish state, and the signs displayed on street corners calling for "Death to Israel!" Time would fail me to tell of the sins of Argentina, Austria, Belgium, Croatia, Denmark, Egypt, Finland, Greece, Hungary, Ireland, Jordan, Korea (North), Lebanon, Malaysia, Philippines (the), Poland, Qatar, Russia, Saudi Arabia, South Africa, Sudan, Sweden, Switzerland, Tunisia, Uganda, Venezuela, Yemen, Zimbabwe—or a host of other countries too numerous to name. But I reiterate what I have said previously, that the reader can, if he is somewhat abreast of his nation's political, religious, and moral attitudes, intelligently utilize the lessons learned from our studies. He can apply the given judgments to specific sins, and foretell with more than reasonable certainty and accuracy, God's determined future for his nation.

AS IT WAS SAID IN THE introduction to this book (page x), the majority of people feel that repentance is for other people, not for themselves; for other nations, and not for their own. It is for this reason that we are hurtling toward the last book of the Bible, called the *Revelation*, meaning the "Unveiling" of Jesus Christ. It is often called the Apocalypse—for obvious reasons to those who have read it—because it is all about the judgment and destruction of the nations. That book would never have been written and inspired by the Holy Spirit if the LORD had not foreseen that most inhabitants of this earth would not repent of their evil ways. Thus this book *SAGA* is a call to both personal and national repentance, a desperate plea for people to change their ways before it is too late, either for them or for their countries. Both man and nations are under severe judgment, but just as the people of Nineveh repented (Jonah 3:4–5) and were saved from judgment, so individuals, cities, and nations today can stave off the judgments against them.

In a number of places the Bible speaks of *"the Day of the Lord,"* or *"that Day,"* but it will not be as simple as judgment falling on a single day and everything goes back to what was before, because the word "day" in Greek is *hemera*, which can mean a single "day," a "time period," or a "lifetime." We also read in *Revelation*: *"in the **days** of the sounding of the seventh angel"* (Revelation 10:7), which make it clear that judgments are prolonged. And just as man is shown to do in *Revelation*, so it is with man today: when catastrophes strike, he curses God but does not repent of his deeds:

> *And men were scorched with great heat, and they blasphemed the name of God who has power over these plagues; and **they did not repent** and give Him glory* (Revelation 16:9).

> *They blasphemed the God of heaven because of their pains and their sores, and **did not repent of their deeds*** (Revelation 16:11).

> *And great hail from heaven fell upon men, each hailstone about the weight of a talent. Men **blasphemed God** because of the plague of the hail, since that plague was exceedingly great* (Revelation 16:21).

Individuals and nations must make their peace with God through His Son Jesus Christ who came expressly to give them life, eternal life. Once man enters that *Day* of judgment it will be all over bar the shouting for most of this world's inhabitants. "But," a reader may say, "God is love, He cannot destroy man because God is love." It was God's love that sent Jesus to die on the cross at Calvary. Jesus is God's atonement for sin. God can only forgive man through the shed blood of Jesus, to do otherwise would mean that God is unjust. The blood of Jesus Christ is the outworking of God's love and it washes away a man's sin. Jesus said:

> *I am the resurrection and the life. He who believes in Me, though he may die, he shall live. And **whoever lives and believes in Me shall never die**. Do you believe this?* (John 11:25–26).

Jesus' question is directed at you, the reader.

THE PAST 50 YEARS HAVE SEEN unbelievable prosperity, and the development of high-technology is unsurpassed in world history. Nations, however, are falling apart, empires are crumbling, disease, famine and war are taking a monumentally massive toll on human life. Men can be propelled into space

Armageddon — Chapter 28

to walk on the moon or among the stars, but they cannot cure the ills of a sick and dying planet.

For every nation mentioned within the pages of this book, Israel has been, or is, the watershed between downfall and prosperity. Israel has also been, and still is, a pawn in a diplomatic game between nations. The objective of the game is to win the political support of the Arab states, and thus gain access to their vast reserves of oil and petro-dollars. Oil not only lubricates the wheels of commerce, it also greases the palms of businessmen, diplomats, politicians and presidents; and decisions are formulated according to the degree of need or greed. Libya's refusal to hand over two terrorists implicated in the blowing up of a *Pan Am* jumbo-jet over Scotland in 1988, brought United Nations sanctions, but according to *U.S. News & World Report*, April 13, 1992: "The oil trade—97 percent of Libya's exports—was excluded from the embargo because Libyan oil is vital to Europe, principally to Germany and Italy" [two members of the G-8—the wealthiest nations in the world]. If Israel had oil or money like the Arab states, the nations of the world would court her also. Israel is only on the verge of extracting oil from its territory today, until it has proven oil reserves and money to burn few world leaders will intervene or even shed a tear if Israel becomes in danger of annihilation.

The nations of the world do not take Israel's God into account when making their diplomatic bluffs and economic calculations. They seem too preoccupied with the enhancement of their own selfish interests at the expense of others. We should ask ourselves: "Where now is Ur of the Chaldees? Where now is Babylon the Great? Where now are the other former empires of the world?" These civilizations lie in ruins—*"haunts of jackals, objects of horror and scorn, places where no one lives"* (Jeremiah 51:37). But Israel lives again on its God-given inheritance, and Jerusalem—the only city with an eternal future—is bathed with golden light, ever expanding, ever more beautiful. Israel has expanded in every direction—in population, in economics, in high-tech and innovation, even in territory. Throughout these pages we have seen that Israel's blessings are a direct result of the promises made to Abraham by the LORD GOD of Israel:

> *By Myself I have sworn, says the LORD ...* **"In blessing I will bless you, and in multiplying I will multiply your descendants as the stars of the heaven and as the sand which is on the seashore; and your descendants shall possess the gate of their enemies***"*
>
> (Genesis 22:16,17).

The Bible tells us that God made this promise to Abraham with an oath, and because *"He could swear by no one greater, He swore by Himself"* (Hebrews 6:13). The Lord swore that Israel would be blessed, and Israel currently leads the world in economic growth. The Lord swore that the population of the Jewish state would multiply, and Israel's population has in creased from 600,000 to 8,400,000 in 67 years. The Lord swore that Israel would possess the cities of their enemies, and it has decisively defeated every combination of nations that has attacked the Jewish state—expanding its territory as a result of each attack.

In the past, many nations have endeavored to annihilate Israel, but they themselves were extinguished. Israel's enemies of today, like Saddam Hussein did, call for the "extermination of the Zionist entity," but it was Saddam and Iraq that got exterminated. Israel's enemies who launched wars against Israel, and lost, apparently forgot that the God of Israel is a Zionist too, and that He has said of Israel:

You are my war club, My weapon for battle—with you I shatter nations, with you I destroy kingdoms (Jeremiah 51:20 NIV).

WHAT OF THE FUTURE? THE BIBLE tells us that many nations will come together to make war against Israel. *"Multitudes"* will gather in *"the valley of Jehoshaphat"* (Joel 3:1–2,12,14). Jehoshaphat—Hebrew *Yehoshaphat*—means "the Lord judges," and few from the nations will survive. And many nations will again array their armies against Israel, assembling themselves for the great battle of *Armageddon*—the final and most dreadful conflict of the age. The name *Armageddon* is derived from the Hebrew *Har Meggido*, meaning the "Hill of Megiddo," which is situated at the southern end of the Jezreel valley. The Jezreel valley—Hebrew *Yizrael*—meaning "God scatters," is known as the graveyard of kingdoms. Many decisive battles have already been fought in this valley, and many kings have died in it. The valley is also known as the valley of Megiddo, and when Napoleon cast his eyes upon it he called it **"the world's greatest battlefield**." It is here that Israel's God, the Lord of armies, will fight the last war against the nations and destroy them like He destroyed the Egyptians, the Assyrians, the Babylonians, the Ethiopians and others, thousands of years ago.

Not every nation will enter into battle with Israel. Some will suffer atomic, chemical, or biological warfare—destroyed by maniacal leaders settling old grievances. Others will die like the Soviet Union—without a single shot being fired, and without Israeli participation. It took 74 years

Armageddon — Chapter 28

from the birth of the Communist empire in 1917 to its death in 1991. The LORD GOD of Israel took five smooth stones of judgment from the river of His wrath—struck the giant between the eyes, and then cut off its head.

TIME International, July 12, 1993, said the "Soviet empire's death" was so abrupt—"No one ... believed it could happen." Abba Eban wrote in *Personal Witness*:

> There has not been a single prediction that could prepare anyone to believe that the Communist empire would end its life in the way that it did.

TIME and Eban had one thing in common—they were both wrong! A good number of Christians predicted the collapse of the Soviet Union. Her godlessness, her attitude toward Israel, and her treatment of Soviet Jewry made her collapse inevitable. I predict total collapse for each of the other 14 nations that have been included in this book. And not for those only, but also for the ones listed at the beginning of this chapter, and others as well. Israel will not be brought to its knees like other nations only because of the LORD's promises, but it will certainly not escape judgment from His hand. Neither will the Church escape judgment, like Israel, it also must be purified. How much time the Church or any particular nation has before judgment falls is known only to the Judge.

IT WAS THE GOD OF ISRAEL that personally struck down all the firstborn of man and beast in Egypt (Exodus 11:4, 12:12–13, 27, 29). It was the God of Israel who personally fought against the Egyptians at the Red Sea (Exodus 14:24–25). And it was the God of Israel who personally brought each individual catastrophe upon Egypt (Exodus 7:17, 8:2, 19, 21, 9:6, 18, 10:4). These calamities were judgments (Exodus 6:6, 7:4, 12:12) inflicted upon Egypt for its sins. And we have shown from the Scriptures in previous pages, the disasters befalling nations today are coming directly from the outstretched arm of the LORD GOD of Israel—as judgments upon those nations. But modem man is like Pharaoh was—hard of heart and dull and insensitive to the voice of the LORD.

When man stops sinning, God will stop catastrophes and wars, but not before. God has made it abundantly clear in the Bible that there will be no further wars when there is no further sin. Unfortunately, the worst wars in the Bible have yet to come. Until Jesus, the *Prince of Peace*, has full reign in the heart of man, the hope of peace is simply a dream that will fade away with the first light of day.

The LORD GOD of Israel went throughout Egypt and struck down the firstborn of every family where no blood had been applied to the doorposts and lintels of the houses. The dwellings of the Israelites, where the blood of the lamb had been sprinkled on the doorways were passed over—there was not a single death. God is about to go throughout the earth and strike down those that do not have the blood of Jesus, the *Passover Lamb*, applied to the doorposts and lintels of their hearts. None should venture out under the angry sky of God's wrath until his heart has been sprinkled with the blood of Jesus—it is the only means of escaping the angel of death—Jesus' blood *"cleanses us from all sin"* (1 John 1:7).

Everything God does is designed to ultimately bring the nations into the knowledge of His Salvation:

> *"As I live," says the LORD GOD, "I have no pleasure in the death of the wicked, but that the wicked turn from his way and live.* **Turn, turn from your evil ways! For why should you die?***"* (Ezekiel 33: 11).

GOD IS GOING TO SEVERELY SHAKE the nations until He gets their attention—the question is, how much shaking will it take? When France was bombarded with hailstones the size of tennis balls in the summer of 1993, the French merely complained that their holidays were ruined. In 1992, the LORD not only sent a record 1,381 tornadoes throughout America, but disastrous flooding in Texas, and devastation in Florida from Hurricane Andrew (winds were registered up to 164 miles (264 kilometers) an hour), which caused an estimated US$22 billion worth of damage. In the summer of 1993, God simultaneously submerged the Midwest under water, sent snow in lieu of sunshine to Colorado, and a merciless heatwave upon the East Coast that took 46 lives—both the flooding and the heatwave were the worst in American history. U.S. weathermen, however, said the weather is inclined to be fickle at that time of year.

The LORD has been manipulating the elements for thousands of years. He might choose to open the floodgates of heaven, or close the valves completely. He might choose to turn the heat up high, or disconnect it altogether—remember, He put the lights out in Egypt:

> *Then the LORD said to Moses, "Stretch out your hand toward heaven, that there may be darkness over the land of Egypt, darkness which may even be felt." So Moses stretched out his hand toward heaven, and there was thick darkness in all the land of Egypt three days*
> (Exodus 10:21–22).

Armageddon — Chapter 28

No man gets the better of the LORD—He had His way with Pharaoh and the Egyptians, and He will have His way with us and our leaders—but how many of us must first die? Floods, droughts, famines, earthquakes, tidal waves, hurricanes, tornadoes, cyclones, typhoons, heatwaves, and freezing temperatures take a large tally of lives every year. Since the beginning of the new millennium "global warming" is believed by many to be the biggest threat to life on Earth, yet we are consistently having record-breaking cold temperatures! Numbers of eminent scientists predict that a mini ice-age will come upon our planet. The weather is doing its own thing. Scientists from all around the world agree that abnormal weather is triggered by a thermal phenomenon known as *El Niño*. Actually, it would all be rather amusing if it were not so tragic. Almost daily, we either read or are told that *El Niño* is the villain of the piece. Now, *El Niño* is Spanish, and the Spanish use *El Niño* when referring of the child Jesus, God's *"only begotten Son"* (John 3:16). Speaking of Jesus the Bible tells us:

For the Lord Himself will descend from heaven with a shout, with the voice of an archangel, and with the trumpet of God. **And the dead in Christ will rise first** (1 Thessalonians 4:16).

We know that when Jesus comes it is all over bar the shouting. But man, including born again Christians, is so obtuse and spiritually bankrupt that he completely misses what the LORD is telling the world. God is telling this world that *El Niño*, **"My Son,"** is coming—that He is on His way!

THE COMBINED TOTAL OF LIVES WORLDWIDE taken by "acts of God" still cannot compete with the numbers that are dying each year from the HIV/AIDS virus. And even AIDS cannot match the millions of lives currently being lost annually to the pandemic of untreatable malaria. According to the May 31, 1993, *TIME International* edition, malaria has even reappeared in Britain, Italy, and Holland, largely among travelers returning from malarial areas. There is also fear that UN peace-keepers who contract malaria—more than 2,500 known cases thus far—will carry the parasite in their blood when they leave and spread it elsewhere. The deadly 2014 Ebola outbreak in West Africa killed more than 11,500 people. Contaminated travelers and medics were also tested positive when they arrived back in their own countries, in some cases they then transmitted the disease to the Good Samaritan medics treating them.

THERE IS A UNIVERSAL FEAR IN the medical world that humanity has entered a global "post antibiotic era" in which antibiotic-resistant superbugs will infect hundreds of thousands of people having routine surgeries like hip replacements, chemotherapy, colorectal surgery, etc. Tens of thousands of patients will simply die the medics say. Influenza is so common that most people simply shrug their shoulders, but many hundreds of thousands of people, mostly the elderly, succumb to the virus each year. The influenza pandemic of 1918 – 1919, known as the "Spanish Flu," was a global disaster and killed many more people than did World War I. Somewhere between 20 and 40 million people died—more people died of influenza in **a single year** than in four years of the Black Death Bubonic Plague 1347 – 1351.

Major diseases which were once thought to have been eradicated are aggressively making a comeback: cholera, tuberculosis, polio, measles, whooping cough, scarlet fever, even bubonic plague that was known as "Black Death" in the fourteenth century. Sexually transmitted diseases (STDs) are reproducing at an almost hysterical rate in the Western world due to its utter moral depravity:

> *God gave them up to dishonorable passions. Their women exchanged natural relations for those that are contrary to nature; and the men likewise gave up natural relations with women and were consumed with passion for one another, men committing shameless acts with men* **and receiving in themselves the due penalty for their error**
> (Romans 1:26–27).

ECONOMIC DECLINE IS NOW PRACTICALLY UNIVERSAL and total financial collapse of some nations appears imminent. Nations, cities, businesses, and individuals are going bankrupt leaving enormous debts. Despair is everywhere, and almost daily one reads of financially related suicides. As far back as May 3, 1993, *TIME International*, reported that eight financial backers of Lloyd's had committed suicide in the preceding four months, Lloyd's—synonymous with insurance for some 300 years—had lost billions of dollars in each of the past two years and stared bankruptcy in the face. Lloyd's said the losses were the result of "**bad luck with hurricanes**" etc. The LORD is shaking the whole earth and nations must lay the blame for its disasters on their sins, instead of on "luck." The 2008 global meltdown—the Great Recession—was due to the unprecedented, unmitigated greed of scores of American executives, who themselves pocketed billions from their schemes while they happily sent millions of people around the world to the poorhouse. And in January 2016 we see the stockmarket crashing again and esteemed financial analysts predicting a financial meltdown worse than the Great Recession. The Bible unequivocally says:

Armageddon — Chapter 28

And there will be great earthquakes in various places, and famines and pestilences; and there will be fearful sights and great signs from heaven. And there will be signs in the sun, in the moon, and in the stars; and on the earth distress of nations, with perplexity, the sea and the waves roaring; men's hearts failing them from fear and the expectation of those things which are coming on the earth, for the powers of heaven will be shaken. Now when these things begin to happen, look up and lift up your heads, because your redemption draws near (Luke 21:11, 25–28).

Shortly before the Babylonian rape of Israel and the subsequent destruction of Jerusalem in 586 BC, God asked a question of His rebellious and sinful people. I now put that same poignant question to my readers:

What will you do in the day of punishment, and in the desolation which will come from afar? **To whom will you flee for help?** (Isaiah 10:3).

Have you, dear reader, made peace with your Judge? Do it now! Tomorrow cannot be assured—only this moment is yours. *"Today, if you will hear His voice, do not harden your hearts"* (Hebrews 3:15), for:

He has appointed a day on which He will judge the world in righteousness **by the Man whom He has ordained**. *He has given assurance of this to all by raising Him from the dead* (Acts 17:31).

The resurrection of Jesus is one of the most attested facts of history—only a fool would choose to disbelieve this. The Bible tells us that *"he who does not believe God has made Him a liar"* (1 John 5:10). To reject the LORD's Word is to reject the LORD Himself. And this will be the measuring line by which nations and individuals are measured:

He who rejects Me, and does not receive My words, **has that which judges him—the word that I have spoken will judge him in the last day** (John 12:48).

There is nothing to fear for the one who is believing and clinging to Jesus. That person is secure in the *"everlasting arms"* (Deuteronomy 33:27) of the One whose *"banner over me is love"* (Song of Songs 2:4).

TWENTY PERCENT OF THE WORLD'S 7.35 billion population ostensibly live under the auspices of "Christianity"—but only eight percent at best have actually been born again. This means that 117.6 million people have Jesus' blood on the doorposts of their hearts, and 7.23 **BILLION** do not.

The harvest is past, the summer is ended, and we are not saved!
(Jeremiah 8:20).

Hear the Word of the Lord, O nations:

> *Thus says the Lord: "Behold, I am fashioning a disaster and devising a plan against you. Return now every one from his evil way, and make your ways and your doings good" ... The Lord will roar from on high, and utter His voice from His holy habitation; He will roar mightily against His fold. He will give a shout, as those who tread the grapes, against all the inhabitants of the earth. A noise will come to the ends of the earth—* **for the Lord has a controversy with the nations**; *he will plead His case with all flesh. He will give those who are wicked to the sword. Thus says the Lord of [armies]: "Behold, disaster shall go forth from nation to nation, and a great whirlwind shall be raised up from the farthest parts of the earth. And at that day the slain of the Lord shall be from one end of the earth even to the other end of the earth. They shall not be lamented, or gathered, or buried; they shall become refuse on the ground"* (Jeremiah 18:11, 25:30–33).

God has been patient, but He will not be patient forever. Nations and people, you have been warned: ***Repent or be destroyed!***

For Your Information

Ramon Bennett, the author of this book, also writes the **Update**, the regular newsletter of the *Arm of Salvation Ministries*. The **Update** keeps readers informed on world events that affect Israel, and also, on the ministry of Ramon Bennett and his wife, Zipporah. An annual donation of $20.00 is

requested for the **Update** to offset production and first class postage costs. The **Update** is also available by eMail in PDF format at $15.00 per year. Amounts given above those stated will be put toward the personal expenses of the Bennetts. PDF subscriptions to the **Update** and any additional donations should be made to **Ramon Bennett** and sent to Shekinah Books LLC at the address given below.

Arm of Salvation (AOS) was founded by Ramon Bennett in 1980 and is an indigenous Israeli ministry dependent upon gifts and the proceeds from its book and music sales to sustain its work in and for Israel and the Jewish people. These are critical times for Israel so financial support is both needful and appreciated.

Copies of **SAGA** and other books by Ramon Bennett (see following pages), together with albums of popular Hebrew worship songs composed by Zipporah Bennett, are available from:

Shekinah Books LLC
755 Engleby Drive
Colorado Springs, CO 80930 U.S.A.
Telephone (719) 645-7722
eMail: usa@shekinahbooks.com.

All payments must be in U.S. funds drawn on a U.S. bank. Alternatively, visit our website: http://www.shekinahbooks.com to purchase, subscribe, and/or donate via PayPal.

Titles by Ramon Bennett

"*WHEN DAY & NIGHT CEASE* is the most comprehensive, factual and informative book on Israel—past, present and future. If you want a true picture of how Israel is falling into Bible prophecy today, look no further. You will want to read this book"

– Freda Lindsay

324 pages – Paperback, or Kindle e-book

RAMON BENNETT has been introduced as "someone who has suffered the trials of Job."

Often verging on the unbelievable, *ALL MY TEARS* IS Ramon's astounding autobiographical testimony; a story of an unwanted, abused child whom God adopted and anointed, and uses for His glory.

448 pages – Paperback, or Kindle e-book

For a descriptive overview or to purchase the above books go to:
http://www.shekinahbooks.com

Titles by Ramon Bennett

GAZA! is an accurate account of the events that led up to, and took place during, Israel's Operation Protective Edge, the 50-day war against Hamas in Gaza in 2014. It is a factual account of what took place, when it took place, why it took place, and the result of it having taken place.

The book shows another perspective—a proper perspective—differing to what was presented on television screens across the world; it gives a different narrative to that told by Hamas-threatened journalists who covered the third round of this never-ending conflict.

134 pages – Paperback, or Kindle e-book

HIStory, the gospels of Matthew, Mark, Luke, and John blended together into a single uninterrupted narrative. *HIStory* transforms the four individual gospels, each with its own color text, into an edifying read for those interested in the full, uninterrupted story of the nativity, life, death, resurrection, and ascension of Jesus Christ. The Color Print Edition shows from where each interpolated piece comes from. Bible Students will find this book fascinating.

184 pages – Paperback, or Kindle e-book

For a descriptive overview or to purchase the above books go to:
http://www.shekinahbooks.com

Titles by Ramon Bennett

Philistine lays bare the Arab mind, Islam, the United Nations, the media, rewritten history and the Israeli-PLO peace accord. **Philistine** will grip you. **Philistine** will inform you. Philistine will shock you. Until you read **Philistine** you will never understand the Middle East—the world's most volatile region.

345 pages – Paperback only

"*VERY INFORMATIVE BOOK FOR THOSE WHO are looking for answers to what is happening in the middle east. Most of what you hear in the news media is such surface stuff and news to steer you away from the truth. God's Word is truth and Ramon Bennett breaks down verses that I've wondered about for years. A very good read, you won't be able to put it down.*"

– William D. Douglas

335 pages – Paperback, or Kindle e-book

For a descriptive overview or to purchase the above books go to:
http://www.shekinahbooks.com

Titles by Ramon Bennett

"**They lead My people astray**, *saying 'Peace!' when there is no peace, and because, when a flimsy wall is built, they cover it with whitewash"*
(Ezekiel 13:10).
Ramon Bennett exposes the peace process for what it is, an attempt to break Israel down piece by piece

367 pages – Paperback. Kindle e-book *coming*

UNDERSTAND the chaos taking place around the world today! **SAGA** is about Israel and Israel's God; about war and judgment—past, present, and future. Nations came and went, empires rose and fell; and God is still judging nations today. A "must read" in light of world events today.

I spent the weekend with Saga—Wow!

237 pages – Paperback, or Kindle e-book

For a descriptive overview or to purchase the above books go to:
http://www.shekinahbooks.com

Book and Music titles by Zipporah Bennett

Return, Daughter of Zion! Zipporah Bennett's testimony and autobiography. Read how Zipporah, a God-hungry Orthodox Jewish girl, found the Reality she longed for. This book, often amusing, will help the reader better understand the way Jewish people think and feel about the "Christian" Jesus.

137 pages – Paperback only

Kuma Adonai

"**Arise O Lord!**" – Songs of warfare and worship

Hallelu

"**Hallelu**" – Dual Hebrew–English songs of worship

Mi Ha'amin?

"**Who Hath Believed?**" Hebrew and Aramaic prophecies in song

The above CD albums contain many of Israels favorite messianic songs!
Hebrew texts, translation, and transliterations printed inside the jackets

For a descriptive overview or to purchase the above items go to:
http://www.shekinahbooks.com

www.ingramcontent.com/pod-product-compliance
Lightning Source LLC
Chambersburg PA
CBHW060821050426
42453CB00008B/523